WENG'S CHOP

Editorials	2
WC Literary Classics: PAINTED SKIN	3
KA-CHA! I GOT SHANGHAIED!	5
Kuei Chin Hung	7
Garko & Kinski: Blood Brothers	10
A Pistolry of Violence	13
El Ranchera Sobrenatural Peliculas	15
Tony Anthony: No Second Banana	21
Bang Bang... Cha Cha Cha	25
Thai Kaiju: Giant Monsters of Thailand	30
Leena Kurishingal Interview	34
DB3 In The Hot Seat	37
Darren Ward Interview	38
REVIEWS!	40
Cult Cinema Under The Gun	55
Indian Horror Film, Part 3	58
The Bookshelf	65

Cover: Leena Kurishingal, model
Brian Harris, photographer

Interior art: Amber Skowronski

December 2012

Brian Harris, Editor & Publisher
Timothy Paxton, Editor & Design

WENG'S CHOP is published quarterly. © 2012 Wildside Publishing / Kronos Productions. All rights reserved. No part of this publication may be reproduced, distributed, or transmitted in any form or by any means, including photocopying, recording, or other electronic or mechanical methods, without the prior written permission of the publisher, except in the case of brief quotations embodied in critical reviews and certain other noncommercial uses permitted by copyright law. For permission requests, write to the publisher, addressed "Attention: Permissions Coordinator," at the address below. 4301 Sioux Lane #1, McHenry, IL 60050, United States

wildsidecinema@comcast.net

Volume #1 / Issue #2 / 1st Printing

A WORD FROM THE EDITORS...

SARAFINA'S STEAMING SUCUK SUPRISE *or* OUR 3RD ISSUE SMELLS OF HAI KARATE!
• Brian Harris (Co-Editor)

Not long ago a friend asked me how in the hell I could write for a periodical and not get paid a dime for it, which is a rather curious thing to ask when pretty much everybody knows you don't get paid shit for writing for anything or anybody, let alone a little fanzine. My answer, as you can well imagine, was sarcastic and offensive, unfortunately he was such a goddamn dimwit and the question so typical of today's aspiring "writer" that I cannot even recall what I said but I'm pretty sure there was a few fucks and shits in there, perhaps one cack-smacker and I'm almost positive I mentioned his mother scrubbed scrote in Turkish bathes. I won't speak for Tim (though I'm sure he would agree) that writing for Weng's Chop isn't about the money or prestige, it's not even about the literary bust-downs that throw themselves at us (is there such a thing?) with panties a'flail, writing for WC is just plain fun. It reminds me that there's still a place in this world for print, whether it's scribbled on paper and xeroxed forty-two times, capturing the spirit of the DIY punk, or written in OpenOffice, laid-out like a pro-mag and sent to the pay-on-demand company to be sold one issue at a time. We do this because we love it, I love it, Tim loves it. Hopefully you love it too. If not, your mother scrubs scrote in hell. Welcome to our third official issue with many more to come! HAPPY HOLIDAYS!

http://boxsetbeatdown.blogspot.com

LOOKING FOR STURDY FOOTING UPON A MIDDLE GROUND...
• Tim Paxton (Co-Editor)

Brian said it all in his editorial. Weng's Chop is not an end-all when it comes to genre analysis, but an exploration into what each author finds interesting and/or is obligated to write about. Granted, this themed issue did have a few folks writing outside their comfort zone (me in particular), and the end result is this text-dense magazine you are now reading. For me, personally, WC embodies everything I love about print.

On a technical side note, I have always attempted to get some sort of standardization when it comes to listing movie, books, magazines, or whatever. As you may imagine, if I made all the adjustments to the many authors' work the end result could have disrupted their compositional flow. I have reset some of the submitted articles and reviews to fit my standardization, but not all. However, for those of you submitting material for WC#3 I'll send you the stats.

All of this may seem to fly in the face of spontaneity and fun. Well, kinda. I am all about the personal aspect of reviews, but I also love as much data as possible to be available to the reader -- casual or seasoned. The deadline for issue #3 (official #4) will be the first week of March for March 31st publication date.

Keep the Peace.

...ABOUT THE CONTRIBUTORS

Lucas Balbo - started his own fanzine (Nostalgia) in the early '80s, then contributed to Shock Xpress and Psychotronic prozines/magazines. Took ten years of his life to write the first directory of Jess Franco's Film (*OBSESSION, THE FILMS OF JESS FRANCO*). Nowadays, he runs his own photo library and collaborate with various DVD distribution companies (http://artclips.free.fr/archives-english.htm).

David Barnes - has his own line of comics and also creates vintage "grindhouse " t-shirts. His work can be seen at zid3ya@yahoo.com and myspace.com@paramere.

Gary Baxter - British born Baxter grew up on a diet of video nasty greats and slasher movie sickness, exploitation excellence and Italian cult gems. When he's not reading about, writing about or watching trash movie madness he volunteers with a group of young wannabe movie makers called Film Junkies. Gary recently got to realize a childhood dream of appearing in a zombie movie, **CONVENTION OF THE DEAD** and is currently working on his own idea for a short film called **TIL DEATH**, to be filmed early 2013.

Stephen R. Bissette - a pioneer graduate of the Joe Kubert School, currently teaches at the Center for Cartoon Studies and is renowned for *Swamp Thing, Taboo* (launching *From Hell and Lost Girls*), *'1963,' Tyrant*, co-creating *John Constantine*, and creating the world's second '24-Hour Comic' (invented by Scott McCloud for Bissette). He writes, illustrates, and has co-authored many books; his latest include *Teen Angels & New Mutants* (2011), the short story "Copper" in *The New Dead* (2010), and he illustrated *The Vermont Monster Guide* (2009). His latest ebooks are *Bryan Talbot: Dreams & Dystopias* and the *Best of Blur* duo, *Wonders! Millennial Marvel Movies and Horrors! Cults, Crimes, & Creepers*.

Danae Dunning - is a goth/metal/hippie chick from Hobbs, New Mexico,USA. Her other interests besides movies are music (just about anything except rap, big band, and polka), writing poetry, and driving people insane. Her first experience in horror that She remember was somewhere in between the ages of 2 and 4 when she saw **FIEND WITHOUT A FACE** on tv. She was scarred for life, but in a good way, LOL. Her mainstay is horror, but she love exploitation, some sci fi and fantasy, even a few chick flicks. And She is the proud owner of Emmett Otter's Jug band Christmas dvd. She is also working on broadening her horizons by exploring the films of The French New Wave.

Phillip Escott - is a British movie lover with a boner for not just the finest trash, but the best art house. Basically he likes anything that shows boobies. When he's not admiring naked bodies he's attempting to make films. He urges/will blow you if you come and watch his 'films'. You can reach Phill through www.facebook.com/441films

Greg Goodsell - recently had his interview with the fabulous character actress O-Lan Jones published in Steve Puchalski's indispensable *SHOCK CINEMA* magazine. Read it today, and let Greg know what you think at gregoodsell@hotmail.com

John Grace - is the co-host of the Damaged Viewing podcast, available on ITunes or at http://damagedviewing.podomatic.com/. He also contributes to Exploitation Retrospect. Mr. Grace is determined to school his young son in the appreciation of all things that make living in this modern world a must. The ways of the Tarmangani.

Brian Harris - can be found skipping the halls of Arborea, pondering the existence of David Lynch and plotting his next foray into the literary world. When he's not dressing up in a cowboy outfit and taping a cut-out of Franco Nero's face to his own, he's furiously masturbating to the sounds of Futurecop. Known for inspiring others, in an almost cult-like manner, Brian marches to the beat of his own drum and prefers the taste of Cherry kool-aid...so will you. You can find four of his books online, if you look hard enough, and he runs a box set blog for his own sadistic amusement.

Mike Howlett - is the author *The Weird World of Eerie Publications* (Feral House) and recently made The Weird Indexes of Eerie Publications available as a made to order book on Lulu and Amazon. There is clearly no hope for him.

Chaitanya Reddy - Man of letters and master of many tongues; Sanskrit, Abugida, and English included. Chaitanya covers many genres in his blog moviemaniac100.blogspot.in.

Steven Ronquillo - is a pretentious know-it-all who looks down on his fellow film fans and refuses to reveal his faves to them unless it makes him look good.

Tony Strauss - has been writing about cinema online and in print for nearly two decades. His existence as that rarest of creature—a movie snob who loves trash cinema (yes, it's possible)—often leaves him as the odd man out in both intellectual and low-brow film discussions. Most movies that people describe as "boring" or "confusing" enthrall him, while the kinds of movies that are described as "non-stop action" usually bore him to tears. He once turned down an offer from Disney for one of his screenplays, and never regretted it for a second.

Dan Taylor - has been writing about junk culture and fringe media since his zine Exploitation Retrospect debuted in 1986. 26 years later the publication is still going strong as a website, blog and – yes – a resurrected print edition. Check it all out at Dantenet.com, EROnline.blogspot.com or Facebook.com/ExploitationRetrospect.

Tim Merrill - is a rabid unrepentant cinephile based out of Seoul, South Korea. He has written for Asian Cult Cinema, and Asian Eye, as well as a number of long lost film rags. When he isn't scouring DVD/VCD shops throughout Asia for out of print treasures, he can be found in his underground bunker hidden deep along the North Korea border watching repeats of Ultraman, and Mario Adorf Euro crime movies.

Tim Paxton - Has been publishing stuff about monsters since 1978, and currently lives to write about Indian films that no one in their right mind would find suitable for human consumption. Has assigned himself the inhuman goal of watching every single film by Kanti Shah. Tim is also assembling and editing a three volume set of his *MONSTER!* fanzine which he will begin publishing in mid-2013.

Amber Skowronski - is a special effects artist and illustrator living in Los Angeles. She is available for commissions and you can find her portfolio at amberskowronski.brushd.com

Pu Songling - is a long dead Chinese author that is required reading for anyone interested in all aspects of Asian spookdom.

Douglas Waltz - lives in the wilds of Kalamazoo, MI where he is experimenting with primitive pottery techniques. His zine, *Divine Exploitation*, has existed in print or online form since 1988 and can be found at divineexploitation.blogspot.com. His recent book, *A Democrazy of Braindrained Loons; The Films of Michael Legge* can be purchased at https://tsw.createspace.com/title/3814218. Douglas would like you to know that all Jess Franco films are good. ALL OF THEM!

Jolyon Yates - is an illustrator and occasional writer for monster mags like Samhain and G-Fan. Storyboarded many commercials (released) and movies (not so released). Currently illustrates Ninjago comics. Can be seen in the James Lew ninja fantasy **TENGU** if the darn thing ever comes out. Will watch anything starring Isabelle Adjani, Randolph Scott or Amitabh Bachchan, preferably all three. Lurks on Facebook and at www.jolyonbyates.com

Dave Zuzelo - is a full time HorrorDad, a full time Media Mangler and a full time Trash Cinema Sponge. He is also a sometime blogger at TOMB IT MAY CONCERN (David-Z.blogspot.com) and enjoys spewing words of sleazy musing across every publication that will have him. Check out his book *TOUGH TO KILL-THE ITALIAN ACTION EXPLOSION* and see just how many exploding huts he can endure, and he'll beg for more!"

LITERARY CLASSICS PRESENTS: 聊齋誌異
STRANGE STORIES FROM A CHINESE STUDIO
畫皮 THE PAINTED SKIN

Written by Pu Songling (1740) • Translated by Herbert A. Giles (1880)

In an attempt to educate the masses, we at Weng's Chop are proud to present the original (albeit translated) Chinese tale that was responsible for at least four Hong Kong fantasy/horror films from the early 1966 to 2012.

At T'ai-yüan there lived a man named Wang. One morning he was out walking when he met a young lady carrying a bundle and hurrying along by herself. As she moved along with some difficulty Wang quickened his pace and caught her up, and found she was a pretty girl of about sixteen. Much smitten, he inquired whither she was going so early, and no one with her.

"A traveler like you," replied the girl, "cannot alleviate my distress; why trouble yourself to ask?"

"What distress is it?" said Wang, "I'm sure I'll do anything I can for you."

"My parents," answered she, "loved money, and they sold me as concubine into a rich family, where the wife was very jealous, and beat and abused me morning and night. It was more than I could stand, so I have run away."

Wang asked her where she was going; to which she replied that a runaway had no fixed place of abode. "My house," said Wang, "is at no great distance; what do you say to coming there?"

She joyfully acquiesced; and Wang, taking up her bundle, led the way to his house. Finding no one there, she asked Wang where his family were; to which he replied that that was only the library.

"And a very nice place, too," said she, "but if you are kind enough to wish to save my life, you mustn't let it be known that I am here."

Wang promised he would not divulge her secret, and so she remained there for some days without anyone knowing anything about it. He then told his wife, and she, fearing the girl might belong to some influential family, advised him to send her away. This, however, he would not consent to do; when one day, going into the town, he met a Taoist priest, who looked at him in astonishment, and asked him what he had met.

"I have met nothing," replied Wang.

"Why," said the priest, "you are bewitched; what do you mean by not having met anything?"

But Wang insisted that 'it was not so, and the priest walked away, saying, "The fool! Some people don't seem to know when death is at hand."

This startled Wang, who at first thought of the girl; but then he reflected that a pretty young thing as she was couldn't well be a witch, and began to suspect that the priest merely wanted to do a stroke of business.

When he returned, the library door was shut, and he couldn't get in, which made him suspect that something was wrong; and so he climbed over the wall, where he found the door of the inner room shut too. Softly creeping up, he looked through the window and saw a hideous devil, with a green face and jagged teeth like a saw, spreading a human skin upon the bed and painting it with a paint brush. The devil then threw aside the brush, and giving the skin a shake out, just as you would a coat, threw it over its shoulders, when lo it was the girl! Terrified at this, Wang hurried away with his head down in search of the priest, who had gone he knew not whither; subsequently finding him in the

PAINTED SKIN (1966, D: Bao Fang)

fields, where he threw himself on his knees and begged the priest to save him. "As to driving her away," said the priest, "the creature must be in great distress to be seeking a substitute for herself; besides, I could hardly endure to injure a living thing."

However, he gave Wang a fly-brush, and bade him hang it at the door of the bedroom, agreeing to meet again at the Ch'ing-ti temple. Wang went home, but did not dare enter the library; so he hung up the brush at the bedroom door, and before long heard a sound of footsteps outside. Not daring to move, he made his wife peep out and she saw the girl standing looking at the brush, afraid to pass it.

She then ground her teeth and went away; but in a little while came back, and began cursing, saying, "You priest, you won't frighten me. Do you think I am going to give up what is already in my grasp?" Thereupon she tore the brush to pieces, and bursting open the door, walked straight up to the bed, where she ripped open Wang and tore out his heart, with which she went away. Wang's wife screamed out, and the servant came in with a light; but Wang was already dead and presented a most miserable spectacle. His wife, who was in an agony of fright, hardly dared cry for fear of making a noise; and next day she sent Wang's brother to see the priest. The latter got into a great rage, and cried out,

3

PAINTED SKIN (1993, D: King Hu)

"Was it for this that I had compassion on you, devil that you are?" proceeding at once with Wang's brother to the house, from which the girl had disappeared without anyone knowing whither she had gone. But the priest, raising his head, looked all round, and said, "Luckily she's not far off." He then asked who lived in the apartments on the south side, to which Wang's brother replied that he did; whereupon the priest declared that there she would be found.

Wang's brother was horribly frightened and said he did not think so; and then the priest asked him if any stranger had been to the house. To this he answered that he had been out to the Ch'ing-ti temple and couldn't possibly say but he went off to inquire, and in a little while came back and reported that an old woman had sought service with them as a maid-of-all-work, and had been engaged by his wife.

"That is she," said the priest, as Wang's brother added she was still there; and they all set out to go to the house together. Then the priest took his wooden sword, and standing in the middle of the court-yard, shouted out, "Base-born fiend, give me back my fly-brush!"

Meanwhile the new maid-of-all-work was in a great state of alarm, and tried to get away by the door; but the priest struck her and down she fell flat, the human skin dropped off, and she became a hideous devil. There she lay grunting like a pig, until the priest grasped his wooden sword and struck off her head. She then became a dense column of smoke curling up from the ground, when the priest took an uncorked gourd and threw it right into the midst of the smoke. A sucking noise was heard, and the whole column was drawn into the gourd; after which the priest corked it up closely and put it in his pouch. The skin, too, which was complete even to the eye-brows, eyes, hands, and feet, he also rolled up as if it had been a scroll, and was on the point of leaving with it, when Wang's wife stopped him, and with tears entreated him to bring her husband to life. The priest said he was unable to do that; but Wang's wife flung herself at his feet, and with loud lamentations implored his assistance.

For some time he remained immersed in thought, and then replied, "My power is not equal to what you ask. I myself cannot raise the dead, but I will direct you to some one who can, and if you apply to him properly you will succeed." Wang's wife asked the priest who it was; to which he replied, "There is a maniac in the town who passes his time grovelling in the dirt. Go, prostrate yourself before him, and beg him to help you. If he insults you, show no sign of anger" Wang's brother knew the man to whom he alluded, and accordingly bade the priest adieu, and proceeded thither with his sister-in-law.

They found the destitute creature raving away by the roadside, so filthy that it was all they could do to go near him. Wang's wife approached him on her knees; at which the maniac leered at her, and cried out, "Do you love me, my beauty?" Wang's wife told him what she had come for, but he only laughed and said, "You can get plenty of other husbands. Why raise the dead one to life?" But Wang's wife entreated him to help her; whereupon he observed, "It's very strange: people apply to me to raise their dead as if I was king of the infernal regions." He then gave Wang's wife a thrashing with his staff, which she bore without a murmur, and before a gradually increasing crowd of spectators. After this he produced a loathsome pill which he told her she must swallow, but here she broke down and was quite unable to do so. However, she did manage it at last, and then the maniac, crying out,"How you do love me!" got up and went away without taking any more notice of her. They followed him into a temple with loud supplications, but he had disappeared, and every effort to find him was unsuccessful.

Overcome with rage and shame, Wang's wife went home, where she mourned bitterly over her dead husband, grievously repenting the steps she had taken, and wishing only to die. She then bethought herself of preparing the corpse, near which none of the servants would venture, and set to work to close up the frightful wound of which he died. While thus employed, interrupted from time to time by her sobs, she felt a rising lump in her throat, which by-and-by came out with a pop and fell straight into the dead man's wound. Looking closely at it, she saw it was a human heart; and then it began as it were to throb, emitting a warm vapor like smoke. Much excited, she at once closed the flesh over it, and held the sides of the wound together with all her might. Very soon, however, she got tired, and finding the vapor escaping from the crevices, she tore up a piece of silk and bound it round, at the same time bringing back circulation by rubbing the body and covering it up with clothes. In the night she removed the coverings, and found that breath was coming from the nose; and by next morning her husband was alive again, though disturbed in mind as if awaking from a dream, and feeling a pain in his heart. Where he had been wounded there was a cicatrix about as big as a cash, which soon after disappeared.

...

PAINTED SKIN (2008, D: Gordon Chan)

KA-CHA! I GOT SHANGHAIED!

• Dan Taylor

Movies can be deep, provoke serious thought and engage us in intense discussion. Movies can incite change and alter the course of history. Movies can cause you to search your soul and wonder if the person you are is the person you can or should be.

Luckily, movies can also provide two hours of pure junk food fun, the cinematic equivalent of inhaling a greasy fast food meal and washing it down with a bucket of soda. And the martial-arts-meets-western comedies of Jackie Chan and Owen Wilson – **SHANGHAI NOON** (2000) and its sequel **SHANGHAI KNIGHTS** (2003) – are about as nutritionally bankrupt but haphazardly enjoyable as cinema gets.

Despite **NOON**'s billing as "The First Kung-Fu Western Ever" the martial arts oater was not a new concept by any stretch. Producers in the 1970s were quick to combine the two then-successful genres, leading to a flurry of East-Meets-West gun-fu flicks like **RED SUN** (1971), **THE FIGHTING FISTS OF SHANGHAI JOE** (1973) with Klaus Kinski and **THE STRANGER AND THE GUNFIGHTER** (1974) starring Lee Van Cleef. None exactly lit the box office on fire and as the popularity of the genres waned so did producers' interest.

By the late 1990s Jackie Chan had done what he'd failed to do with 1980's THE BIG BRAWL (directed by **ENTER THE DRAGON** helmer Robert Clouse); he'd conquered the American box office. No longer just the darling of Hong Kong cinema aficionados and action junkies, imported Chan flicks like **RUMBLE IN THE BRONX** had ignited martial arts ticket sales while the East-Meets-West buddy cop flick **RUSH HOUR** starring Chan and comedian Chris Tucker grossed a staggering $250 million worldwide (and saddled us with the specter of the words "Directed by Brett Ratner" forever).

SHAGHAI NOON riffs on the **RUSH HOUR** formula of the fish-out-of-water-buddy-picture, but transplants the action to the 1880s Western frontier and replaces the jive-talking Tucker with the "aw shucks, did I do that?" stoner rap of Owen Wilson, then best known as one of the oil rig roughnecks in **ARMAGEDDON**.

Opening in the Forbidden City of China, Chan stars as Chon Wang, a member of the palace's Imperial Guard. When Princess Pei Pei (Lucy Liu) is kidnapped by her English tutor (Jason Connery) under the guise of escaping to America, Wang volunteers to accompany his uncle and a trio of skilled Guard members to the US to retrieve her.

When the uncle is killed by a dense desperado in the employ of charming outlaw Roy O'Bannon (Wilson), it sets up an uneasy East-Meets-West alliance as the two must put aside their differences and blah, blah, blah.

Directed by newcomer Tom Dey and scripted by future 'Smallville' creators Alfred Gough and Miles Millar, **SHANGHAI NOON** excels largely – make that "entirely" – due to the strengths and chemistry of its two stars.

I hadn't watched the flick in about a decade before sitting down to check it out for this article and I was surprised at just how lazy and disjointed the film really is. The story lurches from scene to scene, with characters disappearing and re-appearing as plot machinations require, and most of the film's martial arts sequences come off feeling slowed up and dumbed down for mainstream US audiences. (Not surprisingly, Dey's post-**NOON** filmography features duds like **FAILURE TO LAUNCH** and **MARMADUKE**, in which Wilson voices a CGI version of the comic strip pooch.)

All that said, **SHANGHAI NOON** is exceedingly enjoyable on a check-your-brain-at-the-door level thanks to Wilson, Chan and the Gough/Millar screenplay, despite it being packed with anachronisms and inaccuracies. While not all of the action sequences succeed, comedy bits featuring each of the stars – especially Chan's goofy scene getting high with Indians after a rescue and the two stars playing a drinking game while taking baths – are the real highlights of the flick.

By film's end the stars have defeated the bad guys (including an evil marshall named "Van Cleef"), mocked both John Wayne (Wilson's butchering of Chon Wang) and Wyatt Earp (revealed as O'Bannon's real name), trained to modern rock like "Le Grange" and Kid Rock's "Cowboy", spoofed the end of **BUTCH CASSIDY & THE SUNDANCE KID** (1969) and even joined forces as lawmen.

A hit with both critics and audiences, **NOON** spawned an inevitable sequel in 2003's **SHANGHAI KNIGHTS**. Smartly ditching Dey in favor of director David Dobkin (**CLAY PIGEONS, WEDDING CRASHERS**), **KNIGHTS** transforms both O'Bannon and Wang into fish out of water as the action shifts from the Old West to the United Kingdom.

Largely following the blueprint of their **NOON** script, Gough and Millar advance the story six years: Wang/The Shanghai Kid (Chan) is a successful lawman who still pines for Princess Pei Pei while O'Bannon (Wilson) spins tales of their exploits in pulp novels that relegate the Shanghai Kid to the role of ineffectual sidekick.

When Wang's estranged father is murdered by Rathbone (Aidan Gillen) – a member of the British royal family intent on ascending to the throne by any means necessary – Wang's sister Chon Lin (Fann Wong) sets out to find the killer and avenge the murder. Wang and O'Bannon reunite in New York (where Roy waits tables and is a part-time gigolo!) and end up in the UK where they pledge to find Lin, recover the Imperial Seal, save the Empire and blah, blah, blah.

While Millar, Gough and Dobkin smooth out a lot of the first film's rough patches and make **KNIGHTS** a better "movie" their insistence on piling on historical references to groan-inducing levels actually detracts from the film's charms. Along the way we're "treated" to characters that end up being Sir Arthur Conan Doyle, Charlie Chaplin and Jack The Ripper, while O'Bannon inadvertently "invents" Sherlock Holmes and fight sequences evoke everything from the Keystone Cops and Harold Lloyd to Gene Kelly's **SINGIN' IN THE RAIN**. It's like the screenwriters feared they wouldn't get to write a third flick so they packed in every half-baked idea, regardless of whether or not it made sense.

On the plus side, **KNIGHTS** benefits from a strong supporting cast that elevates the action and story above the dumbed-down escapades of **NOON**. Martial arts legend Donnie Yen makes the most of his role as the villainous Wu Chow and has an impressive battle with Chan in the flick's final reel while Aidan Gillen (best known for his roles in *THE WIRE* and *GAME OF THRONES*) evokes the sinister glee of his character's namesake, Basil Rathbone, even engaging O'Bannon in some swordplay inside Big Ben.

So, what's the verdict? While **KNIGHTS** is the better movie of the two thanks to a tighter story, better direction and a stronger cast, **NOON** is actually more enjoyable thanks to a heavier reliance on the chemistry between its two stars. As long as I remembered to check my brain at the door both were perfectly enjoyable diversions from the Eurotrash, slashers, Nikkatsu flicks, and low-budget direct-to-video trash that normally clog my TV screen.

You could do worse. You could watch a **NATIONAL TREASURE** movie.

...

Tony Anthony ... see page 21

AMBER SKOWRONSKI
is a special effects artist and illustrator living in Los Angeles. She is available for commissions and you can find her portfolio at
amberskowronski.brushd.com

FOR YOUR PRIVATE COLLECTION

It's happened! Kronos Productions has completely SOLD OUT of MONSTER! INTERNATIONAL # 1 & 2 and all issues of HIGHBALL MAGAZINE. But you can still get limited copies of #3 and 4 – and the remaining back issues are going fast! Better get yours now - while the short supply lasts!

#3 - Jose Mojica Marins, Possession films. more!

Our MONSTER! #4/HIGHBALL #3 Special Double Issue! Full of Babes and Beasts! Man or Astroman? Flexi Disc! More!!

MONSTER! BACK ISSUES
TIMOTHY PAXTON, CRYPT KEEPER
26 WEST VINE STREET
OBERLIN 44074 OH USA

I enclosed $............for the following issues:

☐ #3 $5.00 PPD USA ☐ #4 $5.00 PPD USA
   $8 PPD WorldWide $8 PPD WorldWide

NAME..
ADDRESS..
CITY...........................ZONE..........
STATE..

U.S. ORDER BY PAYPAL : ORLOF@ OBERLIN.NET
OR U.S. POSTAL ORDERS
INTERNATIONAL ORDERS PAYAPL ONLY

KUEI CHIH HUNG: ARCHITECT OF HK GENRE CINEMA

• Tim Merrill

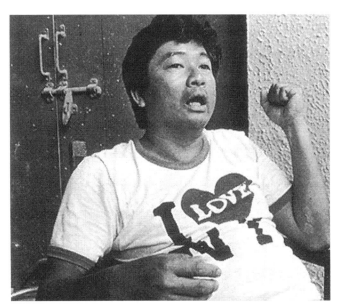

For the uninitiated Cinephile the world of Hong Kong film can often appear to be a deep and intimidating realm. It's often hard to navigate a course as you can start from the high water mark of a Wong Kar Wai film, or plummet into the depths of the cream of the crap of a Godfrey Ho butt nugget. Regardless of whether you look towards the highbrow, or drag your ass in the gutter, you are always guaranteed to find something in the genre that will satisfy the senses. Part of the real joy of wading into this cinematic sea is the discovery of the unknown treasures, hidden beneath the surface. While many are keen to point out the obvious 'must see' films, and mention coveted directors, this barely scratches the surface. There is also a definite line of films, and directors in Hong Kong that that have laid the foundations for Chinese cinema over decades, that continue to stand as the basis from which the films of today are built on.

With over 30 films to his credit director Kuei Chih Hung clearly established himself as one of the prime architects of Hong Kong exploitation cinema. Long before the category III classification was set in place, director Kuei was quickly expanding the parameters of the genre, writing and directing films that would be partially responsible for establishing the notorious rating system that would eventually come in being in the future. It is no line of bullshit to say that if it wasn't for Kuei Chih Hung, and other early directors of his ilk that the whole sordid sub-genre of sleaze that we know as 'category III' would have never seeped into HK theaters.

While largely known for his insane cinematic acid trips into fictional horror and superstition, Kuei was also compelled to portray the true to life dark side of inequality, corruption, and struggle in China throughout a handful of his films. The polarity of his subject matter served to provide Kuei with a wider audience of varying tastes. More importantly, it also showed that his goal was not merely just to shock and titillate, but to also show a true concern toward social consciousness, and justice.

Kuei Chih Hung was born in 1937 in Guangdong China, and even early on as a youth showed a natural interest in film making. Using scavenged 8 millimeter stock, and a basic projector, Kuei was able to put together a handful of shorts in his teenage years. This would eventually lead him enroll in Taiwan's national school of the arts to continue his development as a filmmaker. It would only be a matter of time before Kuei would be invited by the Shaw Brothers to work as an AD (assistant director) within their legendary stable. During his fledgling years within Shaw studios Kuei honed his craft, and learned the essentials through shooting a number of dramatic period pieces, and comedies.

It would finally be in 1973 that Kuei would begin to come into his own, in collaboration with legendary director Chang Cheh. Despite Chang being known primarily for his Wuxia, and Martial Art projects, **THE DELINQUENT** (aka Fen nu qing nian) was anything but. Closer in style to the work of Fukasaku, (primarily, 1972's **STREET MOBSTER**, and 1971 **SYMPATHY FOR THE UNDERDOG**), the film tells the story of a brutal struggle for survival on the grimy backstreets of China. The need to capture the authentic harsh feel of the street and its background was of utmost importance to director Kuei. Shot on location in various brothels, bars, and low income poverty piss holes, one could almost see this as a real life sleazy travelogue through the sordid underbelly of Hong Kong. Part of what makes the film stand on its own is the hyper stylized violence throughout that continues to wallop you like a handful of quarters wrapped in a sock. Although some have compared, **THE DELINQUENT**, to Ozawa's **STREETFIGHTER**, it must be noted that it predates the Sonny Chiba classic by a year. If anything, it was Kuei's early period of working in Japan that influenced his work, which in itself would later ironically influence the Japanese. Regardless of influence, the film clearly showed something that had never been seen before within Shaw studios, as it deviated from the usual Kung Fu fare. Heads are smashed, bones are broken, and bloody faces are rubbed into the filthy streets. Nihilism is the word of the day here, and words are cheap, but life on Kuei's streets is even cheaper. Few films of the time managed to come as close to capturing the true to life anger, violence and frustration of surviving in a concrete jungle of poverty in 1970's Hong Kong. While some directors were merely satisfied with slightly skimming the surface of the dark side, Kuei reveled in it, and showed the only way out is down, with no end reward, but death. Few films in the Shaw Brothers roster compare in matching the levels of sheer bleakness and brutality.

Kuei would soon rebound later in the same year to return with 'Nu ji zhong ying', also known as **BAMBOO HOUSE OF DOLLS**. Despite following the release of Jack Hill's 1971 exploit classic, **THE BIG DOLL HOUSE**, the film must be acknowledged for being primarily responsible for setting the path for future women in prison films to follow. It is quite doubtful that some of the more

notorious releases that were to come such as Jess Franco's, **WOMEN IN CELL BLOCK 9**, or the ILSA series would have ever seen the light of day had it not been for **BAMBOO DOLLS**. While it seems hardly plausible that the Shaw brothers would attach their names to a project of such ill repute, they would continue to show they were not afraid to wade into the sleazy muck of adult exploitation cinema.

Once again, director Kuei plumbs the depths of depravity, and weaves a sordid tale of foreign nurses under the sadistic reign of Japanese imperialists during World War II. Copious amounts of nudity and extreme torture predominate, but while Kuei serves up the standard menu of the obvious scummy tropes, he also does this with his own style and perspective. Most would scoff at the idea of a, 'well shot', women in prison picture, but such is clearly the case here. Behind the debauchery and titillation hides a well-crafted film. **BAMBOO DOLLS** not only sets out to satisfy the unrepentant pervert, but also those in the mood for an action packed prison romp, and succeeds on both parts. On a trivial note, Shaw legend Lo Lich plays a small role as a prison interpreter who falls for the seductive charms of one of the detained nurses.

With his venture into the, 'women in prison' subgenre, Kuei once again inadvertently showed that he was a bona fide trail blazer not only within Hong Kong, but within exploitation cinema as a whole.

For his next film, **THE TEAHOUSE** (Sing gei cha low), released in 1974, Kuei would return to the urban streets once more. Shaw mainstay Kuan Tai Chen plays 'Big Brother' Cheng, a simple tea shop owner who tries to make a meager living in the midst of a criminal cesspool of teenage violence, rape, and disorder. Cheng attempts to deal with the young thugs through a neutered legal system, but to no avail. After several attacks on his family and employees, Cheng finally takes action with the local toughs through violent retribution. While the story arc may sound like your typical Kung Fu joint, such is not the case. Director Kuei plays it straight with, **THE TEAHOUSE** presenting more of an urban drama, and exploring the issues of street crime, poverty and the flaws and limitations of the legal system in China. One can only suspect that the film rang true with Hong Kong Audiences, as it was so popular that it warranted a sequel, **BIG BROTHER CHANG**, a year later. It is interesting to note that Michael Winner's, classic, **DEATH WISH**, was also released in the same year as, **THE TEAHOUSE**, and both play along the same parallel lines of vigilante justice, and retribution. While Kuei easily made the transition from the prison genre to the urban social commentary, his wildest stretch was yet to come.

In 1975, the Shaw brothers would once again wade back into the sleaze pit with Kuei Chih Hung, but this time with a reptilian cast of hundreds in, **THE KILLER SNAKES** (She sha shou). While the Seventies were known for the 'killer pet', run of films such as **BEN, WILLARD, EATEN ALIVE**, and **STANLEY**, nobody cranked up the scaly skeeve factor like Kuei would. Actual cobras, black mambas, asps and even a komodo dragon all run roughshod over an unfortunate cast of human victims. Long before Sam Jackson was crying over CGI snakes on his motherfucking plane, Kuei was wrangling up the real deal, close, personal, and right up in your grill. Unfortunately, as with the case of, **CANNIBAL HOLOCAUST**, real animals were harmed, and killed during the filming, so those with PETA sensibilities are well advised to steer clear.

KILLER SNAKES is the touching tale of a vengeful Young man, and his love for his cold blooded pets. After being beaten, tormented, and humiliated by just about everyone under the sun, our angry lead finds himself compelled to introduce his tormentors to his serpentine family. No space is too tight for our scaly cast, and before you can say, 'step into my orifice', the snakes make their presence known, and leave no 'gap', unoccupied. People are bitten, constricted, and violated by the venomous extras, and it's safe to say that the sale of rubber snakes definitely dropped in China after this sleazy scaly gem was released.

Kuei would go on in the following years to direct a string of sleazy titles including the 'Hex' series of horror films, Corpse Mania (Si Yui), and Killer Constable (Wan ren zan), again with Kuan Tai Chen in 1981. It would not be until 1983, that Chih Hung Kuei would come to direct his most acclaimed crown jewel of bug fuck lunacy, **THE BOXER'S OMEN** (Mo).

While seen by some as an updated companion to the 'Black Magic' series, the film easily transcends all assumptions and comparisons. **BOXER'S OMEN**, was created as the Shaw's answer to the Indonesian horror craze with such films as 1981's **MYSTICS IN BALI** (Leak), and 1983's of **QUEEN OF BLACK MAGIC** (Ratu ilmu hitam). Chinese theater goers both in Hong Kong, and on the Mainland had cultivated a long standing curiosity towards the mysterious practices and beliefs of South East Asia. Director Kuei successfully took some of the imagery and symbolism of the Far East, and mixed them with the spiritual tenets of Buddhism in an cinematic psychedelic hoodoo voodoo cocktail. One can only wonder if someone slipped a nice dose of mountain mushrooms into Kuei's green tea, because he must have been tripping balls as he pieced together this wigged out odyssey.

For those of you not in the know, it's by no means of exaggeration that I say that, **THE BOXER'S OMEN** stands as one of the most mind melting insane collection of scenes ever put to film. Many have said that this is the Asian equivalent of Jodorowsky's, **HOLY MOUNTAIN**, in terms of cinematic psychosis, but that barely scratches the surface. To try to completely convey what happens through the course of 105 minutes in the film is like trying to explain a German scat loop to a troop of boy scouts. It's just something that in all good faith cannot and should not be done. The only way to go

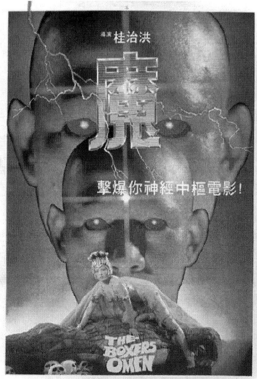

about comprehending the film is to strap yourself in with your glazzies wide open, and let the visual madness pour over your eye sockets like a double dipped purple microdot kiss to the brain.

In a roundabout way, the film follows the standard Shaw brothers plot device of the 'prodigal son', and the quest bestowed upon him to avenge not only his family, but his master. What seemingly starts out as a brutal knock off of the, 'Best of the best', series of films quickly turns into a battle between the spiritual forces of black magic and Buddhism.

The film begins with Bolo Young in the ring playing a Muai-Thai kick boxer up against the Chinese local. After a demonstration by Bolo of his, 'dirty cheating bastard' style of Muai Thai, Chan Wai is paralyzed with a broken neck. Chan's brother, Chan Hung is a local gangster, who is suddenly haunted by images of a mysterious Buddhist monk, via Jedi style. In a promise to his brother to defeat Bolo, and claim revenge, Chang Hung travels to Thailand to challenge him. During his travels, he soon discovers a Buddhist temple, and finally meets Quing Zhao, the Monk that has been plaguing his dreams. Soon Chan Hung learns of an ancient connection to the monk, now a living mummified corpse poisoned by an evil Black Wizard. It has to be noted that the evil Wizard looks like a withered version of Jimi Hendrix, who is skilled in mixing up pea soup poison in the rotting head of a corpse, and commanding an army of spiders to drink it. One incredible aspect of the film is its reliance on bare bones practical effects. The bats skeletons are plastic, and the spiders and various forms of beasties may be made up of puppets and bladders, but goddamn if it doesn't fit the film perfectly in enhancing its wacked out surrealism. Sure, some will scoff at the effects and over all 'cheese' factor, but think again. If you look beyond the budget restraints, and limitations, you can see that Kuei adeptly, 'pulls a Bava', and puts more style and creativity into, **BOXER'S OMEN**, than a handful of films with ten times the budget.

When the Evil Jimi Hendrix wizard gets together with his brothers to battle the young acolyte, shit hits the fan. After digesting raw chicken innards, and yacking them up only to be eaten again, and vomited, they use them in ritual to resurrect the body of an evil queen hibernating in the belly of an actual crocodile corpse.

As Chan Hung does his best to save the soul of the dying monk, and battle the evil wizards, Chan becomes a monk himself, and develops specific techniques and tactics to prevail. During a showdown with the Jimmy Hendrix wizard, Chan adopts the lotus position, and begins to chant. Suddenly, an endless string of Sutra prayers flow across his body like digital code, and act as armor, shielding him from attack. The effect is simple, yet meaningful in projecting the spiritual aspects of the film. This is where, **BOXER'S OMEN**, also shares a connection to, **THE HOLY MOUNTAIN**. Both films are steeped in mysticism, but where Jodorowsky set out to criticize the collective perspectives of religion and spirituality, Kuei attempts to show actual enlightenment, and the pure values contained in Buddhism.

After all is said and done, **BOXER'S OMEN**, is comparable to a night on the skids with a bottle of tequila. Some of it will turn your guts, and many

Troubling times in **THE BOXER'S OMEN**

may bow out early. For those of you with a strong constitution, and in for the long haul, you're guaranteed a wild ride, that likes of which few have seen. I dare you to watch this once, without being compelled to return for another hit.

Although director Kuei died in 1999, he left behind an amazing career, and a wide filmography to be proud of. Today through the efforts of his son, Kuei Beaver Chan, Kuei's films are getting a chance at a second life, through festival retrospectives, and re-releases. To anyone with an inkling of interest in Hong Kong cinema, I urge you to acquaint yourself with the films of Kuei Chih Hung, one of the true progenitors of Hong Kong genre cinema. • • •

BLOOD BROTHERS:
THE PISTOL-PACKED PASTA DRAMAS OF GIANNI GARKO & KLAUS KINSKI

• Dan Taylor

I'm frequently asked about my fascination with iconic actor Klaus Kinski, whose chaotic career took him from *krimi* and Spaghetti westerns to arthouse smashes and exploitation quickies. My stock answer is that even when he's in a film for five minutes it's usually the best five minutes of the whole flick. Incapable of phoning in a performance that even he probably felt was beneath him, "The German Olivier" almost always rose to the occasion.

This intense on-screen presence could not have made Kinski popular with the other actors who frequently turned up as he hopped from one genre to the next, following the money so to speak. Who wants to share the screen with that kind of intensity? Who can match the chops?

In four films together – **IF YOU MEET SARTANA...PRAY FOR YOUR DEATH** (1968), **I AM SARTANA...YOUR ANGEL OF DEATH** (1969), **FIVE FOR HELL** (also 1969) and **THE PRICE OF DEATH** (1971) – Kinski matched wits with Gianni/John Garko a handsome, rugged-looking, theatrically-trained actor who brought a sly charisma and slow-burn that played perfectly against Kinski's icy, but volatile, personality.

Given this issue's Spaghetti/Euro-Western theme I'll take a look at all but the World War II flick **FIVE FOR HELL**, though it may be the best of the bunch.

"I Feel as if a Ghost Were Following Me"

Part magician, part gunslinger and part Angel of Death (with a smidgen of Old West James Bond thrown in for good measure), Sartana ranks right up there with the most iconic of all Spaghetti Western characters. As portrayed by Gianni Garko (and, in one entry, George Hilton) in the series' "official" flicks, Sartana was inspired by Garko's villainous turn as a character named, er, Sartana in 1966's **BLOOD AT SUNDOWN**.

Popular enough that **SUNDOWN** was retitled **SARTANA** in some territories, savvy filmmakers set about to make a series of flicks featuring the character, though they smartly twisted his allegiance from wrong to right. Unfortunately, failure to properly copyright the character led to a series of Sartana knock-offs in much the same vein as Django. The two would even appear together in Miles Deem's 1970 flick **DJANGO AND SARTANA ARE COMING... IT'S THE END** (aka **SARTANA, IF YOUR LEFT ARM OFFENDS... CUT IT OFF**).

And no, I didn't make up that title.

1968's **PRAY FOR YOUR DEATH** is the first film in the official Sartana canon, and begins the love affair the filmmakers had for the comically wordy titles. (My favorite is still 1970's **HAVE A GOOD FUNERAL MY FRIEND... SARTANA WILL PAY**.) Directed by Gianfranco Parolini (credited as Frank Kramer), the flick immediately establishes the mysterious and deadly Sartana as an almost supernatural avenger. Dressed in black and red with a cape inspired by Lee Falk's comic strip hero Mandrake the Magician, Sartana rides a pale horse, his long-range rifle frequently perched atop his shoulder like a scythe.

Little is known about the character and neither Parolini nor the slew of credited writers make much effort to fill in the blanks. Is he a bounty hunter? An agent of the insurance company? A lawman? A card sharp? A mercenary? A ghost? Um, sure!

As is often the case in such flicks we open with a stagecoach being attacked – this time by a gang of marauders led by detached, long-range killer Morgan (icy cold Klaus Kinski). Despite appearing to have been struck by the hidden killer (a frequent contrivance throughout the series), Sartana pops back up and lays waste to Morgan's lackeys thanks to his trusty four-barreled derringer. As he tells one mouthy thug before offing him, "I am your pallbearer".

In terms of character introductions, it's absolutely first-rate and no wonder Sartana/Garko was so popular with audiences. While Clint Eastwood's trend-setting Man with No Name projects an icy, unflappable cool, Sartana exudes far more charisma and charm, as well as a capricious sense of humor that immediately wins you over.

Unfortunately, the rest of **PRAY FOR DEATH** falls into the typically-overplotted Spaghetti Western trap complete with ambushers being ambushed, exponential double crosses, extraneous characters, strongboxes filled with rocks, coffins filled with gold, sweaty generals gnawing on chicken legs and, that old chestnut, the musical pocket watch that strikes fear in the hearts of every villain.

Kinski – who receives the always-deflating "And the Special Participation Of" credit – brings his trademark penetrating stare and devilish smirk to his role as Morgan, the cat-like hitman of Lasky (hammy William Berger, who in a twist of irony, would play Sartana in a 1970 knock-off entitled **SARTANA IN THE VALLEY OF THE VULTURES**).

Garko and Kinski only have a few scenes together – a confrontation in a barber shop and subsequent duel in the undertaker's lair (one of the flick's

best sets) – but the two actors and their characters play off one another nicely. Kinski's clean-shaven, cool-as-ice killer prefers keeping his hands clean as he practices his craft while Garko's dusty, bearded gunslinger isn't afraid to get up close and personal when doing the job. The pair inject the film with some badly-needed sparks and it's unfortunate one of them has to leave far too early.

Spoiler alert... it's not Sartana.

Morgan's departure leaves us with a gaggle of baddies for Sartana to pit against one another, from the wild-eyed Morgan and Frito Bandito-esque General Mendoza (Fernando Sancho) to conniving businessmen Stewal (Syndey Chaplin), Alman (Gianni Rizzo) and their ladies but it's obvious none will be a match for our anti-hero.

"I Am Your Gravedigger"

For 1969's **I AM SARTANA…YOUR ANGEL OF DEATH**, new director Giuliano Carnimeo resolved one of the first flick's biggest problems: NEK or Not Enough Kinski.

In this, the series' second installment, Garko returns as the mysterious Sartana, Frank Wolff from **THE GREAT SILENCE** turns up as Sartana's snitch pal Buddy Ben (replacing Dusty the Undertaker as the hero's sounding board), and the always-reliable Kinski lends his support in a surprisingly good-natured role as a gambling-addicted bounty hunter with the awesome name of Hot Dead. Yes, Hot Dead.

When Sartana is falsely accused of robbing a bank of $300,000 he finds himself with a $10,000 bounty on his head. Not surprisingly, this kind of coin brings enemies, friends and casual acquaintances of the derringer-packing gunman out of the woodwork looking to collect... dead or alive. Traveling the countryside, Sartana tracks down clues, gets into adventures, and kills somewhere around a hundred or so of the most incredibly inept gunslingers ever to strap on a six-shooter.

Unfortunately, the episodic nature of Sartana's travels makes for a storyline that never engages. The flick doesn't so much progress as it meanders lazily and it feels like there are a bazillion side characters all of whom have connections to our anti-hero, yet I never really cared about them. Mostly they were little more than corpse fodder as Sartana gets to the bottom of the faux heist.

Which is too bad because Garko once again exudes an irresistible screen presence as the smug, self-assured Sartana. No cuffs can hold him, no number of gunslingers rattles him, all of which does him a disservice because we never feel like the character is in any danger. It's not unlike what happened to James Bond in many of the post-**GOLDFINGER** outings with Sean Connery and Roger Moore; the character became less of a secret agent and more of an indestructible super-hero whose life never really hangs in the balance.

As for Hot Dead, Kinski is downright charming as the unrepentant gambler who uses his side job as a bounty hunter to fund his addiction. In one of his standout scenes he discovers that the friendly game of poker he's playing on a stagecoach is rigged. When the stagecoach is robbed Hot Dead coolly dispenses with the gunmen and has their bodies thrown aboard so he can stake his game with the bounties on their heads. He even has his own little theme music, though it sounds vaguely like a Christmas carol by way of Nashville.

It's a surprisingly light role for the notoriously high-strung Kinski and makes for an interesting flip-side to other Spaghetti Western entries in his filmography like Loco, the brutal bounty hunter that steals the show in Sergio Corbucci's **THE GREAT SILENCE**.

Unfortunately, it feels like too much time went into coming up with colorful names like Hot Dead, Butch Dynamite, Slim Shotgun and Tracey Three Aces and not enough time on coming up with a good story. While Garko, Kinski and Wolff give it their best, this Sartana adventure comes up a little short.

"Call me Mr. Silver!"

As you may have guessed while reading this article, I am not what you would call a huge fan of Spaghetti/Euro-Westerns. Despite being brought up watching the Man with No Name flicks on local UHF and trying my damndest to appreciate the genre, I've just never been able to get into them. Even the best can be over-plotted to the point of becoming impossible to follow and most rely heavily on plot contrivances that become exhausting after a while. And yet, I love slasher flicks. Go figure.

The best way to get me to enjoy most Euro-Westerns is to dispense with the dreary, shopworn clichés and simply execute another genre in a western setting. For instance, **MAN, PRIDE & VENGEANCE** (1968) spins 'Carmen' through a noir filter while **BLACK KILLER** (1971) has elements of a caper flick flirting around its edges.

But the best of the western mash-ups I've seen has to be 1971's **THE PRICE OF DEATH**, which deftly pulls off a private detective story/thriller/*Giallo* set in the Old West.

Garko is great as Silver, a hot-shot hired gunman/private eye. "Call me Mr. Silver!" he insists more than once in the flick, occasionally slapping the person to whom he's talking. Silver accepts a job from his old pal Jeff (Franco Abbiana), a frontier lawyer with a taste for the bottle. Jeff's latest client has landed in jail, suspected of armed robbery and multiple murders. It comes as no surprise that the client is played by Klaus Kinski, and he infuses Chester Conway – town black sheep – with plenty of flippant, sneering attitude, even in the face of the gallows that are to hang him being built outside his jail cell window.

Silver comes to the town of Applebee Junction to get to the bottom of the casino robbery gone wrong that landed Conway in the pokey. It seems that three masked men burst into the house of loose cards and looser women, killed a working girl and a bartender, then absconded with about $200 in cash. Two members of the trio ended up dead in the aftermath and Conway

11

is the lone suspect in the caper, due in part to the bloody money in his possession, but largely because he's widely reviled by the townsfolk. A long history of drinking, fighting, troublemaking and stealing other guys's gals has left him without many friends. In other words, Kinski was probably the best possible guy to play him.

Naturally, the shifty, good-for-nothing Conway has an alibi for the night in question, but he's unwilling to give up his whereabouts during the robbery. Even to the lawyer trying to save his neck.

Thanks to some quick detective work (he buys the clothes the dead robbers were wearing from the undertaker) Silver deduces that the sheriff couldn't have possibly shot the fleeing robbers and that there's more to Applebee Junction than meets the eye.

While **THE PRICE OF DEATH** could have benefitted from a few less amateurish performances from some of the peripheral townsfolk, the core actors are all great in their parts. Garko channels his inner-Sartana and does a slight riff on the charming two-fisted, derringer-packing rogue who finds himself at odds with the whole town. In their rush to hang Conway for a crime he didn't commit they conveniently overlook the real killer in their midst, not to mention the hypocrisy and corruption running rampant through the town. Kinski plays most of his part from a jail cell but communicates more emotion and range with his eyes and contempt-filled sneer than the rest of the cast together (Garko excluded) could muster. Even when he's facing certain death he has time to flirt with Pollie (Gely Genka), the luscious casino manager who disappears from the film far too quickly.

THE PRICE OF DEATH may have been the duo's final on-screen pairing, but I can't think of a better coda to their all-too-brief collaborative career than this highly entertaining detective western.

It wouldn't be long before Kinski's star-making turn in Werner Herzog's **AGUIRE, THE WRATH OF GOD** (1972) would elevate him beyond the *krimi*, *giallo* and Spaghetti Westerns that had paid his bills for decades, though he'd spend the years until his death in 1991 pinballing between the arthouse and the grindhouse thanks to roles in everything from **NOSFERATU, PHANTOM DER NACHT** (1979) and **COBRA VERDE** (1987) to **ANDROID** (1982), **CREATURE** (1985) and **CRAWLSPACE** (1986).

Garko – now in his late 70s – would appear in a few more westerns, but nothing with the impact of his role as Sartana. Some of his most famous films post-Sartana include the recently released on DVD shocker **NIGHT OF THE DEVILS** (1972), the Henry Silva crime flick **THE BOSS** (1972), Lucio Fulci's **THE PSYCHIC** (1977), Lamberto Bava's **DEVIL FISH** (1984) in which he's reunited with **PRAY FOR DEATH** co-star William Berger, and as a dickish police chief in 1992's **BODY PUZZLE**. Most of the actor's recent work has been for Italian television.

...

Five for Hell (aka Five Into Hell/1969)

William Tecumseh Sherman once said "War is hell". Apparently, he never trained under the watchful eye of Lt. Hoffman (Gianni Garko billed here as John Garko), a gum-chewing, softball "throwing" GI charged with assembling a team of crack soldiers for a deadly suicide mission… as if there's any other kind.

In the flick's goofy pre-credit sequence, Hoffman rides through the training fields, watching soldiers prep for what must be an upcoming war against Cirque du Soleil. They swing past trenches on parallel bars, acrobatically dispatch enemy combatants, and even spring over treacherous barbed wire thanks to handy trampolines.

Hoffman hand picks his suicide squad and ends up with the acrobatic Nick (Aldo Canti), musclebound McCarthy (Luciano Rossi), safecracking Siracusa (Sal Borgese), and Johnny White (Sam Burke), an explosives expert whose glasses and mousy nature make him a natural for the nickname "Chicken".

Their mission? Break into the Nazi stronghold at Villa Verde and get a look at the documents for Hitler's devious "Plan K". With the Allies blocked "at the foot of the Gustav line" details of the plan could save the lives of 50,000 soldiers.

After a dry run that tests all of their trampoline-bouncing, softball-throwing, safe-cracking acumen, the team assembles in their barracks and dances around far more than I suspect was really going on during WWII.

But that's about as far as the lightheartedness of this action-comedy goes and **FIVE FOR HELL** – directed by **IF YOU MEET SARTANA … PRAY FOR YOUR DEATH** helmer Gianfranco Parolini (billed as Frank Kramer) – quickly shifts gears and turns into a surprisingly gritty, tense mission flick.

Helping the squad in their covert operation is curvy double agent Helga

Richter (Eurotrash icon Margaret Lee), a cold and conniving member of the Villa Verde staff who isn't above covering her own ass or exposing it, depending upon the situation.

As if this wasn't enough, **FIVE FOR HELL** (aka **FIVE INTO HELL**) features the great Klaus Kinski in a meaty supporting role as the sinister SS Colonel Hans Muller.

Kinski, who was born to star as a sinister Nazi, lights up the screen as the evil and suspicious colonel who butts heads with General Gerbordstadt (Irio Fantini), the Villa's commandant, and desperately wants to get into Helga's pants, even though he suspects her of being a spy who framed her lover for murder. Kinski infuses Muller with an almost giddy charm as he pursues Lee, finally tightening the noose around her neck until she has no options left.

Though it's a bit of a stretch to buy the obviously Italian stars traipsing around in German uniforms – a fact the script actually addresses in one standoff with SS guards – the screenplay by Parolini and Renato Izzo (from a story by Sergio Garrone) keeps the action moving with enough gun battles, chases and explosions that you're more than willing to suspend your disbelief. By the time the 42% Dirty Dozen begins their assault on the villa you won't care that only two of the members of the squad speak Deutsch (which makes the others wonder if they're spies) or that Garko throws like he's having an epileptic fit.

Thanks to a nerve-wracking villa assault, a willingness to kill any member of the cast, an action-packed finale and great performances from the always-reliable pair of Garko and Kinski, **FIVE FOR HELL** totally delivers. •

FIVE FOR HELL can be found in many cheapo WWII DVD packages and an anamorphic widescreen version has been known to be floating around.

A PISTOLRY OF VIOLENCE: OBSERVATIONS IN BRIGHT RED

• Steven Ronquillo

Since **THE GREAT TRAIN ROBBERY** (1903), the first recorded western film, westerns have always been about "BANG! BANG! I'll shoot you dead!" and "Argh! You got me!" theatrics. For the most part, this article is about the history and major benchmarks in screen violence in the western genre. We have to start with **THE GREAT TRAIN ROBBERY** because it had characters shooting at the gotamn screen, which was quite shocking back in the early 1900s. There were even reports of fainting and panic thanks to that particular sequence, that's how much of an impact the new medium that was cinema had on the movie-going public.

From there we got into mostly goody goody, milk-drinking, shooting from the hip style cowboy westerns, referred to as Oaters. Actor William S. Hart didn't like them at all, he wanted to star in gritty, realistic westerns and he finally got the chance with his final film, **TUMBLEWEEDS** (1925), a film he not only starred in but produced and co-directed as well. The 1968 film **WILL PENNY**, starring Charlton Heston, is basically a remake of **TUMBLEWEEDS** so if you've seen it then you've seen this one. In the original, Hart plays a cowboy at the end of his tumble weed days, looking to finally settle down. Sadly, because of his violent past, he can never really be at home anywhere. In the end he sacrifices his own happiness in order for his lover to have her own happy ending. The film takes place during the great land rush when the west truly died so this is also the first of the "Death of the West" sub-sub-genre films, which became a big focus in a few of the productions I will discuss later in this article.

But sadly back then they were like nowadays, they wanted pop entertainment and not something to make them think so it was a flop, causing Hart to go into retirement. From there we have to go into the '40s and **INVITATION TO A GUNFIGHTER**. Gregory Peck plays a gunfighter who is trying to outrun his past and reconnect with his wife and kid he had to leave once he hit the outlaw trail. But he finds it hard as with his reputation he is either branded a trouble maker and not wanted in the town, or having to deal with every punk with a gun wanting to make their rep taking out the a.no1 badass. The whole movie has him movie around with a paranoid stance as he is always watching over his back. And at the end when he is finally backshot by some young 21 year-old wannabe badass punk he doesn't feel bad but he smiles. And when the kid asks him why is he smiling he says, well now I'm free but you your gonna have everyone who was gunning for me coming after you. You will never have a ounce of peace or a good night's sleep until another pissant like you shoots you down and that is why I'm smiling because I don't have to run any more. If that doesn't sum up why living the outlaw life sucks ass I don't know what does imo.

Next is Sam Fuller's **I SHOT JESSE JAMES** about Bob Ford, the man who shot Jesse James. It's less about the murder than how one bad choice done for the right reason can destroy your life. Bob Ford's choice to shoot Jesse in the back is given lots of homoerotic subtext with lots of innuendo and other subtle touches Fuller put in shows a different side of the cowboy mythos. Fuller always puts in his life experience as a reporter and a WWII vet so to him killing a man is the most horrible thing you can do because it will always stick to you and be a part of your character and life.

But in **I SHOT JESSE JAMES** the real problem is every reason he did it blows up in his face. His girl leaves him, everyone thinks he's a coward and he is reviled and Jesse is made the hero, and most important is the reward he was promised is not given to him and all he has in the end is his regrets. My favorite scene is when in a saloon a traveling song smith starts singing a song about the dirty coward Robert Ford and then realizes that it's the real Robert Ford there so he stops. But Robert makes him keep singing with him realizing where he really stands in the world. It's a nasty bitter pill to swallow but it's another step in western violence history.

Next is another Sam Fuller film **FORTY GUNS**. the hero in this is like a lot of men Sam met in WWII where he didn't kill because of some sense of honor or code, but he didn't kill because he liked killing and when he got the gun in his hands he became a machine killing anything and anyone in his path till he got his target. Sam visualized with a lot of weird shots and the original ending was to be the bad guy pulling the woman in his way but he just shoots through her to kill him killing her to but they made him change it because they didn't want a killer that cold-blooded as their hero. So at the original fade out they put in a shot of the woman supposedly killed in the prior scene. But still this is a brutal slap in the face for western fans and it only got rougher from here.

But for the true next step that was spaghetti westerns we first have to go to the slice of a sword because the spaghetti westerns took a lot of their mood and style from the samurai code of honor and Kurasowa's four samurai films of the '50s set the mold from **SEVEN SAMURAI** pitting desperate men against overwhelming odds to the amoral tone

13

of **SANJURO** and **YOJIMBO**'s heroes, the violent, blood-filled samurai genre paved the way for the path spaghettis would take. And the pioneer wasn't Leone, as many assume, but Sergio Corbucci with his dark and angry westerns.

His earliest violent epic was **MINNESOTA CLAY**, about a gunfighter looking for revenge as he is going blind. Then soon after that he did **NAVAHO JOE** a gory, violent epic that featured Burt Reynolds as an Indian on the warpath. It is perhaps the darkest and grimmest TV spinoff ever made. One also cannot forget his beloved masterpiece **DJANGO**, which sadly never came out over here in the States so we never got the impact of it. Uncut this is a graphic, bloody film with severed ears, a whore whipping and crushed hands. But the semi-happy ending left Corbucci with a sour taste in his mouth, leading us to his next film **THE GREAT SILENCE**.

THE GREAT SILENCE is a movie so violent and bleak there was no way in hell, even in the '70s, it would have received a US release. Even the hero is scarred by violence after bounty hunters cut his vocal chords as a child. As the film starts, a Mormon group has to hide in the mountains as there is a bounty on their heads and they are killed on sight. Enter our hero, Silence, whose modus operandi is goading someone into a fight until they draw their weapon on him, giving him a legal reason to blow their faces off. Hired by the distraught mother of a bounty hunting victim, Silence seeks to kill Loco (Klaus Kinski).

Unbelievably, this film is partially based on a real incident, "The Mountain Meadows massacre." Knowing this you should assume, if you didn't before, that there was no happy ending. The ending of this film is so polarizing that I have had friends call me an asshole based solely on the last two minutes but it's real and ugly, just like life.

Now for Sam Peckinpah, no one writing about violence in westerns can escape **THE WILD BUNCH**, the first splatter western and the best of the death of the west genre.

THE WILD BUNCH is set so far after the death of the west that cars are semi-commonplace and they even talk about planes. The bunch themselves are a group of aging bandits who are doing the only job they know how to do. The opening massacre shows that the laws of the land are getting just as brutal and cutthroat as the criminals are when most of the damage done is to innocent civilians in a shower of gore and blood, unseen in mainstream westerns before.

The remainder of the film involves them trying to get a shipment of guns to a Mexican dictator, hoping to fund their retirement and how it all goes to hell. The finale is one of the most infamously bloody shootouts in cinematic history with a word record for squibs set. I don't think this record has been broken yet, not even by **SCARFACE**'s final squibfest. Needless to say, the whole western film game had changed and nothing would ever be the same again.

Now we are getting into the US gore westerns which were very splattery and can be divided up into two categories,'"Nam is Bad" and "Hey let's just kill some folks and make it bloody as hell!"

The 'Nam wannabe sub-sub-genre involved filmmakers using the western to illustrate their opposition to the war by using the us Indian massacres as a backdrop. I'm going to talk about the two most famous ones:

LITTLE BIG MAN is about Jack Crabbe, a 100 year-old man who claimed to be the only white man to survive Little Big Horn. It is the first of the modern revisionist westerns to show the Indians as the good guys and the white as murderers. There are a few massacre scenes in this movie they aren't as over-the-top as the ones in my next film but they are quite violent. Once you hear the flutes and drums begin to play, signifying a cavalry charge, you know that some kind of ugliness is going to happen. But, unlike my next selection, they don't drum it over your head using a baby's corpse.

SOLDIER BLUE (a.k.a WHITE GUILT: THE MOVIE!), is a nasty mess that builts up to gory and disturbing massacre sequences, sandwiching in 90 minutes of two whites bitching at one another about why being white sucks. This one goes for the gross-out value with rape, disemboweling and, yes, a baby's head being crushed and splattered on a rock. The filmmakers hope to show how much they care for the poor Indians by having one of the whites cry while the other vomits. It's the gore equivalent of showing hardcore sex just to show how bad it is. This isn't as nasty as the last film in my article but its mean-spiritedness surpasses them all. I once read a review which stated that the filmmakers wanted to outdo **THE WILD BUNCH** and boy how did they do it....

The last two films are the "Gorestern" films. They have no point other than doing bloody, nasty scenes and there's not one iota of the stink of white guilt or any other kind of politics in them:

THE HUNTING PARTY is about a noble bandit who kidnaps a rancher's wife because he wants to learn to read and how he gently rapes her into loving him. And then her husband SHOOTS THE SHIT OUT OF THEM. This is all about the killing, like when he shoots off their kneecaps and elbows and just tortures them to death. Slow, sick and nasty this is 20 minutes of pure brutality to cap off 90 plus minutes of boredom. But when it gets sick...wooo boy!

The last is the most insane, gore-filled, brutal western ever made, **CUT-THROATS NINE (CONDENADOS A VIVIR)**! There is no reason for this movie to exist other than "Let's throw around a lot of blood and guts!" and by god they do it right. This movie asks the question, "Why have fights or kill scenes if you can't use a lot of blood in it?" From a simple punch to a hole blown through the chest, this is pure gore-soaked fun. For once, a nasty, mean-spirited, gore-soaked western isn't mean-spirited, which makes it jaw-dropping and damn fun.

Well, that pretty much covers my observation of the evolution of the western film, from brooding to blood-soaked fields. There were a few after some of the films I talked about but I'm going to end my article at this point. I hope you enjoyed it and this article makes you want to check these films out!

...

El Ranchera Sobrenatural Películas del Mexicano Chili Westerns Cine

A brief survey of the Mexican Horror Western
• Tim Paxton

Mexico has always had a long love affair with the dead. That country's fascination with the spirit world can be traced back to Mexico's pre-Christian Mesoamerican roots. Most all of you have heard of the great Aztec nation and its obsession with blood sacrifice. Life, food, sex. Our perception of the Aztecs' culture is based on their underlying belief that there is power in death. Death was instrumental in the perpetuation of creation. Aztec idols and pyramids have wormed their way into the Mexican collective consciousness and worldwide pop culture in general. Skull-faced entities swarm the internet as Day of The Dead Festivals are quickly becoming a popular phenomena (although the equally spooky images of Nepalese and Tibetan skeletons are hip and happening). When the Spaniards demolished the Aztec empire and imposed their own brand of blood religion, Christianity, the conquered peoples mixed and melded their strong ethnic beliefs with the spooky European death art of the Church. A similar amalgamation can be seen with the rites of Haitian Vodou. This is not to say that these cultural roots are directly responsible for the creepiness of Mexico's fantastic cinema, but one can not deny the influence.

Moving on from Social Anthropology to the art of movie making, this article will cover a small scrap of Mexico's love of the Western genre, or more specifically, a macabre sub-genre. This is in no way the definitive word on the subject, but a brief survey; an adulation of the absurd. Before we begin I should give you a not so comprehensive list of Mexican Monster Movies that are most commonly found on DVD (gringo titles): **THE BRAINIAC, CURSE OF THE CRYING WOMAN, THE LIVING HEAD, THE WITCH'S MIRROR, THE MAN AND THE MONSTER, DOCTOR OF DOOM, ROBOT VS THE AZTEC MUMMY** and **THE BLOODY VAMPIRE**.

Westerns are something that the Mexicans clearly enjoy. There have always been big and little screen *rancheras, hacienda,* rural comedies and dramas... so why not mix in the supernatural? Clearly, there are quite a few, and as stated previously, this will not be a comprehensive study. Films such as **MONSTER OF THE LOST SWAMP, BEAST OF HOLLOW MOUNTAIN** and **THE BLACK SCORPION** (both US-Mexican co-productions) are popular examples, and films worthy of lengthy reviews themselves.

Mexican genre cinema comes in two flavors: the urban and the rural. What looks to us as a typical Western would take place in and around rural communities which, for the most part, resemble what could be The West. Cowboys are not always evident, nevertheless the open and dusty feel about such rural locations could almost convince you that many of the films are set in the 1880s. In fact, most of the horror westerns are present day, albeit the 1950s onward. Only a random truck, telephone, or other such modern conveniences clues you in on its placement in time. **LA NAVE DE LOS MONSTRUOS, EL CHARROS DE LS CALAVERAS,** and the "El Latigo," "Latigo Negro"and assorted "Zorro" films reflect this. But I am getting ahead of myself...

So hold on to your sombreros, *mi amigos*, because here's a short survey into the weird world of what I like to call *El Ranchera Sobrenatural Películas del Mexicano Chili Westerns Cine.*

If you're familiar with the upside of Mexican monster movie, then you may think you're in for a feast when ghoulies and ghosties mix it up with cowpoke. It was in the mid-1950s that weary producers, hungry for hits, began experimenting with surreal monster movies. Director Fernando Méndez was very familiar with the Western genre by the time he attempted an early mash-up. Méndez was already making popular Westerns that included **LOS AVENTUREROS** (1954), **LOS TRES VILLALOBOS** (1955); and **LA VENGANZA DE LOS VILLALOBOS** (1956). Those horse dramas aside, Méndez's most impressive additions to the Mexican horror lexicon was an incredible run of terror-based films including the fantastic wrestling monster epic **LADRÓN DE CADÁVERES (THE BODY SNATCHER,** 1957), the blood-sucking Germán Robles vampire series **EL VAMPIRO** (1957) and **EL ATAÚD DEL VAMPIRO** (1958), plus the mind-blowing weirdness of **MISTERIOS DE ULTRATUMBA (THE BLACK PIT OF DR. M,** 1959).

The two films that Méndez made just didn't click for me. There was something missing. I was expecting a hoard of vampires assailing sleepy Mexican villages, screaming peasants, and the undead on horseback. Aaaahhh... no. I'll enlighten you further:

LOS DIABLOS DEL TERROR (1957) is one of the earliest examples of the composite genre to emerge out of Mexico, and the first supernatural film produced in full color. Méndez approached his subject matter rather tentatively. The film looks good, as most of his movies typically do, and the masked "devil riders" are spooky enough to entice a chill or two. It's a pity that the element of horror here is left in the dust. The possible terror took a back seat to caballeros hijinks which included our hero's dancing horse, his goofy side kick, the saloon brawls, and the usual suspects for the remainder of the film. The masked riders that terrorize villagers turn out to be considerably less than supernatural.

His next film was **EL GRITO DE LA MUERTE (THE LIVING COFFIN)** made a year later, but the chills were none the better despite the plot hovering

15

SF zaniness when cowboys battle aliens in **LA NAVE DE LOS MONSTRUOS**

around the classic Mexican ghost legend of *La Llonora*, aka The Weeping/Crying Woman[1]. The film is dull and boring to the point of distraction. Why money was spent on a color film this bad and not on something like the next Western is beyond me.

1957 was a rich year for fantastic and weird films, in both the USA and Mexico, which is why Méndez's film were such a disappointment. In the US we cranked out many of my favorite all time SF/Horror films: **KRONOS, THE INCREDIBLE SHRINKING MAN, 20 MILLION MILES TO EARTH, INVASION OF THE SAUCERMEN, THE GIANT CLAW, THE 27TH DAY, THE UNDEAD, MONOLITH MONSTERS,** and **NOT OF THIS EARTH**. Had I grown up in Mexico I would have experienced a slightly different horror movie boom. Vampires, witches, monsters *and weird westerns*. Director Chano Urueta had his hands full with three "El Jinete Sin Cabeza" movies that fell into this crossover genre.

Director Urueta's unique vision and apparent love of the unusual led him to lens some of Mexico's classiest horror films... and, with **EL BARÓN DEL TERROR (THE BRAINIAC)** in 1962, definitely the weirdest. It took a while, but I eventually tracked down the "Headless Horseman" trilogy; **EL JINETE SIN CABEZA** ("The Headless Horseman"), **LA MARCA DE SATANÁS** ("The Mask of Satan"), and **LA CABEZA DE PANCHO VILLA** ("The Head of Pancho Villa") in the hopes of uncovering something monstrous. Turns out that this trio of films aren't as supernatural as the titles would suggest. The hero of these entertaining tales is "The Headless Horseman", a singing cowboy super sleuth that, along with his silly side kick, battles mysterious monsters and ghastly ghosts. Definitely weird Westerns, but like three Spanish-language episodes of "Scooby Doo," the paranormal threat in all three films turns out to be a disgruntled relative or crafty criminal.

Next up is the rarely seen film **EL REGRESO DEL MONSTRUO**, a 1959 monster Western made by Joselito Rodríguez. This is an honest-to-God monster movie! Rodríguez, like his director brethren, was responsible for all sorts of genre films including monster comedies (**PEPITO Y EL MONSTRUO**, 1957), Luchedore thrillers (**SANTO CONTRA HOMBRES INFERNALES**, 1961), and action dramas such as the "Huracán Ramirez" series. From what I understand, all three feature a Zorro variant known as "El Zorro Escarlata" or The Red Fox. All three El Zorro Escarlata films formed a trilogy which ran more or less in three parts like a serial, each episode just over 20 minutes long. **EL REGRESO DEL MONSTRUO** is the second or third installment to feature El Zorro Escarlata, a handsome hero that happily involves himself in eliminating the supernatural from our daily lives. As with a lot of the *ranchero sobrenatural cine* genre, there is a certain uncertain ambiguity as to the period in which the film takes place. Everything looks like the 1880s until the scientific aspect of the film kicks in.

It should be noted that the source media I acquired for **EL REGRESO DEL MONSTRUO** is from an incomplete print. As the credits role we are presented with "Episodio Segundo: El Esqueleto Viviente" (Episode Two: The Living Skeleton). The film opens as the sinister mad scientist, Dr. Kraken, who had previously discovered the talking skeleton of an undead witch and her monster son, experiments with the undead in the celler of his old hacienda. The monster of the film is a huge bald creature that runs amok and kills and maims the good folk of a local village. Dr. Kraken controls the creature by way of a magical ring which belongs to the witch (á la scientific mumbo jumbo). El Zorro Escarlata catches wind of the evil-doers and sets about to stop the trio of terror. After a series of close calls, El Zorro Escarlata gathers up a group of brave torch toting *caballeros* and leads an attack on Dr. Kraken's secret lab. The scientist and living skeleton perish in a flaming holocaust and the monster dies when the link to his existence, the ring, melts in the flames.

EL REGRESO DEL MONSTRUO is fast paced action, in the classic serial sense of the word, with some tremendous fight scenes (typically where our hero gets his ass kicked severely by the monster). There are some confusing plot issues, but that may be due to my inadequate knowledge of Spanish, or possibly that this film is a sequel to **EL ZORRO ESCARLATA EN LAS VENGANZA DEL AHORADO** (1958) or **EL ZORRO ESCARLATA** (1959). By the way, all three films were made by the one and only Rafael Baledón, director of the exceptional **ORLAK, EL INFIERNO DE FRANKENSTEIN** ("The Hell of Frankenstein", 1960). But since the two other "El Zorro Escarlata" productions are currently considered lost, I've had a hard time verifying the actual order of the films.

If **EL REGRESO DEL MONSTRUO** sounded cool our next feature kicks it to the curb. Director Rogelio A. González's crazy, zany, wacky and wholly absurd **LA NAVE DE LOS MONSTRUOS** (popularly known as "The Ship of Monsters" even though it has yet to get any proper DVD release in the US)

---

[1] A very popular theme in many Mexican films: from early film **LA LLORONA** (1933, "The Weeping Woman", D: Ramón Peón) to the classic we all know and love with **LA MALDICIÓN DE LA LLORONA** (1961, **CURSE OF THE CRYING WOMAN**, D: Rafael Baledón), to newer approaches with **CURSE OF LA LLORONA** (2007, D: Terrance Williams), and the cartoon **LA LEYENDA DE LA LLORONA** (2011, "Legend of the Crying Woman", D: Alberto Rodriguez).

delivers the goods in preverbal spades! A singing cowboy must match wits with two gorgeous alien amazons and a spaceship of killer critters. González was not new to the bizarre as he had a weirdly satisfying ghost comedy the previous year called **DOS FANTASMAS Y UNA MUCHACHA** ("Two Ghosts and The Lady"). The year he made **LA NAVE DE LOS MONSTRUOS** González also created the critically acclaimed **EL ESQUELETO DE LA SEÑORA MORALES** ("The Skeleton of Mrs. Morales") about a sexually repressed taxidermist, his deformed wife and his collection of stuffed animals. Being a prolific director (like many Mexican filmmakers of his generation) González later lensed the rarely seen **DR. SATÁN Y LA MAGIA NEGRA** in 1968, a sequel to the under-rated supernatural thriller **DR. SATÁN** (1966, D: Miguel Morayta).

The film opens on the planet Venus, a world populated by beautiful Amazons. There are no men on their planet, and two courageous females are sent on a mission to gather up as many men as they can from the different planets in our solar system. They pluck the finest example of male bioforms from an odd assortment of populated worlds and put them in cold storage on their spaceship. En route to Venus, an onboard emergency forces them to land on Earth (Chihuahua, Mexico to be exact) for repairs, and that's when the fun begins.

Our sexy ladies (the ravishing Ana Bertha Lepe and Lorena Velázquez, my personal favorite Mexican actress of all time) find themselves on a backwater world with their robot Torr. No sooner than the two amazons are out of their ship, they run into a *charreada*, or singing cowboy. Our hero mistakes them for lost American women and offers to help in anyway he can. In the meantime the monsters on the ship are relocated to a cave for safe keeping.

Besides great musical numbers, you have Lepe and Velázquez as well as a classic line up of monsters: the Dwarfish BEM Martian prince Tawal, the huge cyclopean reptilian Uk from "the fire planet," The arachnid alien Crassus of "the Red Planet," Zok the spooky talking dog skeleton from some unnamed part of our solar system, and finally Torr, the huge robot star of numerous genre films including the absurd classic (and a personal favorite) **LA MOMIA AZTECA CONTRA EL ROBOT HUMANO (ROBOT VS THE AZTEC MUMMY**, 1959; D: Rafael Portillo). Partnering with the sexy Beta (Velázquez), who turns out to be a vampire, the monsters plan on taking over the Earth rather than being carted off to Venus (and not as breeding stock, since the earth men are found to be more desirable). The battle is on!

I am baffled as to why **LA NAVE DE LOS MONSTRUOS** isn't on DVD in the States. The film begs for a proper release, although it is currently available on Spanish language DVD, but, alas, without the option for English subtitles.

1965 saw a few additional entries into the *El cine Mexicano sobrenatural* lexicon including Santo battling **EL HACHA DIABÓLICA** ("The Diabolical Axe," José Díaz Morales), cave dwelling bat monsters in **AVENTURA AL CENTRO DE LA TIERRA** ("Adventures at the Center of the Earth"[2]) and the following Westerns: Vicente Oroná's **LOS JINETES DE LA BRUJA, EN EL VIEJO GUANAJUATO** ("The Witch and the Riders of Old Guanajuato), Alfredo B. Crevenna's **PUEBLO FANTASMA** ("Ghost Town"), and Alfredo Salazar's **EL CHARRO DE LAS CALAVAERAS** ("Rider of the Skulls").

Vicente Oroná's **LOS JINETES DE LA BRUJA, EN EL VIEJO GUANAJUATO** ("Riders and the Witch, in Old Guanajuato") a colorful tale of witchcraft, mysterious riders, bumbling caballeros (you must have a funny sidekick in every film for some reason), and puppet ghosts. Yes, it's a supernatural revenge tale centered around the spectral vengeance of a murdered

[2] A film seen to believed. I can't understand how this failed to get released in the US theatrically or on TV. A group of scientist venture into the bowels of the earth only to be terrorized by bat monsters – incredibly incredible creature costumes at that. There is an English subtitled version on YouTube, though.

puppeteer. Not a great film, although the entire puppet aspect does give the film some creepiness.

The deadly *bruja* in the film is played by the pretty actress Kitty de Hoyos who was a staple in many a Western in the 50s and 60s. Her roles in fantasy films include the SF thriller **AVENTURA AL CENTRO DE LA TIERRA**, the starring role in **LAS LOBAS** ("The She-Wolf", director Rafael Baledón's odd werewolf film), and the ghostly comedy **LOS CUERVOS ESTÁN DE LUTO** ("The Crows are Mourning", D: Francisco del Villar). Director Vicente Oroná's filmography is primarily Western-based, and includes three 1950s "El Látigo Negro" movies that hint at supernatural elements, but don't contain any actual spooks.

Next up is Alfredo B. Crevenna's 1965 **PUEBLO FANTASMA**, a film situated smack dab in the middle of the director's lengthy 150+ filmography. This early western/horror mash up is the one of the best of the cowboy horror films, and so much better than his later "El Latigo" series.

A 200 year old vampire sets out to track down, kill and then drink the blood of assorted bad men so that he can absorb their evil essence. Our monster, a handsome man in black, goes by the name of The Rio Kid and he may or may not be as evil as he seems. But then again, he is a vampire so he has his nice guy routine down pat to cover his ulterior motive: to drain the blood of everyone is a small rural Mexican town. It's up to a Texan gunfighter to try and stop the vampire, although he is mistrusted by spiteful villagers because of his late murderous father.

In fact, our modern era of popular vampire films, wherein bloodsuckers are more than often heroes than villains, the undead gunslinger that appears in **PUEBLO FANTASMA** could have been subject of numerous sequels. **PUEBLO** reflects the director's love of a good looking film that went haywire by the time he was given the job to do handle the first two "El Latigo" films.

The look and feel of **PUEBLO FANTASMA** is classic 60s Mexican gothic with a Western twist. The film oozes with wonderful black and white cinematography thanks to the knowing lens of Fernando Colin, the man who created atmosphere for other many other Mexican horror classics including **ORLAK, EL INFIERNO DE FRANKENSTEIN, EL ROSTRO DE LA MUERTE** ("The Face of Death," 1964 – another weird western), and a heck of a lot of

vampire films (1960-1985). Colin and Crevenna successfully married the two genres without any faults: a dusty Mexican village, a gypsy crone and her sexy daughter, a cowardly gunman looking for redemption, stakes, silver bullets, and a vampire with dagger-length canines. Such Western vampire films are somewhat common in Mexico; they are rare in the US. One such production that comes to mind is Edward Dein's exceptionally odd 1959 vampire Western **CURSE OF THE UNDEAD**, which Crevenna must have seen, or been aware of, as the plot similarities are fairly evident.

If **LA NAVE DE LOS MONSTRUOS** was the science fiction mash-up classic and **EL PUEBLO FANTASMA** was the best Gothic crossover, then **EL CHARRO DE LAS CALAVERAS** ("Rider of the Skulls") is the honest-to-God monster filled horror Western. This is as wild as you'll ever get in any cowboy creature verses throwdown feature. Granted, the film is handicapped due to a limited budget and a head-scratcher of a script, but you can't say that the director doesn't give it his all.

EL CHARRO comes from a long line of monster hunters in Mexican cinema. Luchadore Santo smashed the lairs of vampires and battled other creatures in the early 1960s, while other wrestlers tangled with half-human gorilla creations and other sorts of the living dead. However, none ever approached the level of monster-fueled action as in **EL CHARROS DE LS CALAVERAS**.

Out in the middle of nowhere rural Mexico people are terrorized by a group of monsters whose leader, a headless horseman, is out for blood... literally and figuratively. Luckily a mysterious avenger has ridden into town to smite the evil creatures. El Charro de las Calavares, aka "Rider of the Skulls" is a Zorro look-alike who is aided by his trusty sidekick (and comedy relief), encounters a young boy whose family is the mysteriously associated with ferocious werewolf attacks. The rider tracks the path of the recent werewolf assault (which happens within the first three minutes of the film) to the home of a family under siege from supernatural forces. Sadly, Señor Lobo Hombre turns out to the be the boy's stepfather. The Rider, a professional monster hunter, turns to a local *bruja* (witch) for help. The two unlikely partners arrive at the local cemetery where she works her magic to make a very talkative corpse spill the beans on the whereabouts of the creature. The werewolf is then hunted down and dispatched, but not before the young boy is orphaned after the monster kills his mother.

El Charro adopts the young boy and the trio continue their monster hunting. Next ungodly encounter is with a vampire who resides in an abandoned church. The monster emerges at night to change into a bat and hunt down humans (his first victim is director Salazar in an uncredited cameo). The vampire is a bat-headed creature that sports a fancy cape and even has a large belt buckle with a bat insignia. The monster is determined to decimate the local community, biting young maidens then burying them so they will become his brides. El Charro and his helpers soon dispatch the vampire.

In act three, The Jackal, a headless horseman, raids a small town searching in vain for its head which, by the way, is kept in a box owned by a young woman. The mummified head was originally attached to a bandits that was executed, but the young woman's father kept it for scientific study. The monster is reunited with his head and has plans to take revenge on the young woman

and her family. El Charro intercedes, and after a pitched sword fight the evil is put down and our hero and his two side kicks ride off into the sunset.

EL CHARRO DE LAS CALAVAERAS was the first feature by director Alfredo Salazar, a man who **has** been writing script for spooky features since the mid 1950s. He was the mastermind behind Chano Urueta's **LA BRUJA** (1954), wrote the classic trio of Aztec mummy movies **LA MOMIA AZTECA, LA MALDICIÓN DE LA MOMIA** (both 1957) and the surreal **LA MOMIA AZTECA CONTRA EL ROBOT HUMANO** (1958). Alfredo was the brother of actor, producer, and director Abel Salazar (aka **THE BRAINIAC**), and penned the story and/or the screenplay of other supernatural and weird action flicks including LA **ISLA DE LOS DINOSAURIOS** ("Island of the Dinosaurs", 1968), **LA MUJER MURCIÉLAGO** ("The Batwoman", 1968), and an assortment of the late period Santo vs monsters films from the 70s.

Most of the **EL CHARRO**'s off-set on location sequences grounded an otherwise unreal tale with bouts of super-realism when compared to the obvious of the production values of Estudios Churubusco Azteca. ECA was the major film studio of the day located in the middle of Mexico City. The ratty overcast "day for night" cinematography, sage brush and yucca plants, abandoned haciendas and rancheros and dilapidated graveyards add the required atmosphere for this offbeat thriller. These elements are the most effective during the final gorgeously lensed battle between sword fight between The Rider and the undead bandit. The monster effects in the film is are rather primitive even by the standards of low-budget 1960s filmmaking. The werewolf, zombie, vampire and undead bandito are just stunt men in rubber Halloween masks. Nevertheless, given the way the rest of the film looks, their unreal appearance at least left me with the impression I had just watched the precursor to the zero-budget Indian horror films I so enjoy. The end result is a rarely seen and very effective monster mash. Too bad Salazar's monster hunter never caught on as a film series, I would have loved to have seen more of his adventures.

As a side note, actor Pascula García Peña appeared in a number of westerns, typically playing the cowardly sidekick, boastful coward, or useless assistant. His first starring role was for a film by Chano "The Brianiac" Urueta, called **EL SUPERHOMEBRE** ("The Superman", 1946). Peñaia also showed up as, yep, a sidekick in three earlier weird westerns **EL ZORRO ESCARLATA EN LAS VENGANZA DEL AHORADO** and **EL ZORRO ESCARLATA**, and Rodríguez's **EL REGRESO DEL MONSTRUO**. Fans of stop-film animated monster films saw Peña, albeit briefly, in **THE BEAST OF HOLLOW MOUNTAIN**, and in Edward Ludwig's **THE BLACK SCORPION** (1957).

But I digress... which is an easy thing to do when researching Mexican cinema.

During the 60s there were a lot of action packed monster films. Most of these were luchadore productions where muscular masked wrestlers tackled the undead, paranormal critters as well as invading martians and rampaging robots. The innocence of these films was soon challenged by the right to add "Sexo" into the plots. The Mexican film industry, like its counterpart in the USA, began to see their theatrical markets drying up (thanks to TV and a faltering global economy) and decided to approach their spooky subject matter with a more adult attitude. Although there were supernatural westerns made in the 70s that catered to the old school audience, sex and blood was the new thrill[3].

The 1970s also ushered in what is now formally referred to as the "Chili Westerns" as opposed to the Italian "Spaghetti Westerns." If you are going to pick a food to describe a Mexican Western, then you should probably use something indigenous to the country like Tortilla Western, as chili is typically from the Texas/Arizonia region of the Americas. In any case, these films are usually just as dusty, grimy and nihilistic as their Italian counterparts.

At this point I'm sure your wondering when Alejandri Jodorowsky's **EL TOPO** (1970) is going to be covered. Both that film and his **HOLY MOUNTAIN** (1973) are weird westerns indeed, but not all that supernatural nor do they attempt to be anything but... well, spiritual. Both productions are experimental cinema and definitely don't include monsters other than your usual vile human variety.

---

3 There were alternative "Sexo" scenes inserted into René Cardona's 1968 tame **SANTO EN EL TESORO DE DRÁCULA** ("Santo in The Treasure of Dracula) and released as **EL VAMPIRO Y EL SEXO** (The Vampire and the Sex").

The comic and the film: **EL CABALLEO DEL DIABLO**.

Director Federico Curiel's 1975 film **EL CABALLO DEL DIABLO** ("The Demon Horse") is a fine example of the 70's approach to genre. Curiel, old hand at genre films, was responsible for the Nutrón The Masked Wrestler series as well as Santo films **NUTRÓN, EL ENMASCARDO NEGRO** (1960), the Nostradamus The Vampire series **LA MALDICIÓN DE NOSTRADAMUS** (1960), **LA SANGRE DE NOSTRADAMUS** (1962), **NOSTRADAMUS Y EL DESTRUCTOR DE MONSTRUOS** (1962), the Black Whip series mentioned earlier, and other horror, supernatural, and action related titles.

Mexican folklore through Spanish folklore from the medieval times; these "Caballucos del Diablos" were demons horses mounted by demons. That may be a long reach but it almost fits with this film which I believe is based off a long running series of Mexican sex and horror comic "El Caballo Del Diablo" Mexican which started in the late 1960s. From the few I have seen they are less like Warren Publishing's classically rendered horror of "Creepy" and "Eerie" and more like the pulpy thrills of Eerie Publications' "Witches' Tales" and "Tales of Voodoo." The film stars a ruggedly handsome and totally buff Jorge Rivero who was in the US western **SOLDIER BLUE** (1970, D: Ralph Nelson) as well as in Lucio Fulci's **CONQUEST** (1983). Rivero starred in another strange western **EL PAYO - UN HOMBRE CONTRA EL MUNDO!** ("El Payo - Man Against The World," 1972 D: Emilio Gómez Muriel) and its sequel the bizarre **LA MONTAÑA DEL DIABLO** ("Mountain of the Devil," 1975 Ds: Juan Andrés Bueno and Javier Durán).

Luciano, the sleazy son of a wealthy land owner is found after he mixes it up with a strange black stallion. After the son's body is laid to rest his grieving father prays to Satan to bring his son back. Of course, as anyone familiar with the W. W. Jacobs horror story "The Monkey's Paw" (or the 1972 Bob Clark/Alan Ormsby film **DEATHDREAM**) will know, you don't wish for something that's not meant to be. Luciano returns riding the black stallion, but something's different about the handsome young man. Lucinao enjoys to abusing the hired help, raping the local women folk, and kill any animal or man he can. The boy is pure evil. It's up to his uncle the town priest to stop the demon.

There is definitely a lot of sex in this film; brutal rapes and violent attacks signaling that the days of spooky Gothic vampire chills and rampant monster action have grown short. While there were still a few of the traditional horror westerns being produced in the 1970s (like the "El Latigo" films to follow), productions like **EL CABALLO DEL DIABLO** and Giovanni Korporaal 's **EL DIABÓLICO** (1977) were there to lay ground for their demise.

In **EL DIABÓLICO** an evil gunslinger named Dave, who has ice-blue eyes and a glowing demonic pendant, is raping women, robbing banks and causing all sorts of trouble. He enjoys shooting folks and branding his women with a hot iron after abusing them. Dave is eventually captured by the law, but escapes hanging by using his Svengali-like powers to get a man to shoot the rope at the last second. However, the criminal is shot during his escape and dies... but not before he transfers his Devil-imbued powers to Oscar, the man helped him escape. With the transfer of the demonic pendant and some vague pledge of allegiance to Satan, Oscar leaves the dead man to wreak his own havoc.

Oscar rides a demonic black steed, possesses the cursed iron brand, and the magic amulet of the devil. He meets up with a mute Indian woman who he rapes, brands, and leaves pregnant. After a string of successful killings and robberies Oscar is conscripted into a gang of outlaws headed by a sexy six-shooter by the name of Arizona Jane, steals gold from an old prospector, and eventually returns to the town where this tale all began only to be captured and hung by an angry mob.

Coming at on the end of the Spaghetti western era, this Mexican variant (complete with a very Italian sounding score by Gustavo C. Carrion) was directed by Dutch-born Giovanni Korporaal who was primarily a short documentary filmmaker The film's cinematographer, Xavier Cruz, worked on Juan López Moctezuma's incredible cool **ALUCARDA** that was made the same year.

What better way to end this short survey than return to the fictional character of Zorro. This masked avenger has always been a very popular figure in Mexican media, despite being created by in 1919 by New York–based pulp writer Johnston McCulley. McCulley authored over 60 books on "The Fox" that were immensely popular the world over. Films, TV shows, plays, musical, comics, and websites are dedicated to the character of Zorro and his many clones[4]. The aforementioned "El Zorro Escarlata" The "El Latigo" (The Whip) trilogy ambled into supernatural territory, just barely crosses the line.

This series wasn't the first time a popular hero carried a whip in Mexican cinema. Some titles over the previous decades include includes all sorts of Zorro clones, one of the more popular being "The Black Whip", although he never tangled with mummies or witches that I could find[5]. An older El Latigo film by the name of **EL Ã IMA DEL AHORCADO CONTRA EL LATIGO NEGRO** ("The Ghost of The Hanged Man vs. The Black Whip", 1959, Ds: Vicente Oroná,& Jesús Marín) sounds like a good spooky thriller, but my guess there is nothing supernatural by the time the film wraps up.

[4] Even Spanish director Jess Franco had his hand in the Zorro craze.
[5] For those of you who may have a Zorro fetish here are the titles: **EL LÁTIGO NEGRO** (1958), **EL MISTERIO DEL LÁTIGO NEGRO** (1958), **EL ÁNIMA DEL AHORCADO CONTRA EL LATIGO NEGRO** (1959), and **EL LÁTIGO NEGRO CONTRA LOS FARSANTES** (1962).

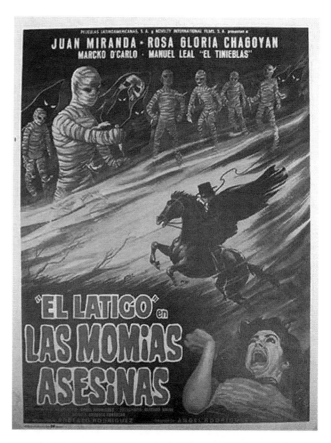

The first two films in the series is by Alfredo B. Crevenna, a director well-versed in the unusual cinema early on in his career with **EL HOMBRE QUE LOGRÓ SER INVISIBLE (THE NEW INVISIBLE MAN**, 1958), **YAMBAÓ (CRY OF THE BEWITCHED**, 1957), **ROSTRO INFERNAL (THE INCREDIBLE FACE OF DR. B**, 1963) and **ÉCHENME AL VAMPIRO (BRING ME THE VAMPIRE**, 1963). So why are the films in this series so lackluster? Resembling more of a TV production rather than a full fledge film series. Their look and pacing is incredibly bland, which is odd considering the lush look and feel of Crevenna's 1980 vampire film **LA DINASTÍA DE DRACULA** (the director's variant on John Banham's **DRACULA** film from 1979).

EL LATIGO (1978) introduces us to The Whip, whose normal day alter-ego is that of a fancy pants peddler of housewares. By day he is a humble and God-fearing friend to everyone, but when evil pops up, he transforms into the whip-baring avenger El Latigo who professes that he's a master of the Occultism and other obscure sciences, and knows how to deal with threats of the supernatural kind. For this first film there is very little in the of weirdness other than El Latigo himself.

For the second outing our hero faces both a gang of evil Satanists and a village full of frightened townsfolk who just at hanging "witches" when it suits them. **EL LATIGO CONTRA SANTANIST** uses the same opening sequence as the first film and what looks like the same shooting location (Tikal, Guatemala). El Latigo encounters the devil worshippers and a bull-headed "Lucifer," and after a few very badly choreographed fights he defeats them. I was baffled as to the ludicrous nature of the film. Alfredo B. Crevenna directed **YAMBAÓ** for Pete's sake. A lot can happen in twenty years, and maybe he was just tired of making good films.

By the time the third film came to be made it must have been obvious that some kind of actual monster had to be introduced to try and keep the audiences interested. For **EL LATIGO CONTRA LAS MOMIAS ASESINAS** ("The Whip Verses The Killer Mummies", 1980) director Ángel Rodrígues Vázquez grabbed the whip and took the series to another level – making the final entry almost as entertaining as a Santos or Blue Demon wrestling monster film. Adding killer mummies was right up Vázquez's alley and his skills as assistant director on **EL HANCHA DIABÓLICA** (1965), **EL IMPERIO DE DRÁCULA** (1967), **LA SOMBRA DEL MURCIÉLAGO** ("Shadow of the Bat," 1968), and the Santo vs the Devil film **ATACAN LAS BRUJAS** ("Attack of the Witch," 1968) provided all the essentials he needed to close the deal.

A gang of evil mummies are out to destroy the families of a local Guatemalan family. One by one the evil undead, under the guidance of a larger killer mummy stalks and murder folks until El Latigo cracks his whip and send the monsters back to hell. The absurdity level is exceptionally high especially when the fights between our hero and the mummies look as of they are staged by a hack. It's a monster tag team match as the lumbering terrors get their mummified butts kicked one by one (with their flashing light bulb eyes and baggy mummy costumes with visible zipper up the back). El Latigo dispatches them by whipping each creature until they explode. Then El Latigo confronts El Grande Momia outside an old mausoleum where the monster was about to sacrifice a young woman. After some well placed snaps of his trusty weapon of choice the big bad mummy explodes into flames.

The series ended there. I was hoping there would have been *EL LATIGO CONTRA FRANKENSTEIN Y LOBO HOMBRE* or even *EL LATIGO Y BLUE DEMON EN LA VENGANZA DE LA LLORONA*. Sadly, no.

There have always been, and always be, room for weird westerns in Mexican cinema. In fact, in writing this article I have uncovered many titles that I had never read anything on. More griss for the mill so to speak. There will always be time to watch and write about the startlingly odd world of Mexican cinema. • • •

NO SECOND BANANA

• John Grace

*For three years, Sergio Leone's Dollars Trilogy ruled the European theatrical markets. As United Artists regionally rolled out the imports in 1967, "Supermanager" Allen Klein, in between handling the Beatles and the Rolling Stones, screened a low budget, Spain-lensed oater titled **A DOLLAR BETWEEN THE TEETH**, directed by Luigi Vanzi. It starred his friend and client, actor Tony Anthony. Anthony thought he had made the worst movie ever. With no partiality to the western genre or even horses, he was baffled by Vanzi's humor and focus of making Tony a different kind of hero.*

Imagine the surprise when Klein and his cohorts laughed throughout the screening and purchased the North American rights for the film with MGM releasing it to compete with the Leone films in 1968 (a note to younger readers, before the advent of cable tv, movies could see theatrical distribution for up to 3 years in most non-roadshow/drive-in/grindhouse markets). Klein retitled the film **A STRANGER IN TOWN**. Marketing would emphasize the mysterious stranger that Tony portrayed, creating the impression to audiences that Tony was playing Eastwood's Joe Monco character(or the Man With No Name if you want to believe United Artists marketing division). Thus began the career of perhaps the most unusual Spaghetti Western hero of them all.

While Clint Eastwood and Lee Van Cleef were tall, imposing men that could walk down main street as invincible pistolmen, Anthony was an average sized, not exceptionally intimidating individual. Eastwood played it quiet cool and was a convincing one man army, but Tony was wisecracking, conniving, shady and frequently a loser of fist fights. He also didn't fit the stereotype of the Western Marlboro man. Like his acting descendant (and later employee) Mickey Rourke, he was a Southerner that many thought hailed from the streets of Brooklyn. Instead of a lean or brawny look, Tony has a babyface and likely stands under 5'10. His appearance suggested a Fedora and Tommy gun, not a cowboy hat and six shooter. Born Roger Pettito in Clarksburg, Virginia in 1937, Anthony's career began as the star of scarcely seen youth dramas for director Saul Swimmer. As for his chosen screen name, one presumes it was better to be redundant than ethnic on the marquee in the 1960s.

STRANGER IN TOWN (1968)· Following the **FISTFUL OF DOLLARS** formula, Tony's Stranger character rides into an abandoned town occupied by an outlaw gang and one citizen, a pretty young mother. Yes, you read that correctly. The town has one citizen with an infant. Director Vanzi had the Stranger sport dyed blond hair and wearing a pink long john top with blue jeans and a serape, very similar to Joe Monco aside from that pink shirt. Vanzi clearly wanted a quirkier hero and knew Anthony wasn't a John Wayne or an Eastwood. The town set is extremely minimal, a ghost town as sparse as the dialogue. The Stranger helps the bandido outlaw gang, led by the always fantastic Frank Kramer (redheaded, ill-fated father in **ONCE UPON A TIME IN THE WEST**, among other memorable turns in the genre) swindle gold from a US army platoon. Then our hero betrays the gang, leading to the gratuitous beatdown of Anthony's character that becomes a trademark of his westerns. Really elongated sequences of sadism vented on our hero in these movies. They beat the tar out of him in a more gratuitous spin on a similar scene in **A FISTFUL OF DOLLARS**. But he escapes, recovers (probably the most unbelievable staple of these films. But hell, you see it in modern "realistic" action films like **TRAINING DAY**), and dusts off his trusty double barreled shotgun.

It wouldn't be a Spaghetti Western without a highly unlikely usage and film-maker ignorance of firearms, and for **A STRANGER IN TOWN**, we have our hero using a shotgun like a sniper rifle. So Anthony spends the final 30 minutes wiping out Kramer's bandidos with his shotgun and wits. For a blatant anachronism, the villains use police action revolvers from the 1930. The type that killed John Dillinger. Perhaps Vanzi had limited access to props, and these pistols were left over from a gangster film of some sort. The film does seem improvised at times, as the finale is our hero's shotgun versus a machine gun with a wheel barrel and track used for advantage. A wheel barrel? Would anybody write that in the script?

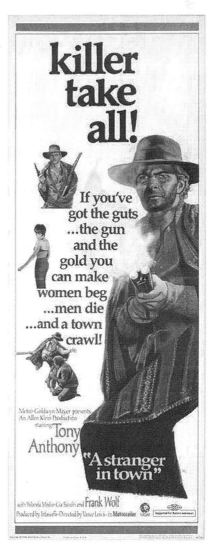

Because this is the 1960s, you have to have a weird, morally inappropriate villain so the bandido gang has a predatory bisexual villainess (played by veteran peplum cheesecake Gia Sandri) who delights in whipping the Stranger after he's brutalized by the gang. She's also predatory to the young village mother. The Stranger kills her by smashing her head against the stone floor. It doesn't play as tasteless as it reads here.

Favorite scene: the great moment where Stranger walks into a dark room suddenly lit up by all the villains' match sticks. A gag worthy of Looney Tunes, and Anthony implies in interviews that the movie's visual hu-

21

mor came from Vanzi.

Laughable when thought about today, the Leone westerns came under fire from critics offended by Joe Monco's lack of morality or fair play(He kills for money! He doesn't fight fair!), leading to square peg reactions like Monte Hellman filming a prologue for the TV version claiming Joe really works for the government. Ahead of that game by half a decade, the twist ending reveals the Stranger was working for the Army the whole time.

The score by Benedetto Ghiglia isn't a bombastic and awesome sweeping work like Morricone, but a catchy, if repetitive punctuation to the movie's visual beats.

A smash hit in theaters. MGM and Klein's company greenlit Anthony and Vienzi to reunite on a sequel put into production before the first film hit US theaters.

STRANGER RETURNS (1968): The first Stranger was fun, but felt improvised. This one is nearly a remake but is a huge improvement, has some well thought-out scenarios and memorable dialogue. The sequel seems to have a script and Anthony clearly knows what he wants to do with the Stranger character. Anthony's sense of humor is more pronounced with much more in the one liners and dialogue department. He's definitely made Vanzi's creation his own, which serves him well when he does the last Stranger film without Vanzi. Also, this is the first of the series where The Stranger's horse is named "Pussy." Not Trigger, Silver or Mr. Ed, but Pussy. I'm sure all the pre-teen boys seeing this at the matinee were snickering between sips of Nehi soda. No longer using a minimal town with one normal resident, this time there is a small population, including a preacher (Marco Guglielmi in a nice character role). In this entry, the scruffy, bandido outlaw gang is led by the imposing Dan Vadis. A veteran muscleman actor from the peplums, a real life tough guy and supra-human athlete, Vadis was part of Clint Eastwood's stock acting crew in the 1970s and 80s. His later descent and early death from drugs were said to be a result of his fearlessness. As the gang leader, he just has to look sneering and tough. No mean feat for the imposing actor. After the obligatory "hero's beatdown" sequence, the Stranger brandishes a four barreled shotgun! As unlikely as it seems to a civilized world, a number of four barreled shotguns have existed, mainly as customized weaponry. The finale consists of the Stranger taking out the gang in elaborate action set pieces that are a bit more creative than the first film. Hell, they may have been storyboarded! Finale was ripped off to inferior effect by Clint Eastwood's **PALE RIDER**, also featuring Dan Vadis as a villain! Cult starlet Jill Banner has a pre-**SPIDER BABY** and **THE PRESIDENT'S ANALYST** supporting role as a village girl. Our unique twist in the epilogue: the Stranger is called "Inspector" and is revealed to be working undercover. However, he is also revealed to be a bit more duplicitous than ethical. The soundtrack marks the debut of Stevio Cipriani's work in the series. His score is excellent, and you'll hum it for weeks after viewing the movie.

While visiting Luciana Paluzzi in Japan as she worked on **THE GREEN SLIME**, Anthony visited the sets of other movies, including a Zatoichi film. A fan of the chambara genre, ideas were sparked for his next two westerns. Why not combine the samurai movie with the gunfighter drama?

SILENT STRANGER (1968) Opens with the Stranger yelling "Pussy" while wandering through snow-covered mountains. Chasing after his horse, in case you skipped the previous review. The mountains turn out to be in Japan. Here it is, the first true Eastern Western, made before **RED SUN** and **THE STRANGER AND THE GUNFIGHTER**. Originally titled **THE STRANGER IN JAPAN**, the action was lensed on location in what appears to be the samurai village set used in many Katsu productions. A village bridge set looks identical to the one used in at least two Zatoichi movies and **BABY CART AT THE RIVER STYX**. The Stranger is hired to retrieve a scroll in the Orient and finds himself caught between two warring factions in a village, one of the movie's many allusions to **YOJIMBO**. He fights and fails against the lead "good" *ronin* in a bamboo versus katana duel. The bad gang is aided by another westerner with a gatling gun, played by Lloyd Battista, a veteran character actor of screen, stage and even radio drama. Beginning with this film, Battista became Tony's collaborative scribe for his best work. And Lloyd always plays a villain. There is no female lead in the film, save for a very young Japanese girl who speaks (dubbed) English and serves as the Stranger's translator for her clan. Interesting that Vanzi does not use subtitles for the Japanese dialogue. We'll guess this was intended to keep the viewer as confused as the hero. Instead, there is mainly narration from the Stranger, a first in the series. He also sings nonexistent songs about money rolling in.

The vaguely-credited Japanese cast contains no familiar faces from the genre. Although Toho-Toei-Daiei production liaison to the west William Ross is credited with working on the film.

There is also the trademark of Tony's quips. Favorite line: after a huge thug claps his hands in a sort of sumo gesture, the Stranger responds "Hey, he speaks Indian, this guy!"

When knife-wielding women in a steambath attack the Stranger, he remarks "Women!" after evading the attack. Our McGuffin bounces between the scroll and the firing pin on the machine. When he kills Lloyd Batista's expat mercenary, he tells him he knows he's a fellow American, because "none of the other indians around here have blue eyes." Interesting thing about the machine gun: in Japan, firearms are banned so filmmakers use electronic guns that fire an orange flash to simulate gun fire. So the gun in this film is not exactly convincing.

In many interviews, Anthony claims the original cut was 20 minutes longer, and MGM shelved the film until 1975 and released the heavily cut version. He says the original cut is the best film he ever made. Truthfully, even the studio cut is still the best film he ever made. The humor, action and pacing work on every level, and it is even more fun for the chambara fan. Unfortunately, the only print I've seen is an even jumpier, cut for commercials version from a TNT cable channel broadcast in 1998. MGM needs to give up the original version and turn it loose!

COME TOGETHER (1971) is not a Western, but Anthony portrays "Tony" an American from Steubenville, Ohio (Lloyd Battista's neck of the woods) working as a stuntman in Italian westerns shot in Spain. This element is rather marginal in the overall film, but there is a fun sequence showing Tony at work, doing stunts in a Mexican bandit outfit. This experimental hippie-ish drama was directed by the star and Saul Swimmer, a veteran filmmaker who directed Tony's early youth dramas before he journeyed to Europe to boost his career. Tony becomes involved with two fellow American girls played by Luciana Paluzzi and Rosemary Dexter. The movie is a bit tough to review because it is one of the post-**EASY RIDER** "young people on a quest for finding themselves" pictures that flooded cinemas for half a decade. I would guess "finding yourself" actually means getting laid as much as possible to the free love generation. It was likely relevant for its time, but seems hokey, shallow and silly by today's standards. Let's face it, the characters are shallow assholes when their collective goal is to have a threesome. What takes four minutes in the average porn video takes a tedious 65 minutes to occur in this flower power vehicle. By the end of the movie you will be rooting for everybody to die. But the movie is not without merit. The threesome has a past: Tony is the only survivor from a platoon massacre in Vietnam, Dexter's character had an abortion and Paluzzi's character...err, well, I guess she has no problem at all. After all, she looks like Luciana Paluzzi. Anyway, the traumatic flashback sequences are effective. The excellent soundtrack was released on Apple Records. There is a hysterical scene where Tony calls his parents in Ohio from his hotel room in Rome. His blue collar father just angrily yells at him for "making pictures with all those queers" in Europe. It's so inappropriate, politically incorrect and likely an autobiographical scene. Though not credited, I got the feeling Lloyd Battista had a hand in the script.

BLINDMAN (1971) is the other film sparked by Tony's trip to Japan. A western version of the Shintaro Katsu's Zatoichi character, Tony's character is a blind pistolman escorting 50 mail order brides through the West. He plays a perpetual cat and mouse game with a bandido gang led by Ringo Starr (as "Candy") and Lloyd Battista. Starr wanted to play a villain and work on shedding the Beatle image. Truthfully, it kind of works here. He should have made more movies in this vein. The gang steals the brides. Blindman tries to get them back. Truthfully, the movie seems structured like a string of Road Runner cartoons, an endless chase.

The formula of the Stranger films is re-used: Blindman is nearly beaten to death by the villains, recovers and seeks righteous vengeance with plenty of one liners. But the odd novelty of a blind hero being a dangerous gunfighter, it is so absurd you don't even question it. Anthony does a better impression of Katsu's mannerisms than Rutger Hauer in **BLIND FURY** or Armand Assante in **BLIND JUSTICE**, two later attempts at westernized Zatoichi movies. He wears bright blue contact lenses to give the impression of blindness instead of rolling his eyes backwards, Katsu-style. The one liners are among his best: "To be blind is a half a man; to be blind, with no money, now that's a bitch." This marks Tony's first collaboration with Ferdinando Baldi, who directs this film with a unique style that complements the star's quirky and unique humor. Notable also as the only Tony Anthony western filmed in a scope aspect ratio, and Baldi uses the frame well to capture the dry, dusty desolation of the American Southwest as portrayed by Almeria, Spain. There is also a bit of nudity and if snobs wanted to accuse the filmmakers of misogyny, they've got a lot to work with here. The formula works and worked great in 1971 because **BLINDMAN** was a huge global hit. A big enough hit to raise the ire of the Medved Brothers, who strangely picked this as one of the 50 Worst Films of All Time in their pre-Golden Turkey book. I think the Medveds just wanted to rip on Ringo Starr for going into acting. Fugg 'em.

GET MEAN (1975): To cash in on the kung fu movie craze, Anthony wanted to make a film where the Stranger ends up in Ancient China via a timewarp. When ABCKO's financing only allowed for the Stranger to be timewarped to a Spain inhabited by Moors and Vikings, **GET MEAN** became the final and oddest of the series. Hired to escort a princess to Spain, (which the Stranger says he is ignorant of Spain's location), he loses the princess, ends up in blackface(don't ask), is captured and served up like a pig(apple in mouth, the works) as a feast for cannibals and says "Bullshit" for a one liner. There's a gay villain referred to by our hero as "little sister." After much abuse from the villains, the Stranger dusts off the trusty 4 barrel shotgun from **THE STRANGER RETURNS** and shoots every villain within a 15 mile radius. And he utters the film's title before he starts blasting away. Baldi's style with the Stranger formula is different than Vanti, with far less usage of the music score to punctuate scenes. The music, credited to Fabio Frizzi, Franco Bixio and Vince Tempera is mainly a banjos and a moog. Hate to sound square, but it reminds me of Bernie Leadon's "Journey of the Sorcerer." I'm losing it.

Lloyd Battista plays one of the villains and also co-wrote the script. Anthony told Spaghetti Cinema's Bill Connolly that money was being smuggled into Spain to produce the film, so what would an Allen Klein production be without ABCKO's legendary financial shenanigans (i.e. The Rolling Stones' run in the 1960s, the Beatles, the myopic handling of the Cameo Parkway label, the treatment of Alejandro Jodorowsky, etc.).

At a party screening of **GET MEAN** for a group of zine veterans like Bob Sargent, Mark Clark, Bryan Senn and Bruce Holecheck, it was remarked that the movie was reminiscent of **ARMY OF DARKNESS**. Certainly with the ongoing frustration and abuse of the hero in various fantastic situations and the timewarp gimmick, it wouldn't be hard to believe that Sam Raimi saw this at a Michigan drive-in in 1976.

COMIN' AT YA! (1981). We're all tired of the return of 3-D in today's movie cinemas, but you can credit and blame Anthony for the format's comeback in the 80s. After an unsuccessful pitch for a Stranger team up with a Taiwanese gung fu movie star from the producers of the 3-D martial arts epic **DYNASTY**, Anthony decides to make his own 3-D western. After a disastrous attempt to film **COMIN AT YA!** was aborted, due to frustrations with the 3-D technology and financing, Anthony took a temporary hiatus from movies, only to meet with Xerox executives willing to develop a workable 3D process and invest in **COMIN AT YA!** One of those executives was Gene Quintano, who rewrote the script and later had a prolific career in Hollywood writing terrible movies. Baldi is back at the helm, so **COMIN AT YA!** reuses elements from **BLINDMAN** (kidnapped brides) and the Stranger elements(much abused wisecracking hero, dusts off a shotgun for the coup de grace on the villains), and Quintano assumes the usual Lloyd Battista role as a heel. The quality of writing in Tony's movies really dropped when Quintano replaced Battista as Tony's collaborator. It is disappointing and not nearly as entertaining as the earlier westerns. To exploit the 3-D gimmick, gratuitous shots of spoons, beans, infant buttocks and other nonsense are constantly thrust at the camera and pad out the film's already tedious pacing. At least it has the lovely Victoria Abril as Tony's kidnapped bride, before she became the only reason straight men watched Pedro Almodavar's movies.

COMIN' AT YA! was a surprise box office hit in 1981, sparking a short-lived 3-D revival that gave us the likes of **FRIDAY THE 13TH PART 3, PARASITE, JAWS 3-D** and **SPACEHUNTER: ADVENTURES IN THE FORBIDDEN ZONE**. Thanks Tony. Really.

If seen in a theater in the 3-D format, it is enjoyable for the gimmick. If you watch the disastrous Rhino DVD, which uses an outdated 3-D process for video, the movie comes off poorly. Anthony warned Rhino Home Video that the more recent 3-D format developed for the film wouldn't technically work for their version, but he was ignored. The result was the muddiest transfer to DVD in home video history. Ironically, it is now out of print and goes for ridiculous prices on Amazon.com. Drafthouse Films acquired **COMIN AT YA!** for a limited re-release and remastered the 3D effects, changing some effects via sepia tone. I was lucky to see it on the big screen at a festival screening and it worked very well. But the new release flopped in theaters, Tony bought the movie back from Drafthouse Films and is not currently planning a home video release.

Tony later followed up **COMIN' AT YA** with the dull Indiana Jones-meets-Topkapi knockoff **TREASURE OF THE 4 CROWNS** for Cannon Films. It underperformed, causing Cannon Films to cancel plans for a 3-D space opera *ESCAPE FROM BEYOND*. Tony Anthony and Baldi collaborating on a tribute to 1930s Sci-fi pulp stories? It just might have worked! Tony's last theatrical film credit was as a Producer on Zalman King's **WILD ORCHID**.

Unfortunately, all titles reviewed have a scattershot and dodgy availability on home video. **A STRANGER IN TOWN** and **THE STRANGER RETURNS** are annually broadcast on Turner Classic Movies, and there are bootleg DVDs around the usual gray market outlets. **THE SILENT STRANGER** is rarely broadcast, unfortunately. **COME TOGETHER** is available from Something Weird Video. **BLINDMAN** is available in a variety of shady versions, but the best is said to be the Koch dvd released in Germany some four years ago. I have yet to see a DVD print of **BLINDMAN** that looks truly remastered. Allen Klein's estate has reportedly remastered the film and was working on a Tony Anthony box set for the dvd market, but no official announcement has been made. Copies of **GET MEAN** have been ported from an old PAL release from either the UK or South Africa. Co-producer Ron Schneider is selling a widescreen DVD of **GET MEAN** off his website www.getsmean.com. I haven't seen his version, but reportedly the quality is good.

Anthony hasn't given up the exploitation ways. He recently co-authored with old partner-in-crime Lloyd Battista a book about basketball's Olympic Dream Team to compete with other NBA Dream Team books released in 2012.

I learned a lot about Tony Anthony's career thanks to an excellent 3 part audio interview available athttp://thecinemasnob.com. Also, Bill Connolly filled in some details from his interview with Anthony in the exhaustive Spaghetti Cinema fanzine. • • •

BANG BANG...
...CHA CHA CHA

An Indian Western Primer • Tim Paxton

The Western genre has been considered by many critics and historians to be a unique development of American cinema, not unlike Jazz to American music. There are the classics to be sure: **STAGECOACH *(1939)*, HIGH NOON *(1952)*, SHANE *(1952)*, THE MAGNIFICENT SEVEN *(1960)*, BUTCH CASSIDY AND THE SUNDANCE KID *(1969)*,** *and others. But as unique as the Western was to Hollywood, countries all the world over wanted to share in the fun.*

The Italian-based "Spaghetti Western" genre lasted roughly from 1965-1977. During this period, the Italians really churned them out, producing around 200 films. It follows, then, that the Western genre would also appeal to other cultures, such as the movie-hungry audiences of India. The Indian film industry covers all the major film producing states: Andhra Pradesh, Assam, Bihar, Gujarat, Haryana, Jammu and Kashmir, Karnataka, Kerala, Maharashtra, Manipur, Orissa, Punjab, Tamil Nadu, Uttar Pradesh and West Bengal[1], the three biggest being Andhra Pradesh (Telugu), Tamil Nadu (Tamil), and Maharashtra (Hindi). With all those industries each producing hundreds of movies a year, you would think that there would have been a great many Indian variants on the Western as well. But that was not the case. Less than twenty Westerns that I know of were produced between the early 70s to mid 80s, when the *annual* average of films produced in Indian cinema was around 1000 films[2] a year.

The Indian Western comes in three distinct flavors. The first that developed was the "Masala Western". "Masala" comes from the cuisine popular in South Asia, not unlike Italy's "Spaghetti" and Mexico's "Chili" variations. And like the complex Indian dishes that the genre is named after, the films are a mix of action, comedy, drama, romance, and music – which accounts for a lot of Indian cinema, Westerns included.

Next is the "Curry Western", which is a harder-edged variety of the "Masala". The third is a wilder brand which is often called "Daaku" meaning "Bandit". (A sub-genre of this third branch is known as the "Jungle" genre, which will be covered in a future issue of *Weng's Chop*.)

That said, I present this rather bare bones account of these oddities, and, as per the usual disclaimer in my articles, I am in no way an expert on Indian cinema. The many and varied facets of Indian culture fascinate me. India is a beautiful country from what I can tell, and I am particularly taken by its cinema. As of writing this article I have sat through at least 200 Indian films; the majority being without the benefits of English subtitles as the preferred manner of collecting video in India is on the crude low-quality digital format known as VCDs. Few of the films I have watched for review have ever been on DVD with the possible benefits of subtitles.

Film locales are just as barren and forbidding as their Hollywood or Italian counterparts. Many of the films are shot in the valleys and rocky deserts that surround the foothills of the Himalayas. The film **SHOLAY** was shot on the Deccan Plateau in the south-eastern part of Karnataka, whereas **MERA GAON MERA DESH** was filmed around Rājasthān, located in the north-west of India. This region comprises most of the area of the Thar Desert (near the Pakistan border), a place as beautiful and rustic as the badlands of Almeria in south-eastern Spain, where a many a Spaghetti Western was shot.

The very first Masala Western is the 1970 film **MOSAGAALAKU MOSAGAADU** ("Cheater of the Cheaters") from Telugu director K.S.R. Doss, a man who enjoyed mixing up the genres and dishing out insanity. The film ushered in the modern Western in India. As with most of the productions that followed, this one takes place in the modern era, despite all the hallmarks

Mosagaalaku Mosagaadu, 1971

of the classic Western motif. Doss was the first director to tackle the genre, and did so with such gusto as to influence almost every film afterwards. Odd thing about **MOSAGAALAKU MOSAGAADU** is that it was also the first Telugu film dubbed into English under the title of **THE TREASURE HUNT**, although I have no leads into finding a copy of that... or the Telugu edition for that matter.

PISTOWALI (1972) is the wildest of the early Doss productions, with all the song and dance, shoot 'em, beat 'em, and love 'em plot concoctions thrown about to keep any jaded critic off his or her game long enough to fully enjoy its lunacy. The action is frenetic, often to the point of entering a surreal territory, reminiscent of a vintage Warner Brothers cartoon. Somewhere in the badlands of 1970's Andhra Pradesh, a young woman (Jyothi Laxmi) is enjoying life with her family. She sings and dances, while frolicking at waterfalls, riding horses, and beating up bad guys. Her bold and brash attitude soon comes to the attention of a group of train robbers who don't care much for her busting up their bar and abusing their gang members. In a move they will soon regret, the bandits kidnap and kill her mother, setting in motion a brutal retribution.

That's pretty much the plot. Simple and to the point, with a few twists and turns (and great musical interludes). It also had a tragic ending that took a few viewings to figure out what was going on. The majority of **PISTOLWALI** is chock-full of what you would expect from a Masala film. Drama, melodrama (lots of that), comedy, and surf rock based pop tunes[3] that perfectly accompany Jyothi Laxmi's wild "Southern Bombshell" style of dancing. Whether she is shaking her money-maker while soaking wet in a skimpy bathing suit or beating the crap out of some villains to an exciting soundtrack of manic strings and bombastic horns, Laxmi is the main reason to watch the film.

---

1 http://en.wikipedia.org/wiki/Cinema_of_India
2 A very conservative number tallied from various sources.

3 Score assembled by one Sathyam aka Chellapilla Satyam, a popular musical director and composer for Telugu and Kannada cinema from the 1960s through the 1980s.

Doss made a career out of having strong, forceful women in his films. In her frenzied existence, the film's brutal cowgirl wastes no time smashing her male opponents into pulp with her fist or filling them full of holes with her six-shooter. Laxmi appeared in a number of Doss's female-centric Telegu revenge films including **JAMES BOND 777** (1971), **PILLA? PIDUGA?** (1972), and **RANI AUR JAANI** (1973). Her actions are echoed in many of the director's later films starring Silk Smitha, including **TOOFAN RANI** (1985) and **BADLA AURAT KA** (1987). One could see this protagonist as the embodiment of the Goddess Durga as she dishes out vengeful female wrath on stupid men.

The entire forceful woman theme in Doss's and other Indian directors' films is an odd one. It's not as if women have a lot of rights in India, or haven't only recently acquired them. There have always been Indian movies that have strong female leads, but most of them have been (and still are to some extent) powerfully *passive* roles. Consider the female leads in western films like **GONE WITH THE WIND** (1939) or **ERIN BROCKOVICH** (2000) and the way they dealt with their crumbling worlds. These women didn't get their way by engaging in violent throw-downs every ten minutes as in **PISTOLWALI**. A similar theme has been popular in Japanese cinema and anime for decades wherein strong-willed heroines clash with androids, vampires, and other such violent forces in an otherwise (still) male-dominated society. This type of heroine has entered mainstream American media culture in films such as **THELMA AND LOUISE** (1991) and the **ALIEN**, **UNDERWORLD**, **RESIDENT EVIL** franchises, etc.

PISTOLWALI director Doss was not someone to throw away a good idea, and remade one his 1970 Telegu smash hits, **ROWDY RANI** (which is reported to be the first heroine-oriented action film in India) in 1972, as **RANI MERA NAAM**. In the original version, "Rowdy" Rani is a woman who plans to kill the four thieves who murdered her entire family in her childhood. The film that was made two years later is a more extreme, Western variation on the same plot. I have yet to track this film down (something that is not unusual in this line of work). Alas, if K.R.S. Doss was such an important director in the development of Telugu cinema, you would think that a collection of his films would have been released on DVD. Doss created around 100 films in his long career, but was there a retrospective of any kind after his death in 2012? Nope. Sad.

Since **RANI MERA NAAM** and **ROWDY RANI** are nowhere to be found on VCD, DVD, or YouTube, I'll have to lean on another Doss Western, **GUNFIGHTER JOHNNY**, which was also made in 1972. **GUNFIGHTER JOHNNY** is a Hindi remake of **MOSAGAALAKU MOSAGAADU**. In this film, Doss concentrates more on the manly aspects of the traditional Western as the hero, Johnny, partners up with a criminal named Naganna to help a young woman, Radha, defend herself against a small army of bandits. Seems that these bad guys are out to steal a treasure that Radha's family is

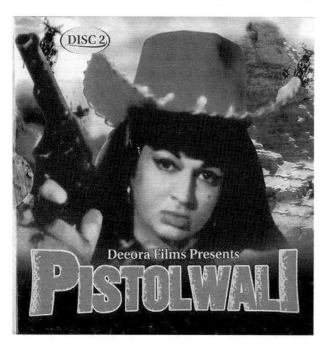

in charge of safe-keeping. Against all odds, Johnny, Nagaana, and Radha square off against the thieves. In the meantime there is always time for savage beatings, gunfights, and musical numbers.

GUNFIGHTER JOHNNY isn't as insane as **PISTOLWALI**, but it is a better film overall. Doss makes the most of the wonderful geography of his native Andhra Pradesh. He loads the film up with dramatic chases and fanciful musical numbers lensed in green valleys, the plains of the Eastern Ghats, and the low scrub badlands and sandy dunes of the Deccan Plateau. The acting is less broad as in his earlier films, and the musical numbers are much more accessible.

The score for the film was written by P. Adinarayana Rao and is without a doubt one of the best non-Italian Spaghetti Western soundtracks this side of anything written by Ennio Morrcione, Piero Piccioni, or Stelvio Cipriani. In fact, there are snatches of melodies from Sergio Leno's "Dollar Trilogy" worked into the score throughout. And nothing nails it like the second musical number when Radha and Krishna (aka "Johnny") frolic about in a snowy mountainside to Rao's re-imagination of a Morricone theme. Visual nods to the Leon films also permeate **GUNFIGHTER JOHNNY**, thus sealing it for me as Doss's best. It's fun, violent, silly, wacky, and very, very entertaining if you are into Spaghetti Westerns as much as I am.

It is fun to note that Doss denies that his films were in anyway inspired by Hollywood oaters and Spaghetti Westerns. During a 2009 interview he was asked about some of the clearly obvious borrowed elements. Doss answered, "No, it's not! Arudra [a screenwriter] adapted the cowboy theme to suit Telugu nativity and we made it accordingly. Only one scene was taken from that film, Arudra said. In fact, I have not seen the English film in question even till date!"[4]

I'm sure that Doss is referring to **GUNFIGHTER JOHNNY**'s openly and unashamedly ripping off of Leon's **THE GOOD, THE BAD, AND THE UGLY**. One fine example of this tribute to the Italian film is when a worse for wear Naganna enters a gun shop after spending a few horrible days in the desert, hellbent on getting himself a weapon. His picking and testing of various guns mimics Taco's famous scene and even includes the gunman shoving the store's "Closed" sign in the shop owner's mouth. I don't believe Doss for a minute that he wasn't aware of Leon's film, considering it was the most popular of the Dollar Trilogy. There are other bits and pieces of mimicry throughout, but that fact doesn't bother me in the least, as it only it adds to the pleasure of watching this two and a half hour epic.

---
[4] http://www.telugucinema.com/c/publish/stars/interview_ksrdas.php

K.S.R. Doss may have broke ground in India, but his films, as popular as they were regionally, didn't reflect any significant major shift in cultural attitudes. There have always been some form of strong female beings in Hindu religion, but rarely in Indian culture. The goddess Durga, Kali, and other mother deities possess a powerful, angry and very vengeful aspect. Few Indian film directors took Doss's extreme view on female vengeance, and those who have (Kanti Shah for example) are never produced as what is considered a mainstream movie. Actresses in the majority of Indian films are still passive objects of desire or good daughters, mothers, and sisters that follow the rules the masculine culture has set out for them[5]. Their roles are more passive-aggressive than outright confrontational, and the hyper-violent role of avenger never really caught on as it has in other countries.

If the technicolor clothing, broad acting, female vengeance, funky musical numbers and hard-to-follow historical references aren't your cup of tea[6], then you may want to consider a more straightforward Western with **MERA GAON MERA DESH** (D: Raj Khosla, 1971).

As mentioned earlier, Masala has always been a part of Indian cinema in one form or another. As a friend once told me, "I think comedy is just part of the mix in India, isn't it? It's what's seen as 'commercial'. And they have this idea that if you put something for everyone in there, then you'll get a bigger audience. They don't really understand genre. Even the Ramsays put daft comedy scenes in their films." Luckily for us, Khosla tones down the zaniness of Doss's comedic lexicon in exchange for **MER GAON MERA DES**'s realism and brutality without sacrificing entertainment.

Trouble maker and small-time crook Ajit is jailed for theft, only to be released after six months in the care of Major Jaswant Singh, a one-armed good-natured officer of the law for the sleepy rural town. City boy Ajit has a tough time at first getting used to the agrarian environment, but eventually he falls in love with village chief's daughter, Anju, and the idea of settling down begins to suit him.

Of course this can't happen, and 45 minutes into the film we meet Thunkar and his gang of *dacoits* ("bandits"). The *dacoits* assault local townspeople, setting in motion the deadly remainder of the film. When Anju's father is murdered by the thugs and Ajjit is viciously beaten by a man on horseback (in a scene that would have fit in any Spaghetti Western), then it's high octane Western action from here on out. Of course, the action is punctuated every so often with fancy musical interludes by the brilliant soundtrack duo Laxmikant-Pyarelal. Their score is spiced with a twangy guitar lick here and a funky organ there, once again referencing popular themes by Ennio Morrione.

At the same time that Khosla was working on his interpretation of the American West, Tamil director C. M. Kanran released two of his films back to back.

The Tamil film industry is the second largest in India, sometimes called "Kollywood". As with the popular term Bollywood (the name commonly used to refer to the Hindi-language film industry, which combines Bombay and Hollywood), Kollywood is a portmanteau created from combining Kodambakkam, a residential neighborhood in the city of Chennai (the capital city of the Indian state of Tamil Nadu) where the main Tamil studios are, and, of course, Hollywood. Although made in 1972, a time when most films were produced in full color, Karnan's films **GANGA** and **JAKKAMMA** were filmed in black and white, due to a variety of studio limitations.

JAKKAMMA

Karnan's **JAKKAMMA** is probably as pure an Indian Western as you can get. There is little of the manic Masala mix that infused with the bloodthirsty nuttiness of Doss' **PISTOLWALI** and **GUNFIGHTER JOHNNY**. Instead the film is more of a typical Tamil melodrama about rural cow herders and the hard times they face when bandits raid their stock, steal their women, shoot their men, and smash up their villages. All is lost, or so it seems, until one angry woman decides to pick up a gun and take a stand against the bandits.

Karnan's films feature less of appearances of the "savage" Naga tribesmen[7] that plagued **PISTOLWALI** and **GUNFIGHTER JOHNNY**. Instead we have more of the traditional Indian outlaw genre heavily influenced by the Italian love of Mexican *banditos* as protagonists.

JAKKAMMA sports some impressive outdoor cinematography. exploiting the stunning beauty of Tamil Nadu, with its wide open plains, gorgeous skies, and rugged terrain. This is probably as close as any studio ever got to capturing the essence of the American West without even trying. C. M. Kanran's producer didn't have to build any fancy "outdoor" sets, just set up the camera and let the lens drink in all the beauty.

The songs featured are in a more classical/traditional vein than a 70s pop hit, although the soundtrack does sport the occasional nifty electric surf guitar hooks among the tablas, sitaars, etc.

If you want a film with the goofiness of **PISTOWALI** mashed up with the realism of **MER GAON MERA DESH**, then you have my all time favorite Indian Western: Bollywood director Narendra Bedi's 1973 epic **KHOTE-SIKKAY**. Of all the films mentioned thus far, this is the closest you'll get to an official unofficial remake of an American Western. A group of ne'er do wells come to the aide of a dusty rural town against a band of cut throats and thieves.

---

[5] Monica Motwani, The Changing Face of the Hindi Film Heroine, G Magazine Online, 1996
[6] A few of film by K.R.S. Doss included references to the British invasion of Amarvedu at the time of Bobbili war in South India, circa 1750s.

[7] The Nagas are an actual group of people from Nagaland, a state in the far north-eastern part of India, and have always been treated as the country's token wildmen. Most often in films the Nagas have been villians or "noble savages", seen running aorund in feathers and loincloths hunting snakes and stealing women, or as country bumpkins good only for comic relief. Pretty much how the Indians were treated in American film.

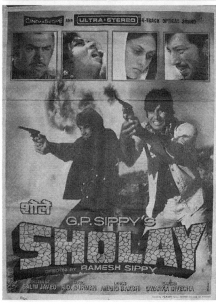

KHOTE-SIKKAY is a forerunner of yet another emerging sub-genre, the Curry Western. Gone is a lot of the playfulness of the lead, replaced by the development of a grim anti-hero *daaku* or *dacoit*. The *Daaku* Western slips even further into the realm of bad boy territory two years before Ramesh Sippy's groundbreaking smash **SHOLAY**. **KHOTE-SIKKAY** features Indian action super star, Feroz Khan as a mysterious Johnny Cash "man in black" look-alike horseman who is hunting down a vicious bandit named Jhanga. Jhanga has murdered too many innocents and it's up to "The Horseman" to stop the monster. Khan cuts a dashing figure as he shows up unexpectedly throughout the film at crucial plot twist accompanied by the theme to **A FISTFUL OF DOLLARS**. Kahn made a career out of playing characters inspired by Mr. Clint Eastwood's lone gunman in the Dollar Trilogy.

Meanwhile we're introduced to another major player, Raju (we know this because the same Morricone theme is played), when he's accosted on the street by some thugs and easily dispatches them with his kung fu skills. Raju meets with his brother Ramu, and they team up with Danny, the cool-as-a-cucumber card shark, to figure out how to handle the bandits. À la **THE MAGNIFICENT SEVEN**, a team of rag tag folks are gathered, including Bhaggu the Romantic, Jaggu the YoYo King, Bhaghu the Giant, and Rani, a local prostitute with a heart of gold.

Despite the lengthy 182 minute run, there is nary a dull moment. Our group assembles at Ramu's village where their help is less than appreciated by the fearful townsfolk. Luckily for them, the Mysterious Horseman shows up to help prepare the village for the final showdown with the bandits. He sings the catchy tune "Jeevan Mein Tu Darna Nahin," pumping up the bravery of the entire village. It goes without saying that there are wonderful dance numbers by R. D. Burman. The soundtrack is bouncy and very enjoyable, even with the blatant theft of Morricone's compostions along with Nito Rota's theme from Francis Ford Coppola's **THE GODFATHER** (1972). Other winks and nods include Jhanga's use of a pocket watch to torment his victims (from **A FISTFULL OF DOLLARS**), and an assortment of other scenes.

KALA SONA is a 1975 Hindi film from director Ravikant Nagaich, and again stars Feroz Khan as yet another rebel with a cause. India is so vast and has immense stretches of seemingly barren scrub land that you can be in your office in a major city one moment, and a short distance away riding your horse in a dusty rural village the next. I imagine this is what makes this modern, present-day Indian Western so believable. In this film, Kahn is a big city lawyer who ventures into the outback and encounters assorted troubles when he encounters... yes, bandits. **KALA SONA** takes an even harder edge than **KHOTE-SIKKAY,** and finds itself further away from the Curry Western and deeper into Daaku territory.

Buy the time **SHOLAY** (D: Ramesh Sippy) rolled into production, the Masala craze had fallen by the wayside, its violent, surreal, silliness passé due to the popularity and rise of the Daaku genre. **SHOLAY** was released in 1975 to underwhelming reviews and was expected to tank. Turned out that this "Curry" Western was a sleeper hit that soon became a super smash and then went on to being one of the biggest grossing Indian films of all time. Of course, few in the US ever heard of the film, and the DVD released in 2003 by Eros received little fanfare and love, as it was the government-approved, edited, pan and scan version, and none of the songs were subtitled.

There is little that I can add to the overwhelming monster that is **SHOLAY**. Director Sippy took what could have been a run-of-the-mill daaku (featuring plot elements shamelessly borrowed from **MER GAON MERA DESH** and **KHOTE-SIKKAY** – but then that's the essence of a lot of Indian cinema), and created a classic.

In a plot following **MER GAON MERA DESH**'s, a retired police officer conscripts two convicted but lovable rogues to help in capturing a dacoit chief and his crew, who are terrorizing a small rural town. You kind get the drift. What made **SHOLAY** such a hit wasn't just the film's epic scope and its incredible soundtrack (by musical genius R.D. Burman), but its two super stars, actors Amitabh Bachchan (who would later take Bollywood by storm in the 1978 film **DON**) and Dharmendra. It's one of the few insanely great Indian films that you can easily find. But buy the director's uncut DVD if you can find it!

The 1980s ushered in an odd time for the Western in India. Rakesh Kumar made **JOHNY I LOVE YOU** in 1982, a romantic thriller with Western overtones. After the death of his wife, a bandit decides to go straight. However, he is pulled back into the fold when his son becomes involved with the daughter of a rich man. It's a convoluted mess, but that's not all that unusual since, well, it is an Indian film. Also out that year was Narendra Bedi's **KACHCHE HEERE** which follows the well-worn tale of a young man who is out for blood. As the survivor of a blood-thirsty purge of his family, this young man must match brawn and brains with a horrible bandit. In the film, our protagonist also tangles with a Bollywood producer for good measure. The Western angle is tenuous at best.

Just when you think that the genre has breathed its last, director Harush Shah does a decent job of reviving the Curry Western with **ZALZALA** (1988). **SHOLAY**'s Dharmendra stars in this rural action adventure film about a man in search of a golden temple dedicated to Shiva. He encounters bandits and a love interest. By the time **ZALZALA** was released, the Masala and Curry Westerns were pretty much history and the Daaku genre was firmly in place.

Again, for some odd sense of abuse, I am including a film by that master of Indian no-budget cinema, Mr. Kanti Shah. Shah started his career with the blockbuster melodrama action film **GUNDA** in 1985. Since then he, along with his brother Krishan Shah, a few other less notable directors, his crew and actors have churned out over 100 productions under the moniker of Pali Films and a few other loosely associated studios. Shah's style is The Static Shot, letting his team ham it up before cutting the next static shot – then to the next, etc., while canned music as soundtrack is never ending.

The closest Shah has ever gotten to a Western other than the dozen or so Dacoit movies or "Daaku/Jungle" films he made with his wife, the bodacious Sapna Tanveer, would be his **DUPLICATE SHOLAY** (2002). From what I can gather a "Duplicate" in the title gives Kahn liberty to take a popular film and remake it without any legal action as a parody. He did the same thing in 2003 when he mauled Rajkumar Kohli's 1979 film **JANNI DUSHAMN** under the imaginative title of **DUPLICATE JANNI DUSHMAN** (see review on page 58).

The past few years have seen a nostalgic return to genres once considered too quaint, trite or passé to treat with any respect. I was very surprised when the 2011 Telugu film **SRI RAMARAJYAM** became a regional hit. This was a seriously glorious rendition of an old skool mytholoical by the Telugu director Bapu. Bapu successfully reinvented a cherished national genre that had grown tired and repetitive. The same can be said of the Masala Westerns, which have had a sort of mini boom in the past few years.

Traditional Indian Westerns were revisited in 2009 when **QUICK GUN MURUGUN** moseyed out of Tamil Nadu and immediately fell on its face. The film was savaged by most critics who just didn't get it in my opinion. I had major misgivings about **QUICK GUN MURUGUN**, but I am glad to say that the film was a joyful nod and wink to the bygone genre. Director Shashanka Ghosh's blantly "hip" style has slightly skewed the genre in such a manner as to make it accessible to today's internet savvy audiences. **QUICK GUN MURUGUN** has all the hallmarks of a Tamil cowboy film, from the flamboyantly attired pencil mustached hero to the grungy, loud-mouthed bandits ... but with great cinematography and a witty script that keeps everything fresh and highly enjoyable.

The film opens as a cowboy named Quick Gun Murugun is gunned down by some villains. He is then carted off to *Yama Loka*, the afterlife, by a *Yamadutas* demon. In *Yama Loka* he petitions to be reincarnated as soon as possible so he can return to Earth to protect a village of vegetarian peasants (and their sacred cows) from the hungry beef-eating *dacoits*. Once he does make it back to Earth he must face down the bandits while protecting the village and the woman he loves.

The film flopped, but has had some success reincarnated on DVD, especially since the release retains the original Tamil/English/Telugu/Hindi mixed language version, rather than being badly dubbed into Hindi. There are even English subtitled whenever Tamil is spoken. Typically I hate Indian comedies, but **QUICK GUN MURUGUN**, with its wonderful fantasy elements of the bureaucratic afterlife (similar in a feeling to Tim Burton's **BEETLEJUICE**), and obvious nods to a half a dozen Hollywood, Spaghetti, and Masala Westerns, had me loving it.

IRUMBUKKOTTAI MURATTU SINGAM is another Tamil cowboy flick from 2010 which stars the popular Indian actress Padmapriya. In it she's a gun wielding village woman fed up with rampaging *dacoits*. I have yet to track down a copy of this film, so all I can say is that is looks darn good! Apparently this film has numerous references to past famous Italian (Clint Eastwood), Hollywood (John Wayne), and Indian Westerns (**SHOLAY**, **GANGA**, and others). The film was a major regional hit for director Chimbudeven, so maybe more Westerns are in his future ... and ours.

I can only hope. • • •

> ***Disclaimer****:*
> *The terms I have bandied about, Masala Westerns, Curry Westerns, the oft confusing Daaku and Dacoit Westerns are not concise genres. If any of you have better definitions, please feel free to write. I love letters.*

Special thanks to Cara Romano who is a diehard fan of **PISTOLWALI**, Chaitanya Reddy for translation assistance, Natasha Morrow, and especially Todd Stadtman for his eye-opening blog **diedangerdiediekill.blogspot.com**

THAI KAIJU:
A SKETCHY INTRODUCTION TO GIANT MONSTERS IN THAI CINEMA

• Jolyon Yates

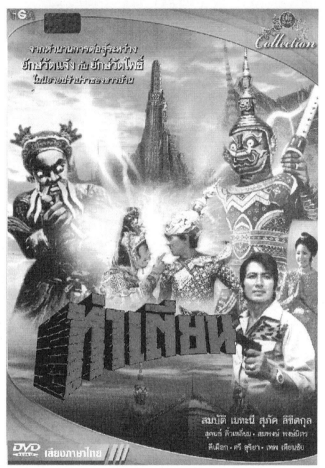

DVD cover for **TAH TIEN** (1973)

Until the last decade little of Thai cinema has reached western theatres, though many a western film has been shot there, including **THE MAN WITH THE GOLDEN GUN** (1974) and **REVENGE OF THE SITH** (2005). It was the location for **CHANG** (1927), a documentary on a family versus the fauna of northern Thailand, or Siam as it was known until 1939, by Merian C Cooper and Ernest B Schoedsack of **KING KONG** (1933) fame. Thailand's own giant ape movies were to come with those featuring Hanuman of the Ramakien, the Thai derivation of the Hindu epic Ramayana, in which the ape fights alongside Phra Ram against the monstrous forces of Thotsakan. Hanuman had featured in Mythological movies of India since as far back as **SATI ANJANI** ("The Birth of Hanuman", 1922), and was the subject of Thai animation pioneer Payut Ngaokrachang's second short, "The New Adventures of Hanuman" (**HANUMAN PACHON PAI KRANG MAI**, 1957), a 20 minute fantasy with an anti-communist message made in collaboration with Japanese animators and the US Embassy of Bangkok. Often human sized, Hanuman can grow into a colossus big enough to carry a mountain.

However, the first Thai giant monster movie would be **TAH TIEN** (1973), which presents Yak Wat Chaeng (or Yuk Wud Jaeng/Yak Wat Jang depending on how one romanises the name). *Yak* (aka *Yaksha*) are the fierce guardians, *dvarapala*, of the *Bot*, the assembly hall for monks in a Thai Buddhist *Wat*, temple, in which the main image of Buddha is kept. Wat Chaeng itself is now known as Wat Arun, short for Wat Arunratchawararam Ratchawora-mahawihan, and there are two guardians, both from the Ramakien. The white one is Sahassa Decha (aka Sahassateja). The green one, the movie star, is the aforementioned Thotsakan. Yak Wat Chaeng has bulging eyes, indicating rapt attention to the words of Buddha. The movie title, literally 'flattened dock', is the bank of the Chao Phraya where it flows past the Grand Palace in Bangkok, and the leveling is said to have been caused by the combat of the two giants whose temples, Wat Arun and Wat Pho, lie across the river from each other in this district. Wat Pho contains a 46 metre long reclining Buddha, who keeps himself above the feud.

In the prologue of the movie Yak Wat Chaeng stomps a temple thief into the ground with his foot and a *krabong* staff. Chaeng is represented onscreen by a 15ft figure with a simply articulated lower jaw and moveable eyes and arms, and a pair of Chaeng size boots for close-ups of thief stomping. The scene introduces three characteristics of Chaiyo Productions monster movies, firstly how bloody they are, secondly how darn chatty the monsters can be; the thief is pounded, spraying the red stuff, as Chaeng laughs, then Chaeng delivers his remarks, a bit late for the enlightenment of the wrongdoer. Thirdly, as was common in Asian exploitation cinema, several familiar pieces are filched for **TAH TIEN**'s soundtrack, here Gustav Holst's 'The Planets' and some covers of Ennio Morricone Western themes, although there is also a jolly song about the temple guardians over the opening credits. Chaeng returns after 92 minutes involving a frog woman, a snake man, two suitmation dragons (possibly the Thai creature, Hayra), a wide-mouthed gorilla and a man-eating crocodile. The latter two scenes introduce other staples of Chaiyo: topless women being ogled and/or groped, and crocodile attacks. Chaeng takes human form for a while, but his financial dispute with fellow guardian Yak Wat Pho (aka Yuk Wud Pho) spins out of control and they become giants. Flame from Pho's hand brings down a helicopter, water from Chaeng's mouth floods a bridge. There is some use of miniature scenery but in most shots the stiff figures are wheeled about in front of Bangkok streets, more like a scene of dueling parade floats than a monster showdown. After a few minutes the warriors are pacified and return to being statues.

Chaeng returned in **YAK WAT JANG WU JUMBORG A** (1974, aka **JUMBORG ACE VS THE GIANT, GIANT AND JUMBO A, JANBORG A TAI GIANT, YUK WUD JAENG POB JUMBO A, YUK WAT JANG POB JUMBO A, TITAN AGAINST JUMBO A**, and others as shall be told…), and the water starts to get a little muddy here. Beware crocodiles.

Popular culture in Thailand has had a long standing relationship with that of Japan, at least as far back as its first movie theatre, the Japanese Cinematograph built in 1905. In the late 1930s, the pro-Japan military dictatorship decreed the making of propaganda films, shot on 16mm, and the surplus of this stock after the war became material for a film production boom. 16mm colour reversal film yields particularly vivid hues, a distinctive palette in the fantasy films of the 1970s.

By that decade superhero shows had become hugely popular around Asia, primarily the series from Tsuburaya Pro, which had been in business since April 12 1963. Around this time the studio was visited by Sompote 'Sands' Saengduenchai on a Thai government scholarship to study cinematography, and once back in Thailand, Sands founded Chaiyo Productions and made **TAH TIEN**. *Chaiyo* means 'Triumph' or 'Bravo' and the logo is a pair of *Qilin/Kilen*, a horned chimera of good omen. In 1973 Sands made a licensing deal with Noboru Tsuburaya, whereby Chaiyo owned Thailand television broadcast rights to the first six Ultraseries and 'Jumborg Ace' (January

17th ~ December 29th 1973, 50 episodes). They also made a deal to produce two monster movies sharing their characters. 22 years later, just after Noboru's death, Sands would approach Kazuo Tsuburaya and begin a series of claims about not only ownership of the Ultra franchise worldwide, but also having suggested the Ultraman character in the first place. Unfortunately as of this writing it is Chaiyo, and not Tsuburaya, which has made the Ultraman and Ultra Seven series available on dvd in the US. For a report on the affair please read the article 'Legal Victories for Tsuburaya Productions' on SciFiJapan.com.

Tsuburaya Pro had already contributed to monster films of South East Asia, starting with Foo Hwa Cinema Co Ltd of Taiwan's **TSU HONG WU** (February 18 1971), the undoubtedly true story of the first Ming Emperor Zhu Yuanzhang, with monster special effects directed by Koichi Takano. Takano's footage, not all of which made it into the final cut, was recycled for the sequel released December 31st that same year, **A STORY OF LOU BO-WEN**, directed by fellow Japanese Namio Yuasa, who had been film making in Taiwan since the mid 1960s. The scenes also appeared in **SEA GOD AND GHOSTS** (LONGWANG SAN TAIZI, 1977), **THE FAIRY AND THE DEVIL** (1982), possibly the **SAKYAMUNI BUDDHA** films c1980 and Korea's **THE FLYING MONSTER** (BICHEONGOESU, 1984), which also sampled from Tsuburaya's ultrahero television shows.

'Jumborg Ace' the series deals with Naoki Tachibana, a Cessna pilot who fights invaders from Planet Growth, with powers granted to him by Kain of The Emerald Planet. When he yells "Jum Fight!" the plane becomes the jumbo cyborg of the title. A more heavily armored android, Jumborg 9, is introduced in episode 27. The leaders from Growth are Antigone (episode 1-13), Madgone (13-32), Satangone (32-46) and the supreme leader, Demongone (46-50), who has male and female faces. Appropriately enough, given what will happen to the show, Antigone is named after the daughter/sister of Oedipus.

In the movie, Yak Wat Chaeng, Yak Wat Pho, Jumborg Ace and Jumborg 9, with the aid of the Earth patrol Protective Attacking Team, fight various creatures commanded by Demongone and Jum Killer, a robot which defeated Ace in the series. We are flung in and out of scenes, the bulk of which are from the television series, with little regard for narrative or continuity, but I think the main plot line concerns Jum Killer stealing a crystal from a three-headed beast, which has Godzilla's roar, in a cave beneath Wat Arun. The crystal is used in a diamond solar beam weapon set up on either Mars or The Moon. Chaeng and Jumborg fight the villains on Earth and at the beam weapon site. This time around, all the giants are portrayed via suitmation, with stiff dolls for flying scenes. Chaeng's staff can extend, fire energy bolts and throw up a force shield. On this occasion Chaiyo made it through a superhero movie without bloodshed, nudity or crocodiles.

The film was then bought for release in Taiwan. Roughly 30 minutes were retained, and about 50 minutes of new footage added, directed by Chen Hun-Ming (aka Chen Hong Min) and starring Wen Chang-Lung (some sources give Yen Chiang Lung and Man Kong Lung). The original 'Jumborg A' series starred Naoki Tachibana as... Naoki Tachibana. This edition was released as **HUA XING REN** or **MARS MEN** in 1975. It had made so much money by this point, $144,230 from a budget of $45,000, that the Taiwanese team produced another giant guardian versus space monster film in 1976, **ZHANG SHEN** (WAR GOD, aka **CALAMITY**). Wen Chang-Lung was also in the Taiwan re-edits of three Kamen Rider movies, known locally as **SUPER RIDER**.

The 84 minute feature was dubbed and re-edited as **GLI UOMINI DI MARTE** (The Men of Mars) in Italy, and ran between 92 and 100 minutes. Jumborg Ace is referred to as "il giganto roboto Americano". Italian posters credit direction to Seika Den. When it reached Turkey the film was known as **MARS ADAM** (Mars Man/Men). By the 1990s the Taiwanese/Thai/Japanese palimpsest had reached France, where the original script was ignored, a French dub was imposed, and it was released as **LES HOMMES D'UNE AUTRE PLANETE** (The Men of Another Planet). It is this version which played at the Fantasia Festival 2010 in Montreal. One country where the Jumborg movie has not been shown to date is Japan.

Footage was recycled in Sompote Sands' final movie **KING-KA KAYASIT** aka **MAGIC LIZARD** (1985), although the star here is a rollerskating man-sized frilled lizard which can fly when it spins its frill like helicopter blades. As in many of his movies, Sands also reuses footage from his own film **CHORAKE** (CROCODILE, 1981, aka **JORRAKAY, HORROR OF THE CROCODILE, GIANT CROCODILE: BLOODY DESTROYER**) which itself recycled footage from the Thai & South Korean film **AGOUI GONGPO** (HORROR OF THE CROCODILE, 1978) and Sands' disaster movie **PAEN DIN WIP-PA-YOK** (aka **PANDIN WIPPAYOKE**, 1978).

Returning to 1974, Sompote Sands and Tsuburaya Pro teamed up for the second and last time, legally, with **HANUMAN AND THE 7 ULTRAMEN** (**HANUMAN POB JED YODMANUD** or **NOOMAAN BUAK JET YAAWTMANOOT**), directed by Shohei Tojo.

Hanuman the ape hero from the Ramakien carries a three bladed weapon, the *trisoon*, a weapon of Shiva originally named the *trishul*. This can be transformed into a *krabong* club and fire energy weapons. Hanuman can fly when he assumes the pose of a *devata* angel. He is also prone to scratching himself and dancing about in the manner of his depiction in *khon* dance dramas and *nang* puppet theatre performances.

MARS MEN credited here as a "Shochiku Film"

VCD cover of **PHRA ROD MEREE** (1981)

Mangkapon & friend

THE NOBLE WAR (1984), Hanuman front & centre

GARUDA (2004)

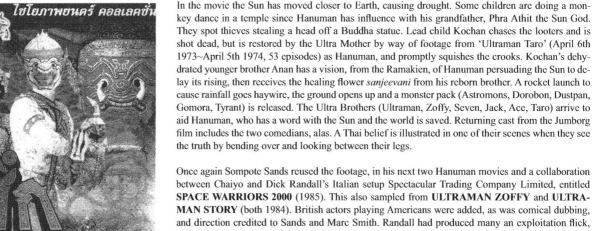

KA KEE (1980) carried by Garuda in *devata* pose

In the movie the Sun has moved closer to Earth, causing drought. Some children are doing a monkey dance in a temple since Hanuman has influence with his grandfather, Phra Athit the Sun God. They spot thieves stealing a head off a Buddha statue. Lead child Kochan chases the looters and is shot dead, but is restored by the Ultra Mother by way of footage from 'Ultraman Taro' (April 6th 1973~April 5th 1974, 53 episodes) as Hanuman, and promptly squishes the crooks. Kochan's dehydrated younger brother Anan has a vision, from the Ramakien, of Hanuman persuading the Sun to delay its rising, then receives the healing flower *sanjeevani* from his reborn brother. A rocket launch to cause rainfall goes haywire, the ground opens up and a monster pack (Astromons, Dorobon, Dustpan, Gomora, Tyrant) is released. The Ultra Brothers (Ultraman, Zoffy, Seven, Jack, Ace, Taro) arrive to aid Hanuman, who has a word with the Sun and the world is saved. Returning cast from the Jumborg film includes the two comedians, alas. A Thai belief is illustrated in one of their scenes when they see the truth by bending over and looking between their legs.

Once again Sompote Sands reused the footage, in his next two Hanuman movies and a collaboration between Chaiyo and Dick Randall's Italian setup Spectacular Trading Company Limited, entitled **SPACE WARRIORS 2000** (1985). This also sampled from **ULTRAMAN ZOFFY** and **ULTRAMAN STORY** (both 1984). British actors playing Americans were added, as was comical dubbing, and direction credited to Sands and Marc Smith. Randall had produced many an exploitation flick, including Sands' own **CROCODILE** and the awesome **FOR Y'UR HEIGHT ONLY** (1981) and **PIECES** (1982), so respect due. When **SPACE WARRIORS 2000** made its way to US television, Tsuburaya got word and the film has never been seen again, legally.

In 1979 the negative of **6 ULTRA BROTHERS** was flown to Japan, edits were made, including a new title song performed by Isao Sasaki, and it was released as **ULTRA ROKU KYODAI TAI KAIJU GUNDAN** (*6 Ultra Brothers versus The Monster Army*) during Golden Week (late April to early May). There was another Chaiyo cut of **6 ULTRA BROTHERS** in the 1980s, **HANUMAN vs 11 ULTRAMAN** (**HANUMAN POB SIB ET YODMANUD**), editing in footage of four more Ultrabeings, Leo, Astra, 80 and Ultra Father.

Following the financial success of the Ultraman collaboration, Sands suggested to Toei that their heroes could also be teamed with Hanuman. Toei declined, but Sands proceeded anyway. **HANUMAN AND THE 5 RIDERS** (**HANUMAN POB HAR AIMODDAENG**, 1974) teams the ape with Kamen Riders 1, 2, V3, X and Rider Man, courtesy of Chaiyo copies and footage from the movie **FIVE RIDERS vs KING DARK** (**GONIN RAIDA TAI KINGU DAKU**, 1974).

King Dark, the arch enemy from 'Kamen Rider X' (February 16th~October 12th 1974, 35 episodes) launches a monster army on Thailand. Interspersed amongst the Rider footage we see Yommaban/Yama/Phra Yam, lord of *Narok*, Thai Hell, send a trio of crooks back to the mortal world. Insert temple banditry/dead child/Hanuman's revenge from the previous film. Once the monsters have been dispatched, King Dark has a kidnapped scientist create a gang of men with creature heads, a pig, a fish, a frog, a chicken and so on, but they fall to the Riders too. As a last resort, King Dark becomes a giant, so Hanuman turns up again and the final fight is on.

The Thai footage is garish and gory, particularly the Narok scenes. In the Hell of Adulterers people are forced to climb a tree of thorns, and the final shots of the film detailing the crooks' fate is incredibly bloody. As is usual in Sands' films, there is child killing, excreta to the face, naked women, comical transvestism (the *katoei* is a fixture of Thai entertainment) and pilfered music, including the Gort theme from **THE DAY THE EARTH STOOD STILL** (1951) and a cover of The Jackson 5's 'Never Can Say Goodbye'.

In the following decade Chaiyo continued its Mythological films. The title beauty of 1980's **KA KEE** is snatched from a royal court by Garuda, the bird man ridden by Vishnu, here portrayed as a man with wings and a bird helm. The Mythological Musical stars popular leading man Sorrapong Chatree (also in the zombie/werewolf/magic movie **JING JORK PHEE SING** aka **POSSESSED BY THE FOX**, 1985, and the historical fantasy **THE QUEEN OF LANGKASUKA**, aka **PUEN YAI JAN SALAT**, 2008). Garuda's energy weapon has Tsuburaya's maser cannon sound effects, which also turn up in **PRINCE ROT & PRINCESS MERI** (**PHRA ROD MEREE**, aka **NANG SIB SONG**, **PHRA RODASAN** etc, 1981), previously filmed in Cambodia as **PUTHISEN NEANG KONG REY** (1972). This is the tale of twelve sisters abandoned by their destitute parents and fallen into the hands of *yaksha* and their shape-shifting leader Santhumala. With the aid of a friendly male ogre they escape and soon catch the eye of a local king, who marries them all. Santhumala, whose true form is a giant *yaksha* with massive bare breasts, appears to the king as a beautiful woman, so he makes her his Number One Concubine and the pregnant sisters are sealed in a cave. Santhumala gouges their eyes out, although Phra, the youngest, gets to keep one of hers. The starving sisters then have their babies, and before you can say "Anthropophagus The Beast" their hunger is assuaged, except for Phra's child, whom she names Rothasen. The friendly ogre frees him, and grows breasts to suckle him, even when he becomes adolescent. Rothasen feeds the sisters on the proceeds from his cockfighting, and eventually marries Santhumala's daughter Meri. Rothasen finds the sisters' eyes in a jar and rides off to restore them, which breaks Meri's heart. It is hard to decide which is more disturbing, the eye gouging, the tearing up and eating of the baby, the cockfighting or the boy pleasuring himself with the ogre's nipples. I suspect the Disney version would have more songs.

The next Hanuman film from Sands was **THE NOBLE WAR (SUK KUMPAKAN**, 1984), based on episodes from the Ramakien. It features Thotsakan's brothers Phipek, who has defected to Hanuman's side, and Kumpakan, who feels bound to fight for Thotsakan, although he knows the cause is wrong. Hanuman's uncle Sugreep/Sukhrip becomes a giant red six-armed ape god who attacks the city of Longka. Kumpakan becomes a colossus and floods the home of the Vanara (ape people), so Hanuman enlarges to dislodge him. The Vanara get attacked by a crocodile, Hanuman takes the form of a bloated animal corpse, and the Sun God sequence from **6 ULTRA BROTHERS** is reused. The movie ends with Kumpakan's final battle against Phra Ram. The performances are in the manner of a khon drama; movement is a stylized dance, and the unmasked performers never move their mouths. This was the last giant monster movie to be produced by Chaiyo, and although big beasties continue to be popular in Thailand, except for commercials and homegrown superheroes like 'Squadron Sport Ranger' ('Kabuan Gaan Sabpordta Renje', August 6th ~ November 29th 2006, 16 episodes) they moved further away from the Japanese model.

GINSENG KING (aka **THREE HEAD MONSTER**, 1989) involves a three-headed ogre, a nazi zombie and the humanoid vegetable of the title. The hero is aided by monolithic colossi named Giant Eyes and Giant Ears, probably inspired by Qianli Yan and Shunfeng Er from the 'Journey To The West' story. The poster for **CHANG-ANG HUANG KHAI** (aka **PHI SONG NANG**, c1990) depicts two giant *naga* serpents, the reincarnations of sisters drowned in the Mekong, although if this is the same film as **HEAVENLY SPELL** then the creatures in the movie are much smaller. **THE PRINCE, THE WITCH & THE MERMAID (PHRA APAI MANI**, 2002) is a mythological tale based on an epic poem by Sunthorn Phu, featuring a giant sea witch named Nang Phiswa Samut/Pisua Samudr, previously filmed (1976-9) as Thailand's only cel animation feature by Payut Ngaokrachang and his team.

Thai titans entered the digital age with **GARUDA (PAKSA WAYU**, literally 'Wind Bird', 2004). A creature resembling the mythological birdman is disinterred and goes on the rampage in Bangkok. It contains the most blatant anti-miscegenation in a monster movie since **THE X FROM OUTER SPACE** (1967). Director/writer Monthon Arayangkoon has since made the horror films **THE VICTIM (PHII KHON PEN**, 2006) and **THE HOUSE (BAAN PHII SING**, 2007).

Giant spiders turn up in **PEESARD MANGMUM SAO** (1990) and **DEATH WEB** (2005). Giant snakes in **THAI GIANT KING COBRA (NGOO YUK PHAYA MAE BIA**, 1993), **BOA (BOA… NGUU YAK!**, 2006) and in two movies directed by Preaw/Pleo Sirisuwan, **VENGEANCE (PHAIRII PHINAAT PAA MAWRANA**, 2006) and **THE SCOUT (BIT PI-POP TA-LU LOHK**, 2009). A giant octopus, crab and turtle guard treasure in the pirate fantasy **SALAD TA DIAW KAB DEK 200TA** (aka **SALAD TADEAW**, 2008).

Less prosaic creatures appeared in a couple of comedies. In **THE SPERM (ASUJAAK**, 2007) aliens enlarge one spawn of a chronic onanist into a giant. In **COOL GEL ATTACKS (KRADEUB**, 2010) the country is invaded by blue cyclopean medicinal gel packs which can become the size of a bus.

Many Thai movies of the last decade are available on Region 1 DVD. I purchased the Tiga label releases of the Chaiyo titles from eThaiCD. Check your player can handle Region 3, and choose DVD over VCD if you can, the quality is better. The Chaiyo titles are cropped, scratchy, have no subtitles or dubs, let alone chapters, menus or any extras, but it is amazing they are available at all.

Information was gathered from online sources by fellow Thai-illiterates, so trust it accordingly. Thank you very much to those intrepid authors and the film experts who helped me directly, especially Timothy Paxton and Mang-

HANUMAN vs 11 ULTRAMAN (1984?)

kapon, who inspired this article. Mangkapon's monster character has appeared on television shows like Thailand's Got Talent, where he performed with his monster band, and creates and wears monster suits for films and commercials.

References
Books (Japanese titles translated)
Bangkok Nancy Furstinger
Complete Manual of Ultraman 3rd edition Tsuburaya Production
Culture in Thailand Melanie Guile
Eiji Tsuburaya: Master of Monsters August Ragone
Encyclopedia of All Monsters & Monstermen 1977 edition Keibunsha
Encyclopedia of Indian Cinema Ashish Rajadhyak & Paul Willemen
The Heritage of Thai Sculpture Jean Boisselier
Indian Mythology Jan Knappert
The Making of King Kong Orville Goldner & George E Turner
The Sculpture of Thailand ed. Theodore Bowie
Superhero Chronicles B Media Books Special
Tales from Thailand Supaporn Vathanaprida
Thailand in Pictures Stacy Taus-Bolstad

People
John Paul Cassidy (web spelunker extraordinaire)
Keith Aiken (Scifijapan)
Mangkapon (monster)
Yasutaka Nakanishi (translator)
Timothy Paxton (editor of Monster! International)
August Ragone (Master Monster Scholar)
Pete Tombs (author of Mondo Macabro)

Websites
And You Call Yourself A Scientist
Cinehound Forum
Clubdesmonstres
Die Danger Die Die Kill > Thai Style Kaiju
Enlejemordersertilbage.blogspot
eThaiCD
Fantasia Festival 2010
Henshin Hall of Fame
Kaijuphile.com > Rodan's Roost > Obscure Kaiju
Kavinman.blogspot
Mangkapon
MJSimpson.co.uk
Nanarland [French]
NinjaDixon.blogspot
Robert Hood's Giant Monster Film List
Schoolgirl Milky Crisis
Scifijapan
Siaminterhero.blogspot
Stomp Tokyo
Superheroes Lives
Tars Tarkas.net
Teleport City
Thai Film Journal
Thai Toku
Thai Worldview
Unknown Kino
Warauna Kiken (Susie Arabia)
Worldweird Cinema
WtfFilm
Youtube

WENG'S CHOP COVER MODEL
Leena Kurishingal

Brian Harris: Hey Leena, thanks for taking time out of your busy schedule to talk with WENG'S CHOP about you and your career! We're truly appreciative of the amazing photo shoot you did for our cover. Let's talk about your decision to get into the world of film and modeling.

Leena Kurishingal: Absolutely, twas great fun. Well, I guess a lot of the decision was simply embracing what was already there. It's been a yearning and a curiosity that's been with me since I was a child, doing stupid things that would make my mother and sister say, stop it or your face will freeze that way...unfortunately it was something I also fought for a long time because of fear and no one to encourage this kind of lifestyle. Or role models that looked like me doing it. Which created a long and varied path, including film school and some rock bottoms that finally pushed me to do what I felt inside. And I have to say, it made it a lot easier to think if I die tomorrow, I will be happy. No stone unturned, no misery of regret, even if it isn't as perfect as my dreams. It's still a work in progress :) Ultimately, it was overcoming the fear to be happy and fulfilled. I love people and what makes them tick, and understanding that and myself well enough to portray it is the ultimate challenge.

BH: What have been some of the pros and cons, that you've experienced, while working in the independent film industry?

LK: The cons are probably talked about a great deal more than the pros, generally speaking: minimal budgets, beginner crews, non-sequitur schedules..and all of that can be really true and difficult to deal with, mostly because of that mini-budget. But there are some definite pros involved I've seen. Everything is in the hands of the people on that set. Though it can be helpful, having 'names' involved isn't the only thing people are concerned with. The degree of catering to someone else's interests before your own vision just isn't there, as it is with large productions. There aren't as many people telling you 'no'. There's a lot more room to play and make magic. And frankly, some of those crappy cons circumstances are what allows for great bonding to happen with your intimate cast and crew -a great pro of independent films I've experienced first-hand. Sometimes it's like surviving a war together. Of course we all like a paycheck and some prestige, so...we look towards the large apple.

BH: You've also done a little voice-over work, is that correct? What do you like about voice-over work and have we heard anything you may have done?

LK: That's right, a voice over audition awaits me after this interview, actually. Voice overs are fun because you really get to play with the language and manipulate it, and find the challenge in expressing all these crazy emotions and notions, with just your voice. It lets you really feel the piece and find what brings it to life. I find there's also the guilty pleasure of just emoting. And no one sees you trying to emote a foolish storm in the recording booth while doing it. That's a plus, haha. Films not included, a Banco Popular radio advertisement I did would probably be the most notable to date, in addition to many corporate videos.

BH: What are some of the films you've starred in, especially in leading roles, and what are your thoughts on those films?

LK: Some of the early gems, like **FAST ZOMBIES WITH GUNS** and **THE LONG DECEMBER** were more action based and visual. They definitely have a special place in my heart because I helped on the production side making them. 100% was given by everyone and at the time, they were mostly fueled by the dream part of making films, not yet the business part. And I do think for the amount of resources, both were solid pieces. I got the opportunity to explore some really big, interesting characters that would not automatically be cast with my ethnicity. They let me do the best part of acting -which is creating someone completely different than yourself. In the past few years, I've stepped away from that type of genre some to explore more every day characters that suffer day to day conflicts, find internal growth, etc. Not so much guns, zombies and karate chops... the last particular couple of projects, **PROMISE LAND** and **INDIAN EXPRESS** (both currently in post), exemplify this. They deal with very real world problems of immigration, family ties, and what it takes to be happy. I'm very proud to help offer those stories to people looking for answers

themselves. And it has also been interesting exploring my own cultural background as an Indian-American. Having been born and raised in the US, I have found I've sought out more of my heritage 'playing' an Indian in some of these projects, than I ever have in my life otherwise. I've gotten a lot from it.

BH: Have you done any modeling? What attracted you to do modeling and how difficult is it to remain relevant in the industry?

LK: Oddly enough, you find modeling is just part of the working actor's bag of tricks. Being on the shorter end and all, I never saw myself as a model, and still sometimes am thrown by the term, but the need is out there to represent everyone. Particularly with the nature of advertising these days, with real people and real voices being sought. I guess I stay relevant simply by morphing gracefully into each new demographic I fit. I think the jobs find you. There was a good while when I did shoots for a lot of student loan companies, wearing a backpack as the college student or diversity spots. Now young and corporate has found me, so I invest in suits, lol. Every now and again, I'll do some wonderful portfolio or promo shoots, like *WENG'S CHOP*, where there's a lot more room to be artistic and stylized, and then you can be a little more out of the box. It's just a different acting muscle.

BH: Can you give the readers, both men and women, some tips on pursuing their goal of acting and/or modeling?

LK: Go in being realistic. Know it's an endurance game. As someone told me, success in this field is not linear, so be prepared for it all, if you really love it. That being said, get the proper training from people who know the ins and outs of what you want to do -might save you a little time. Don't be afraid of a 'day job', because you need money to make money. You are investing in the business of yourself constantly, with classes, professional pictures, and personal upkeep. Definitely get experience doing whatever projects you can, so you can make the connections for the next projects down the road. Help others along the way ... and learn to find a positive attitude. It's your own personal journey, and there's no way to get through the constant rejections of this field, without being able to take care of yourself mentally and emotionally. Still working on it myself.

BH: Is getting you to come back for another cover shoot, perhaps even a spread in the mag, a possibility?

LK: I'm already intrigued! Maybe so ... ;)

Big thanks to Leena Kurishingal for taking the time out for the photo shoot and for this interview! If you'd like to know more about Leena visit her at: leenakurishingal.com

Photo credits: (page 34) from the film **WAYWARD**, photo still, Photography by D. Antoine Dixon, othreeproductions.com; (page 35 top) from the film **THE LONG DECEMBER**, photo still, Photography by Jessica Sladek, jessicasladek.com; (page 35 bottom) Professional shot by Photography by Zöe McKenzie Photography, zoemckenziephotography.com; (page 36) photo Brian Harris.

35

5 DEADLY QUESTIONS FOR SIFU DB3

Interview by Brian Harris

Brian Harris: Hey David, thanks for taking the time out to do this short interview, we really appreciate it. So, WENG'S CHOP stands out from other zines for a few reasons but one of the biggest has been the distinctive look, created by you. Talk to us about your your passion for art and how it started for you.

David "DB3" Barnes: Thanks Brian. My passion for art started at 5 years-old when I drew my first Mickey Mouse, without tracing, back in the day. Walt Disney, The Little Golden Books as well as ''Sesame Street, gave me my blueprint to create and draw. My passion began to grow bigger once I received my first LEGO set for building castles, in my pre-teen years. Later on I graduated to animation and comic books by the time Middle School rolled around. "VOLTRON" was the first cartoon show where I had no picture to copy his look. Every time the show would air, I would painstakingly draw each part, little by little every day, just to make sure I captured every detail. I didn't have a VCR to record the episodes so I had to draw the parts by memory. Ha ha!

BH: Your style is extremely unique, how did you develop it. There's seems to be all kinds of influences there.

DB3: My unique (crazy) style started off by being not having room..which is..I always did my artwork on large formats, like cardboard, poster paper.. it didn't matter. I illustrated all the U.S. Leaders witnessing the BILL OF RIGHTS being signed, in the 5th grade, and won a $100.00 gift certificate for art supplies. My single lines started to get thicker and broader with detail because the art supplies I had were just crayons and pastels. No top-notch pencils, like they have now. When the crayons ran down, I used what was left of them, and used two fingers to finish up whatever I was doing. My art teachers use to show me how to draw with my right and left hand. It was very

crazy training back in the 5th grade.

BH: When you're working on a specific illustration, do you listen to music or throw on the TV for white noise? If so, what do you listen to or watch?

DB3: I listen to everything. Rock music is my ultimate tool for creating. Classic R&B is good for adding color sources. Hip hop works best for me when I'm experimenting outside my comfort zone.

BH: Have you ever considered getting some work together to pitch to some of the t-shirt companies out on the web?

DB3: I have never given it much thought, to pitch my designs to t-shirt companies because they always come and go. I'm not too fond of fads, especially in clothing, at all. The funny thing is...I never considered doing t-shirts in the first place. It was my fans who pushed me to develop an idea to do it. I think it's too much of a costly business, so I just do it only for collectors, because people in general think my art isn't commercial enough to sell. I've learned many lessons when it comes to a fickle audience. Don't please 1,000 haters, please only the 500 who care and the 300 who show support. Ha ha ha!

BH: What are some of the favorite pieces you've done and why are they your favorites?

DB3: Wow. What are my favorites that I have created up until now is impossible to choose. But I do have a Top 5:

#1 - CHOW YUN FAT from **THE KILLER** in my photos gallery at ''ORICONN'S WALL OF VISION.'' It's my ultimate statement and one of the very few where I only added two colors to a very menacing and direct picture.

#2 - **DEEP THROAT** because it's my first classic porno piece for a film that one one ever dared to create.

#3 - **THE 5 DEADLY VENOMS** because it's the ultimate kung fu film. No other artist has been able to illustrate the characters in their signature styles.

#4 - **DRIVE IN MOVIE** promo teaser. I love this one as a direct homage to my childhood Influences.

#5 - **FRIDAY THE 13TH**. It's a strong runner up because I didn't focus on the infamous money shots, I focused on the feeling of the film. Truly classic.

We at *WENG'S CHOP* would like to thank David for his amazing artwork, giving nature and dedication to cult cinema. You can check out more from DB3, as well as seek him out for your own projects by contacting him through Facebook at: facebook.com/davidoriconn

DR. DEATH'S DAY OF VIOLENCE:

Interview with Filmmaker Darren Ward

• Gary Baxter

During the summer, I took a 9 week course in radio production through the YMCA, the outcome being a show of up to an hour long going out on their Christian radio station. It was a no-brainer for me to do something on film and having already become aware of him [Darren Ward] through the internet I quickly contacted writer, producer and director Darren Ward in the hope of getting an interview with the man who had worked with 2 of my all-time favorite actors, David Warbeck and Giovanni Lombardo Radice.

Luckily for me Darren said yes and was kind enough to send me signed copies of his films, **SUDDEN FURY** and **A DAY OF VIOLENCE** so that I could prepare my questions and get as good an interview as possible. Darren was also kind enough to invite me to his home to conduct the interview, so armed with a mini-disc recorder and my questions ready my friend Jaymz and I hit the road, buzzing with excitement all the way.

Now, as prepared as I was nothing could have prepared me for just how laid back Darren was, he was more than happy to share his story and as a result I ended up with an in-depth, career spanning interview as well as gaining a huge insight into the world of independent film production. If you'd like to hear the full radio show you can find me on Facebook and check it out through Soundcloud, for now though, here's a little taster of what went down:

Gary Baxter: *So Darren, let's start at the beginning. You've been making films for a while now, how did you get started?*

Darren Ward: Well, I left school in 1989, I was 16 and my local video rep said a couple of his mates were making back yard movies, they were in their 20's. We met up and we really gelled you know? They were doing extravagant gore and I realized I wanted to direct. We made around 15 to 20 shorts between 89 and 91 and they've worked on every movie I've done

since and gone on to have great careers, Alistair Vardy has gone on to do pyro for **LOCK, STOCK AND TWO SMOKING BARRELS**, **SNATCH**, **BEHIND ENEMY LINES**, loads of Seagal movies and is now working on **DIE HARD 5** and Stuart Browne has done make-up for the new **BATMAN**, **SNOW WHITE AND THE HUNTSMAN** and **PROMETHEUS**.

*Tell us about your first feature **SUDDEN FURY**.*

Well, it was a long shoot due to funding issues and getting everyone on set at the same time due to other commitments so it took around 2 years to finally get done. It was based on a short I'd made called **BITTER VENGEANCE** which I'd sent to the British Amateur Video Awards and it got highly commended by the judges so I thought let's make a feature. I re-shot it, expanded the story and it did its thing, it really took off in Germany and was labeled a cult film there, the fanboys loved it and for a film that cost £15,000 (roughly $25,000) to make it's done okay. There are things I did then that I wouldn't do now for instance it's quite dialogue heavy but considering the kind of independent films that were being made at the time all the action sequences really helped it stand out so in that respect I'm still quite happy with it.

The film tells the story of gangsters fighting to control the trade of cocaine in the South East and the bloodshed that ensues, something that's still happening today in local news. Is that something you were aware of at the time of writing and did it play a part in inspiring this tale?

Well basically my inspiration mainly comes from having grown up with video nasties and Italian cinema, the horror, the Giallo and the Poliziotteschi and at the time I'd just got into the Heroic Bloodshed style films of John Woo and Ringo Lam which is why you get a kind of mixed genre of gangsters versus gore! You know, I thought I'd make my first feature an action film rather than a horror because I didn't wanna be bogged down with all the make-up and effects but I ended up putting loads in anyway as I didn't want everyone just getting shot. As a result you have people getting disemboweled, blown up and one guy gets a hand saw in the neck while one of David Warbeck's scenes has him putting a blow torch to the faces of a couple of goons in homage to Fulci's **CONTRABAND**.

While we're talking about Fulci do you have any particular favorites from old school Italian horror?

DEEP RED, ZOMBIE FLESH EATERS, CANNIBAL HOLOCAUST, CANNIBAL FEROX, CANNIBAL APOCALYPSE, pretty much all the Argento and Fulci stuff, I just saw them all really! I used to sneak down Sunday Morning and my dad would've left them lying around, so rightly or wrongly I was about 8 or 9 years old when I was first watching and I was always fascinated by how the make-up effects were done, I've always wanted to be involved in making films and originally I wanted to be a special effects artist but getting back to your question I'd never turn my back on Italian cinema, it's provided with some great inspiration and like the old directors I take an idea from here, an idea from there and I've been able to make the kind of films I like to see.

*Let's talk about the late, great David Warbeck, a regular face from the glory days of cult film. How did you get him on board for **SUDDEN FURY**?*

38

Just by chance really! I was at a theater in London for Eurofest, it was an all weekend thing and I was on my last legs wondering when my train home was and there he was in the bar. I approached him and told him I was making a film and that I'd written a part specifically for him (which I hadn't!) and he was up for it so I went home and wrote his part and he was excellent. He based his character Pike on Charlie Kray after seeing a photo of him so he was wearing slightly too small suits to make him look gangly and he really went for it. Of course by the he was quite ill and he never actually got to see the final cut as he passed away before filming ended. He did get to see rushes of his scenes and when Sage Stallone came over to get a commentary for Grindhouse Releasing's **THE BEYOND**, David was more than happy to show him them. But you know, you see these people in films growing up and then they're in your movie, it's unbelievable and a great privilege too, and to think that he almost became James Bond at one point! It's a shame the way that situation turned out but at the same time if he had taken over for Roger Moore I might never have got to work with him.

Nick Rendell is lead actor in both SF and ADOV, how did he get involved?

Nick is a good friend, he'd never had any acting training and one day I just said I want you to be in my film and that was it. You know, he's a natural, he's got great presence and he rises to the challenge of whatever I throw at him 110% every time. He teaches full in London and his grubby little secret is he's shot and killed all these people in my films, his students think it's great!

Let's move onto A DAY OF VIOLENCE, the tale of Mitchell, a debt collector who stumbles on £100,000 ($160,000) while on a routine collection which then leads to a very violent 24 hours. The film starts with Mitchell dead in a morgue telling his story through voice-over, did you feel maybe you were taking a bit of a risk giving away a vital piece of info like the hero dying right at the start?

Not really, I mean, there's a twist and it's quite a powerful twist and by the time you realize why what's happened has happened you've almost forgotten he dies anyway. Ultimately it adds weight to the final outcome and it's been really cool seeing different audience reactions, I had one guy calling me a bastard because the film had made him cry! The film continues to do well, it's just received its first US release and I'm currently planning the German Blu-ray release.

I think it goes without saying there is some great gore effects in ADOV, particularly the castration by garden shears and some awesome gun fights provided by Alistair and Stuart. As mentioned earlier you've worked with Giovanni Lombardo Radice, one of my favorite actors and once again he's killed on screen in stylish fashion, was he easy to get for your second feature?

Yeah, he was great! I found him online a while ago when everyone still used Myspace and he was very quick to get back to me and we stayed in touch, I told him I'd worked with Warbeck and I sent him the script and he loved it, he loved the emotional content. Originally he was going to play Boswell but it wasn't possible due to time restrictions and travel expenses so he agreed to play Hopper, he was an absolute gent, full of great stories and he brought a lot to his character and I'm pleased to say he'll be back for my next film, **BEYOND FURY**, in a feature roll.

Will that be a sequel to SUDDEN FURY?

Yeah, it'll follow the story of Walker and expand on his character as he's got older, Nick will be reprising his role, Barbara Cupisti is coming out of retirement for a feature, and possibly Bobby Rhodes from DEMONS 1 and 2. It will also finish up my crime trilogy, I'd always had in mind doing three crime films and then going onto do a full blown horror, I've got a few scripts to choose from.

In closing, what are your thoughts on on-screen violence?

I've always been against censorship since I was young you know, it was always about getting the uncut version of this film or that film so as for the violence I'm all for it, while I'm not a fan of so called torture porn and find films like **A SERBIAN FILM** a bit too much I've always been of the opinion that if you don't like what you're watching switch it off. What's the point in complaining about something you've seen when you've got the choice not to watch in the first place? And the BBFC seems to be more relaxed and attitudes are changing, I remember meeting Craig Lapper and said I that having ramped up the gore I thought for sure **A DAY OF VIOLENCE** would be cut and he told me it had been bought to his attention but there wasn't a problem.

Thanks very much for taking the time to chat to me Darren, it's been great.

You're welcome Gary.

If you enjoyed this interview and want to know more about Darren I strongly recommend checking out the full 59min radio version. Next time in Weng's Chop I'll be talking about my experience as an extra in the forthcoming independent British zombie comedy, CONVENTION OF THE DEAD, as well as an interview with the film's director Kelvin Beer.

Check out Darren Ward and his films at www.giallofilms.com

...

REVIEWS...

Yûreisen: Zempen and Yûreisen: Kôhen

Review © 2012 Stephen R. Bisstte

YÛREISEN: ZEMPEN (some sources translate this as "Zenpen") and **YÛREISEN: KÔHEN**, both from stories by Jiro Osaragi, were (despite the evocative titles) primarily samurai adventures with superstitious characters but only vague (and completely bogus) supernatural touches. Nevertheless, **YÛREISEN: ZEMPEN** will be of interest to Japanese horror devotees for one striking element.

Less then 17 minutes into the first of these two Toei Company Ltd. features, the demon mask western audiences associate with 鬼婆/ **ONIBABA** (1964) makes its startling appearance—般若, the classic Hannya mask from Noh theater, embodiment of a jealous female demon or being. There are actually two matching demon masks, worn by two mysterious figures who haunt the abandoned ruins of the so-called "demon mansion" our naïve hero Jiromaru (a very young looking Kinnosuke Nakamura, who was 25 at the time) explores while searching for his estranged uncle. The revelation of the first mask, dramatically framed by the bright scarlet inner lining of a kimono held as a frame for the demonic visage, is among the most memorable images in the entire film. Once the masks are off, though, the rumors of demons are abandoned: the masked pair turn out to by the Princess Yuki (Yumiko Hasegawa) and her lovely attendant Chacha (Hiroku Sakuramachi, making her screen debut at age 20), spied by the boyish Jiromaru amid one of their furtive midnight secreting of Yuki's family treasure to safe keeping beneath the floorboards of the crumbling estate.

Much like the American B westerns with borderline genre components, **YÛREISEN: ZEMPEN** and **YÛREISEN: KÔHEN** are sure to disappoint those seeking supernatural chills, as both features are rather prosaic widescreen color action programmers (much like the majority of big-screen American westerns at the end of the 1950s and beginning of the '60s). The titular ghost ship finally surfaces in the final minutes of the first feature, providing the cliffhanger teaser.

After its opening, in which the ship Kannonmaru and its skipper Jubei are lost at sea in a savage storm, leaving only the first mate Shinbei (aka "Gramps") the sole survivor, **YÛREISEN: ZEMPEN** is a land-locked traditional samurai outing. Despite Shinbei's dire warnings, Jubei's son Jiromaru, who has no love for the sea, heads off with his dog Shiro for the city of Kyoto, intent on finding his Uncle Gorodaiyu and becoming a samurai and (in time) a general. He instead finds a city in ruins, plagued by constant warfare in the wake of the despotic Matsunaga Danjo's overthrow of the Ashikaga Shogunate. In league with the rich Uncle Gorodaiyu, Danjo has imported rifles to use against the starving citizenry. Meeting first the peasant Oniyashi, who directs Jiromaru to the "demon mansion" where the lad meets Princess Yuki and Chacha, the lad bonds with the bandit Samanosuke (handsome Ryutaro Otomo) before finally meeting his Uncle Gorodaiyu and brutal cousin Saemontaro. The boy eventually abandons his samurai dreams as he realizes Yuki, Samanosuke and their rebel allies "were much nicer people than Matsunago Danjo and his uncle" (to quote Part 2's Nippon Golden Network subtitled synopsis), and joins forces with Samanosuke and his militia to rescue Princess Yuki from Danjo's clutches in the climactic melee. Shinbei handily appears with his ship, in search of Jiromaru, and they all set sail together to escape Danjo's army.

While western audiences were justifiably intoxicated with the international breakthrough hit 七人の侍 / **SHICHININ NO SAMURAI** / **SEVEN SAMURAI** (1954), films like **YÛREISEN: ZEMPEN** were far more typical of the genre in their native country. Japanese audiences flocked to these just as Americans filled hard-tops and drive-ins to see the steady studio torrent of westerns, and it must be said that despite the resources Toei provided for this movie (including four working ships for part 2), the same studio was lavishing far greater resources on their more fantastic samurai features (like Tadashi Sawashima's **NINJUTSU GOZEN-JIAI/TORAWAKAMARU** "The Koga Ninja", 1957) and multi-feature adventures (Kokichi Uchide's **SATOMI HAKKENDEN**/"Eight Brave Brothers", 1959, comprised of three features). It is very much a programmer in budget, scope, narrative, characters, pacing and its occasional battle sequences. The B-western ambience is strong, emphasized throughout by Jiromaru's greenhorn manner and his constant canine companion Shiro.

If **YÛREISEN: ZEMPEN** is a leisurely-paced B-western in samurai trappings, the second feature **YÛREISEN: KÔHEN** is essentially a pirate adventure on the high seas with some Jules Verne elements. The perky Shiro is nowhere to be seen, as picking up on the heels of the first installment, the second opus opens aboard ghost ship—wherein Jiromaru finds rotting bodies in its hold, and his hysteria mounts as he finds all his friends dead on the deck—in what quickly turns out to be nothing more than a fever dream. Once that's out of the way, Jiromaru, Samanosuke and even Oniyashi espouse their new devotion to the sea, but before they can set sail Princess Yuki and Chacha are tricked into boarding the pirate vessel Konjinmaru and kidnapped by the scarred pirate "Boss." Shinbei mobilizes a ship, which he dubs the Sumiyoshimaru, making Jiromaru the skipper, and the good guys set sail after the pirates to rescue Yuki and Chacha.

The ghost ship Kannomaru drifts back into the action a half hour into the film; when the pirates fire upon the vessel, it imperiously sails beyond them, and returns fire with a single enigmatic cannon shot that tops the pirate's main sail mast.

Incensed, Boss doggedly follows the wake of the Kannomaru and is told of a mysterious uncharted isle named Naked Island, though local nautical lore marks it as a cursed place and refers to it as Ghost Island. Suspecting the Kannomaru docks there, Boss sets out for Ghost Island, with our heroes in hot pursuit. The final act resolves the mystery of the Kannomaru, Ghost Island, and the real fate of Jiromaru's father Jubei, building capture upon escape, betrayal upon betrayal in true serial fashion, and culminates in a rousing climax.

Completely eschewing any existential, philosophical or serious baggage, **YÛREISEN: KÔHEN**'s provides something comparable to the Errol Flynn actioners and the horns-and-swords excitement of Richard Fleischer's **THE VIKINGS** (1958), which was an international hit one year after **YÛREISEN** and sparked a cycle of "Norse Operas" (to lift New York Times critic Bosley Crowther's flippant term for Fleischer's movie) that continued to play into the 1960s. Pirate movies were popular in Japan, too, including future Toei efforts like Tadashi Sawashima's **KAIZOKU BAHANSEN**/ "The Pirates" (1960). It's all here, at a modest scale comparable to the Italian viking movies (like Mario Bava's **GLI INVASORI/ERIK THE CONQUEROR**, 1961), bringing all three ships—the pirate Boss's, the Sumiyoshimaru, and the Kannomaru—into conflict, and all parties meet their fate on the Verne-like "mysterious island."

It's almost impossible to find anything in English about this pair of companion features, and many online sources (including imdb.com) completely garble the titles. The entertaining but unremarkable widescreen color duo was efficiently directed by Sadatsuga Matsuda (aka Sadaji Matsuda, here credited as "Teiji Matsuda"), working from Katsuya Susaki's adaptation of the novel by Jiro Osaragi. Osaragi's novels and stories had been popular source material for almost 50 Japanese features lensed from 1924 to 1965, including Matsuda's **KOJIKI TAISHÔ** (1945), but they were fading in popularity at this time; **YÛREISEN** was one of the last five adaptations.

1957-58 was an incredibly busy year for director Matsuda, who directed at least two other features in this period, including 任侠清水港 / **NINKYÔ SHIMIZU-MINATO** and what some refer to as Japan's first Cinemascope feature, **OHTORI-JO HANAYOME**. Matsuda is renowned today among some circles for his final two features, the Shôchiku Eiga studio "female Zatoichi" movies めくらのお市 地獄肌 / **MEKURANO OICHI JIGOKUHADA / TRAPPED, THE CRIMSON BAT** and めくらのお市 みだれ笠 / **MEKURA NO OICHI MONOGATARI: MAKKANA NAGARADORI/CRIMSON BAT, THE BLIND SWORDSWOMAN / WATCH OUT, CRIMSON BAT!** (both 1969), but there's much confusion in English language sources about Matsuda's filmography (I welcome any corrections). He was among Toei's sturdiest craftsmen, entrusted with their popular Tange Sazen/ "The One-Eyed Swordsman" (1958-61, starring Ryutaro Otomo, fresh from Matsuda's Ghost Ship films) and Shingo's Challenge film series (1960-63, all starring Hashizo Okawa) as well as all-star samurai extravaganzas like **O-EDO SHINCHININSHU**/ "Seven from Edo" (1958), **NINKYO NAKASENDO**/ "Gambler's Code on the Nakasendo"/**ROAD OF CHIVALRY** (1960), etc. All accounts note Matsuda began making films in the silent era, working as a cinematographer and assistant director before co-directing **RAIDEN** (1928) with the "father of Japanese cinema," Shozo Makino, who directed over 200 films between 1908 and 1928 (**RAIDEN** was Makino's final feature). Matsuda's first solo director credit was **KOJIKI TAISHÔ** (1945), and his fleeting association with horror and mystery films began with **SANBON YUBI NO OTOKO** (1947), the first cinematic adaptation of a novel by Seishi Yokomizo entitled *Honjin Murder Case* (later remade in 1976 as **HONJIN SATSUJIN JIKEN/ DEATH AT AN OLD MANSION** and for Japanese TV in 1992 as *Honjin Satsujin Jiken*). Thus, Matsuda was the director whose work launched over 30 adaptations of Seishi Yokomizo's novels, including Kon Ichikawa's recent **INUGAMIKE NO ICHIZOKU/THE INUGAMIS** (2006).

Matsuda adapted two more Yokomizo novels, **YATSUHAKA-MURA** (1951) and **AKUMA GA KITARITE FUE O FOKU** (1954, from *Akuma ga Kitarite Fue o Fuku*), but found his comfort zone directing straightforward samurai adventures. Just before tackling the two-feature **YUREI-SEN**, Matsuda helmed the samurai epic 赤穂浪士 天の巻 地の巻 / **AKÔ RÔSHI— TEN NO MAKI; CHI NO MAKI** (1956, another Jiro Osaragi story credit based on the often-filmed 18th century national legend of the 47 Ronin, or the Akô Vendetta) for Toei Kyoto studios in 1956 from a screenplay by the prolific Kaneto Shindô—who less than a decade later directed 鬼婆 / **ONIBABA**. No wonder that demon mask in **YÛREISEN: ZEMPEN** looks so familiar (note that Matsuda also directed another version of the 47 Ronin legend entitled 赤穂浪士 / **AKÔ RÔSHI**, 1961).

Though it's hard to comment on any visual subtleties given the inadequacies of the sole available English-subtitled transfer, cinematographer Shintarô Kawasaki's contribution to **YÛREISEN: ZEMPEN** avoided any overt stylization and making optimum use of the locations and studio sets (the lush green Jiromaru and his dog move through en route to the demon mansion is beautifully composed). **YÛREISEN: KÔHEN** is tougher to assess, as the transfer renders its many night sequences on the ships, on the island and at sea at times incomprehensible, through no fault of the original filmmakers. Kawasaki and Matsuda had been working together since **KOJIKI TAISHÔ**, and continued to right through to the **CRIMSON BAT** movies. The cast is solid throughout, with ingenue leads Kinnosuke Nakamura and Hiroku Sakuramachi ably supported by Yumiko Hasegawa's Princess and familiar male stars and character players like Ryutaro Otomo, Ryunosuke Tsukigata, and the marvelous Denjirô Ôkôchi (the original one-eyed, one-armed swordsman of Yamanaka Sadao's excellent **TANGE SAZEN YOWA: HYAKUMAN RYO NO TSUBO/TANGE SAZEN AND THE POTS WORTH A MILLION RYO**, 1935; Akira Kurosawa's **NO REGRETS FOR OUR YOUTH, MEN WHO TREAD ON THE TIGER'S TAIL**, both 1945, etc.).

Still, it's that first glimpse of the Hannya demon mask, framed in blazing red, that will outlast every other element of this viewing experience. Minor? Yes. But such is the fleeting magic of cinema for some of us; these are the odd associative images I live for. Given the immediate connection between director Matsuda and then-writer Kaneto Shindô (who may have seen **YUREI-SEN** if only to see what the director of his earlier script was up to), one cannot help but wonder if that image—two robed female figures, one with a torch held aloft, the other bracing her arms around the demon mask to perfectly frame it with the scarlet inner lining of her clothing—could have possibly been the catalyst for **ONIBABA**, one of the finest Japanese horror films ever made.

Currently available from Kurotokagi Gumi (http://www.kurotokagi.com) in "TV Broadcast quality" only.

JAPAN, 1957. Director: Sadatsugu Matsuda

Tiki Terror on the Isle of the Hungry Zuni Fetish Dolls:

Hell Island aka Attack of the Beast Creatures

Review © 2012 Stephen R. Bisstte

The only film from screenwriter/cinematographer/co-editor Robert A. Hutton and first from director Michael Stanley (who much later helmed the community theater comedy **DOING AGATHA**, 2008) is a color made-in-Connecticut curio echoing the early 1960s black-and-white efforts of that state's homegrown horror pioneer Del Tenney (**PSYCHOMANIA/VIOLENT MIDNIGHT, ZOMBIES/I EAT YOUR SKIN, CURSE OF THE LIVING CORPSE, HORROR OF PARTY BEACH**, etc.) and a bit of that same era's made-on-Long-Island Jack Curtis/Arnold Drake sf-gore opus **THE FLESH EATERS** (1964). That's an association sure to whet the appetite of exploitation fans, and I'm happy to report this efficient, unpretentious and long-neglected 'lost' film amply rewards rediscovery.

Shot in and about Fairfield and Stratford, CT in the early 1980s (though most sources list it as being released in 1985, the film itself and its original poster are copyright 1983), this apparently enjoyed brief theatrical play (if nothing else, a regional debut) under the title **HELL ISLAND**, as one-sheet posters of the film under that title exist. Brooklyn-born, NYC-based exploitation distributor Joseph Brenner acquired the film just before the dissolution of his venerable Joseph Brenner Associates' theatrical distribution operations. Brenner successfully spun similar genre fare into boxoffice gold from the 1950s well into the late '70s and early '80s. Almost to the end, Brenner scored with stateside release of British fare like Pete Walker's **FRIGHTMARE**, Italian imports like **TORSO, AUTOPSY, ALMOST HUMAN** and **EYEBALL**, the hilarious Shaw Brothers sentai **INFRA-MAN**, and domestic sex-and-violence exploitation like **GINGER, THE ABDUCTORS**, etc. By 1983-84, the corporate consolidation of theatrical distribution increasingly shut out independents like Brenner, and the proliferation of suburban multiplex theaters and closing of venerable rural drive-in and urban grindhouse venues put paid to the market for indy exploitation. Voluntarily abandoning the distribution game when he no longer found it profitable or enjoyable, Brenner reluctantly dumped **ATTACK OF THE BEAST CREATURES** direct to video in the US via Western World Video and landed some foreign video distribution (confirmed in Australia and Germany). That was the first and last wide release the film ever enjoyed.

Though it's highly unlikely Hutton and Stanley's film would have scored at the boxoffice, it's livelier fun than many low-budget films Brenner handled. Given Brenner's skill with trailers and ballyhoo, it would have been interesting to see what he could have done with it in a riper marketplace, and the film itself would have been a delightful big-screen experience with a raucous urban audience patient enough to make it to the film's frenzied ravenous puppet-dwarves-on-a-rampage setpieces.

The film unreels like an Eerie Publications horror comic story, and proves to be just as malicious in its cliché-riddled mischief. The year is 1920, and the offscreen sinking of a luxury cruise ship leaves a lifeboat adrift in the North Atlantic Ocean carrying a clutch of well-dressed passengers, two crewmen and one officer (Robert Nolfi as 'John Trieste,' our nominal hero). The survivors wake to find themselves beached on an unknown shore. Diane (Lisa Pak) is first to shriek upon finding one of their lifeboat companions inexplicably bloodied and barely conscious. After the sketchiest of characterization – the eldest male, Morgan (John Vichiola), is a belligerent boor; the gentile Mrs. Gordon (Kay Bailey) has never been away from her husband of 20 years "for so long" – and fleeting glimpses of inexplicable shadows (visible only to the viewer, not the castaways), the ship-

41

wrecked passengers leave their wounded fellow traveler Bruin (Robert Firgelewski) alone on the beach, having "made him as comfortable as possible," to go bumbling about the inland forest.

After tentative snatches of conversation (more vague characterization), crew member Philip (Frank Murgalo) finds a patch of apparently safe edible berries, and we're given more teasing glimpses of twitching brush, furtive undergrowth movement and something peeking at the castaways from behind a tree. In short order, Pat (Frans Kal) discovers a pond and plunges his hands and face in, desperate with thirst – but it's acid, not water! In the film's first burst of bloodshed, his throes of agony plunge him further into its lethal shallows. Responding to his shrieks of pain, Diane (of course) finds him face-down in the bubbling acid. While John, first mate Case (Robert Lengyel) and crabby ol' Morgan hang back to bury what's left of Pat, Philip leads Cathy (Julia Rust), Diane and Mrs. Gordon to forage for desperately-needed food. While picking berries, Mrs. Gordon is bitten on the hand by an unseen animal. John and Case return to the beach to find Bruin's skeleton picked clean; they decide it best to hide this from the others. Clearly, something inhabits the island – rats, they speculate, though the speed with which Bruin's body was devoured is almost inconceivable – but they've yet to grasp the danger they're in.

By nightfall, the castaways gather around a campfire and weigh their options as the friction between John and Morgan escalates and romance between John and raised-on-an-Iowa-farm Diane blooms. While the rest sleep, Cathy (Julia Rust) spots a pair of glowing eyes in the darkness; before she wakes the others, she is terrified as the eyes multiply into a glowering horde – which quickly attacks. Amid the frenzy, Morgan is badly bitten in the thigh and Cathy manages to hurl one of the savage creatures into the fire, sending it screaming into the night ablaze.

After fighting off this initial raid, the mauled and bleeding survivors decide their best option is to gather food and get back to the beached boat once the sun rises. Come dawn, we see the tiny red-skinned, long-haired brutes push the lifeboat into the waves. As the castaways prepare to brave the forest again, they have no idea they are now trapped on the island and at the mercy of the ravenous subhuman tribe, already mobilizing against them…

I don't want to give away anything more, as all the fun to be had here involves the insane setpieces in which the toothy puppets attack the increasingly bloodied cast. None of it is the least bit convincing, but its all executed with deadpan conviction. Whether you greet this mayhem with glee, laughter or utter disbelief matters hardly at all; some will find it too impoverished and tedious and simply give up, but fuck 'em if they can't take a joke. The single-minded determination to make the most of the increasingly dire plight of its castaways amid the feeding frenzies of the patently phony but marvelously malicious puppets was and remains the film's greatest virtue.

Screenwriter Robert A. Hutton designed the critters, voiced by Christopher Hutton, and Robert Firgelewski (the first victim of the creatures) handled the mechanical special effects. They work wonders with their meager resources. The scarlet, goggle-eyed monsters are clumsily animated (all live-action puppetry, literally in the field), but there are a lot of 'em and they are run ragged: tearing through the brush with arms stiffly pumping, leaping about, perching on and dropping from tree limbs, swarming, opportunistically striking with a bite-and-run tactic, and sinking their choppers into arms, legs, necks and faces at every opportunity. At one point, as Mrs. Gordon enjoys a bath alone by a pool of fresh running water, Hutton and Stanley recreate the famous Alfred Hitchcock **THE BIRDS** sequence by the school, only here it's the red devils gradually massing in the treetops. The 'ah fuck it' audacity of these sequences – despite the lack of money or fancy special effects, the cast (gamely holding the dolls and thrashing around to simulate being under attack) and crew go for broke – is in and of itself intoxicating.

The tribe of carnivorous creatures are clearly inspired by – actually, wholesale ripoffs of – the Zuni fetish doll concocted by special effects expert Erik von Buelow[1] for Dan Curtis's celebrated adaptation of Richard Matheson's "Prey" as the third story segment "Amelia" in the made-for-TV classic **TRILOGY OF TERROR** (originally broadcast March 4, 1975). Curtis revisited the Zuni doll puppet's antics in **TRILOGY OF TERROR 2** (broadcast October 30, 1996; the doll returned in the "He Who Kills" episode), which was great fun, but there's no denying the grander conceit of an entire island tribe of the feral monsters. They attack like land piranha, and their resemblance to the Curtis/Matheson Zuni puppet only enhances the loopy allure and spectacle of their cartoony ferocity. The film also bears some superficial resemblance to the Peter Fonda curio **DANCE OF THE DWARFS** aka **JUNGLE HEAT** (also 1983), directed by Gus Trikonis (**MOONSHINE COUNTY EXPRESS, THE EVIL, TAKE THIS JOB AND SHOVE IT,** etc.), based on a novel by Geoffrey Household, which featured a tribe of reptilian subhuman pygmies. That listless affair remains far less entertaining than Hutton and Stanley's spare adventure.

All that duly noted, **ATTACK OF THE BEAST CREATURES** is most evocative of a Pre-Code horror comic story, specifically the Pre-Code "Black Death" that was reprinted in black-and-white in the Myron Fass Eerie Publications title *Weird* #12 (October 1966), supplanting that tale's island-bound nest of giant carnivorous ants with the screeching flesh-eating humanoids here. Once the little bastards have cast the lifeboat adrift and marooned the castaways, the clock is ticking – and however ludicrous the little buggers are, the tension does ratchet up over the final hour. It is, if nothing else, an effective low-budget survival tale with a novel central menace.

Part of the fun (as usual in such fare) is the inane dialogue exchanges and obvious inadequacy of means the script inadvertently emphasizes. At one point, John and Case ponder the "tropical" nature of the island, completely out of place in the North Atlantic; but they've been wandering a sparsely wooded New England forest, peppered with saplings, mossy ledges, and rocky brooks and streams. These locales are painfully similar to the Connecticut locations in Wes Craven's **LAST HOUSE ON THE LEFT** (1972, shot right next door in and around Redding and Westport, CT; they're all southern CT locations roughly in the same area) and are not by any stretch of the imagination "tropical." At another point, Phil claims to have vet training, and that Mrs. Gordon's bite looks like no animal bite he's ever seen – what?? Actually, it looks like every bad movie fake animal bite ever seen. Such absurdities are par for the course.

It must be said all concerned play the adventure straight, which makes everything work. Despite the amateurish acting and long stretches of wandering the woods (which are nonetheless more

---

1 Czech-born von Buelow (born July 1922; died in Zürich, Switzerland November 2002) also created the miniatures for Bert I. Gordon's final pair of H.G. Wells 'giant animal' opuses, **THE FOOD OF THE GODS** (1976) and **EMPIRE OF THE ANTS** (1977). Though his admittedly minor work is sadly forgotten and neglected, his imaginative puppet design and effects for the Zuni fetish doll have earned him a place in the genre hall of fame.

interesting than similar stretches in Jess Franco's faux-jungle movie opuses), Stanley's direction is for the most part efficient and effective, Hutton's lensing and cutting is solid and at times quite ingenious, and John P. Mozzi's score is typical of its era, incorporating synthesizer, guitar and percussion to atmospheric funereal effect throughout. Though imdb.com and other sources list a 104-minute running time, the film actually clocks in a little over 82 minutes (Mozzi's score continues past the end credits closing) and its highly unlikely there was ever a longer cut, unless Brenner trimmed more listless scenes (but 22 minutes worth?) from the only extant version.

Director Michael Stanley has enjoyed some genre celebrity in recent years, including an appearance at the Eerie Horror Fest (in Erie, PA) in 2006. Interest in his solo horror film hasn't achieved cult stature, but give it time. **ATTACK OF THE BEAST CREATURES** has yet to enjoy a DVD release, but its big-box vhs video release is still fairly affordable and available via online venues. That'll change, too. Recommended, for those who can savor the paucity of performances and production means and enjoy this no-nonsense, straightforward regional genre gem for what it is.

USA, 1983/85. Director: Michael Stanley

"MIND THE DOORS!"
RAW MEAT

Review © 2012 Stephen R. Bisstte

MGM's 2003 DVD release of **RAW MEAT** (original UK title: **DEATH LINE**, 1972) finally rescued a long-unavailable masterpiece of the revisionist British horror scene of the 1970s. This sleeper was a personal favorite of the drive-in flicks I caught during their initial run, a harrowing, heartbreaking tale of a lone cannibal stalking the London tubes for prey -- and a new mate -- as a dour police inspector (Donald Pleasence in one of his best roles) doggedly uncovers the truth behind the cannibal's existence that the authorities would prefer remain (literally) buried.

Though rarely seen since its early 1970s circuit, **RAW MEAT** proved influential, precursor to **C.H.U.D.** and the never-properly-released NY indy **MOLE**, along with a small torrent of subway horror movies that hit about five years ago.

RAW MEAT was another of the early 1970s AIP releases that fused American and Brit creators: the feature directorial debut of Gary Sherman (who went on to direct **DEAD & BURIED**, among others), starring David Ladd (child actor of **THE PROUD REBEL** and **A DOG OF FLANDERS** fame, later producer of **SERPENT AND THE RAINBOW** and other films), and produced by none other than New Yorker Paul Maslansky (producer of two early Michael Reeves projects -- **CASTLE OF THE LIVING DEAD**, which also debuted Donald Sutherland as an actor, and Reeves' debut feature **THE SHE-BEAST** -- and John Hough's **EYEWITNESS** aka **SUDDEN TERROR**, before returning stateside to direct the zombies-vs.-gangsters gem **SUGAR HILL** and eventually produce the Bruce Lee scripted **CIRCLE OF IRON** and the **POLICE ACADEMY** series, among others).

There are a few tenuous thematic links with another seminal American-director-directing-UK-mayhem classic, Sam Peckinpah's **STRAW DOGS**: the events kick off when American Alex (Ladd) and his Brit girlfriend Patricia (Sharon Gurney) find a man unconscious on the steps of the tube; Alex wants to ignore the downed man, believing him to be a passed-out alchoholic, but Patricia insists they get help. Returning with a Bobby, Alex finds the body gone, but he has now been linked with the disappearance and Patricia can't shake her concern for the missing man and their culpability in his disappearance. Like David (Dustin Hoffman) in **STRAW DOGS**, Alex does all he can to ignore the situation, but is inextricably drawn into inevitable confrontation with violence on the 'home turf' of the bestial 'Man' (character actor Hugh Armstrong, given his best showcase, and delivering an indelible performance on par with Richard Wordsworth's in **THE QUATERMASS XPERIMENT**), with the life of/bond with his partner Patricia at stake. But I don't want to inflate those indeed tenuous links; this is hardly **STRAW DOGS** underground, and is in fact one of the most unique of the 1970s British horrors, and one of the best cannibal horror films ever made.

The 'third world' of this particular cannibal film is literally the underbelly of London: the 'Man' is the last survivor of generations bred beneath the streets of London when a collapsed tunnel during the construction of the tubes trapped workers underground, and it was more cost-efficient for the company responsible to write them off for dead than to mount a rescue operation. Feeding on each other and whatever they could find -- including hapless contemporary Londoners stranded in tube stations -- and incestuously breeding until the death of the 'Man's pregnant 'Woman' (June Turner) leaves him the last of his sorry kind. Thus, a potent genre metaphor for the true 'underclass' emerges, embodied in Armstrong's scabby, shaggy, sorrowful primal man, who lives Sawney-Beane like in the rot-and-rat infested squalor of their charnelhouse burrow, and wanders the tracks -- the only world he has ever known -- seeking food for himself and his dying mate, a mate after her passing, and mouthing the only words he knows: "Mind the doors" (the oft-repeated phrase warning subway riders to be cautious departing the tube cars, and the first line of dialogue heard in the film).

It's one of those succinct, brilliant mergers of narrative simplicity and potent metaphor (of the UK class system's lowest conceivable common denominator) that lends such a primal punch to this unpretentious, elegantly conceived, and powerfully executed thriller, which remains director Gary Sherman's (and producer Maslansky's) best film. While UK genre directors like Michael Reeves and Gordon Hessler were laboring to bring the no-nonsense energy of US directors like Don Siegel to the fold, Sherman accomplished the feat with his first film.

Sherman (who also wrote the story, skillfully scripted by Ceri Jones, her only credit on record, as far as I can see) effectively crosscuts between three narrative threads -- Alex and Patricia's involvement, the 'Man's plight, and the police procedural of Inspector Calhoun (Pleasence) and his Detective Sargeant (Norman Rossington) -- drawing them together for a stunning final act. The strength of this weave is only fueled by the potent genre setpieces: the long, leisurely, malingering pan across the fetid corpse-strewn 'nest' of the 'Man' and 'Woman' as we first awaken to their situation; the attacks in the tube, one of which is genuinely terrifying and horrifically violent; the mix of terror and pity the climax evokes as Alex, Patricia, the Man, and Inspector Calhoun are drawn together in the darkness of the abandoned tunnels.

Compare the sole 2003 MGM DVD extra -- the AIP trailer -- to the feature, and you can see how beautiful a job MGM did. The trailer is somewhat

43

faded and peppered with speckling; the feature transfer remains crisp, sharp, and absolutely sterling (the slightly dingy nature of the color was how the film was shot). Long available only as dupes, or via transfers of the UK PAL video release (from Carlton's The Rank Collection; #30370 60163), the darkness much of **RAW MEAT** takes place within was forever muddied further by transfers and dupes, rendering many of the film's most indelible sequences (including that pan across the cannibal's home) barely discernible.

One other key point about **RAW MEAT**:

Seeing it *clearly* for the first time since I saw it on the drive-in screen over 30 years ago, I'm amazed by how detailed the makeup and art direction/production design remain. The attention to detail in the environment the 'Man' lives within tells *much* of the story; it's an approach to the genre that was considered innovative when Tobe Hooper and Ridley Scott (with **TEXAS CHAINSAW MASSACRE** and **ALIEN** and **BLADE RUNNER**) wielded it, but here it is masterfully realized.

The introductory shot of the 'Man's den is a quiet, stunning 360-degree exploration of the place, which at the time impressed most viewers for its gruesome detail: indeed, the gore quotient is still disturbing as hell. But the shot completes itself, and then drifts (with a rise in the musical score, heretofore in this sequence stilled by the sound of dripping water, a muffled heartbeat from a still-living but comatose victim, and the scuffling of rats and soft rustling of maggots) into the 'bedroom' of the 'Man' and his suffering 'Woman.' We see the tenderness between them, and their hideous conditions -- riddled with unhealed wounds, sores, and ravaged by disease and malnutrition -- before the camera continues *out* of their den and into the vast chambers of the abandoned underground station-in-progress. As this movement continues, the soundtrack swells with new sounds, which we come to realize (as the camera arrives at its destination, the ruins of the cave-in that trapped the forefathers of the 'Man' below) are the sounds of the past: the digging workman, the collapse of the roof, the finality of their fate.

It's a brilliantly conceived and realized sequence, and quite remarkable for its time *and* our own.

Furthermore, when I assert that the film was influential, I failed to note its influence on Robert Burns' staggering sets for **TEXAS CHAINSAW MASSACRE**. The details of the sets and setpieces in **RAW MEAT** are so layered that their meanings are gradually unveiled as the film unspools its nightmare -- and some of those details are surprisingly moving (as the 'Man' lays a trinket on the body of his 'Woman' in the final act, the camera moves over the many bodies laid to rest about her that we've already glimpsed earlier -- and we realize ALL of them have some item laid on their chests, tender memorials from previous survivors to their loved ones). Rarely had horror and pathos been so delicately textured; most horror film sets boasting such attention to minutia did so for mere atmospherics, not narrative density.

RAW MEAT is an unsung masterpiece, and MGM's DVD provides a rich testimonial to its previously-hidden substance (via decades of poor dupes and cut prints). The 2003 DVD release of **RAW MEAT** -- it's first US release in any format since its AIP theatrical run and truncated re-release -- was very welcome, and *highly recommended*. Track it down, while you still can.

UK, 1973. Director: Gary Sherman

CHASING THE KIDNEY STONE
(Jakten på nyresteinen)

Review by Brian Harris

As I slowly scanned through hundreds of films on Netflix's streaming service looking for something out of the norm, something I hadn't already seen, when I came across an odd-looking little film called **CHASING THE KIDNEYSTONE** [sic]. This Norwegian-made television film for children, written and directed by Vibeke Idsøe, was apparently acquired by Aaron Spelling's Spelling Films International for worldwide theatrical distribution. Garnering a generally positive critical reception, the film and its creator went on to be nominated in 1997 for the Fantasporto film festival's Grand Prix of European Fantasy Film in Gold as well as winning a Méliès d'Argent award at the Fantafestival in Rome. Despite prestigious honors and critical accolades, the film seems to have fallen through the cinematic cracks and into obscurity, a place that cinemaphilians are well acquainted with.

Following in the footsteps of Twentieth Century Fox's '66 sci-fi classic **FANTASTIC VOYAGE** and Joe Dante's hair-brained **INNERSPACE**, Idsøe's **CHASING THE KIDNEY STONE** introduces the viewers to young Simon, his grandfather and a talking teddy bear as they prepare for a very special engagement in which Simon's grandfather is to reunite with the Jazz band he played for as a young man. Instead of elation and anticipation though, the old man is melancholy and withdrawn, still pining over the loss of his beautiful wife over 30 years prior.

That night, Simon is awoken to the sound of groans as his grandfather tosses and turns, unable to rest due to agonizing pain. Concerned that his grandfather may need medical attention, he turns to the wisdom of his stuffed animal, who suggests they mix up a magical potion to shrink the boy and allow him to enter the senior citizen's body and seek out the cause of his discomfort. Willing to do anything to help, Simon agrees and is soon reduced to the size of a speck. Making his way in, through the mouth, Simon encounters a host of bizarre, eccentric entities including taste buds, bad breath, white and red blood cells, the vocal chords and more! Teaming up with a white blood cell named Globule and an organism from the lungs named Alvéole, the trio journey through the organs in an effort to track down rumors that calcium may be building up a kidney stone, with an eye on killing grandfather! They'll need water and determination in order to dissolve the stone but how is one to find water in a man that has not cried in over 30 years?

CHASING THE KIDNEY STONE is an obscure and beautiful gem of a children's film, one that deserves a fully-loaded Blu-ray Disc release from someone, somewhere in the world. As it stands right now there only seems to be two out-of-print R2 releases, one from Norway and one from France (renamed **SIMON IN THE LAND OF BLOOD**), both on DVD. Without over-hyping the film too much, my initial thoughts on this production were,"This is fucking awesome!" Imagine my surprise and dismay after seeing it when I discovered that, for some strange reason, this film had no release! It looks quite good on Netflix, I can't complain, but this is one of those bizarro films that cult cinema fans enjoy having in their collection.

The dub was on point, the voice talent were all great actors, but the real star of **CHASING THE KIDNEY STONE** is the award-winning special effects work by David Estern and Martin Grant, the latter having done effects work on André Øvredal's **TROLLHUNTER**. The look and feel of this film reminded me of something one might expect from Cronenberg (**NAKED LUNCH**) and Nishimura (**TOKYO GORE POLICE**), it had this highly textured, stylized production design with gorgeous colors. Combined with outrageous characters, breathtaking costumes and elaborate sets, this has to be one of the coolest children's films I have ever laid eyes on, especially one made for television. I'm left wondering just how much more interesting this film would have been to me had I been able to see it in its original Norwegian, subbed in English, with an HD transfer. Don't take my word for it though, load it up on your queue and check it out.

Norway, 1996. Director: Vibeke Idsøe

THE LEGEND OF LA LLORONA
(La Leyenda de La Llorona)

Review by Brian Harris

While out for a rambunctious night of trick or treating in the eerie village of Xochimilco, siblings Beto and Kika run afoul of the legendary Mexican ghost known as *La Llorona* (The Weeping Woman) as the specter slowly makes its way through the back alleys, wailing and mourning the loss of its beloved children. Unbeknownst to Kika, the racket she's making has attracted the monster and Beto's decides that his only chance to save his younger sister is to distract the ghost and call it to himself, which he does successfully. The chase is now on as Beto flees in desperation through the village and into the forest, with La Llorona close behind and Kika not quite sure what's going on. It's not until both siblings meet on opposite sides of a river does the little girl realize the danger lurking behind her brother. And then, in an instant, Beto and La Llorona are gone!

Elsewhere, a balloon-powered ship floats through the air on its way to Xochimilco, manned by a group of well-known ghost-busters lead by a brave young boy named Leo San Juan. Leo and crew have been asked by a concerned priest to visit the village and try and help rid the poor townsfolk of the accursed denizen that snatches their children. Leo (the orphan), Don Andres (a ghostly Spanish knight), Alebrije (a brightly colored dragon) and two adorable Dia De Los Muertos sugar skull children named Moribunda (Dying) & Finando (Deceased), are well acquainted with the supernatural after having defeated the witch, La Nahuala, years prior. With the on-again, off-again help of their gifted ghost guide Teodora, the gang hopes to track La Llorona and rescue the children from whatever nefarious end she has planned for them, unfortunately a mid-air mishap during a freak storm causes their balloon ship to capsize, separating the group.

With good luck on his side, Leo nearly lands right in Kika's lap while she trolls the river in search of her abducted brother. The others in the group aren't quite as lucky though as they land smack dab on La Isla de las Munecas (Puppet Island)! While Leo is nursed to health by Kika's mother, and filled in on the specifics of La Llorona and her quest to locate her deceased children, Don Andres and the others must fight their way through hordes of demonic puppets, lead by an evil enchanted hand-puppet named Pecas (Freckles).

In order to stop La Llorona, she must be reunited with the long lost graves of her deceased children but first Leo must come to terms with the loss of his own mother and the others must break the curse that Pecas has brought to La Isla de las Munecas!

Wow, what a delightful animated film! From beginning to end, **LA LEYENDA DE LA LLORONA** is heavily steeped in the culture and folklore of Mexico. From La Llorona herself to the dragon Alebrije (a form of bright colored Mexican folk art) to the Dia De Los Muertos sugar skull children, this cartoon overflows with the rich heritage and proud traditions of the Mexican people and it's spooky to boot! I was genuinely excited and entertained while watching as well as challenged to spot the influences in the characters and situations. There wasn't a single thing I disliked about this production with the exception of feeling completely lost, as if I'd been plunked down in the middle of an ongoing story filled with established characters. Interestingly enough, it turns out I was!

LA LEYENDA DE LA LLORONA is actually the 2011 sequel to a highly successful 2007 animated feature entitled, **LA LEYENDA DE LA NAHUALA**. Talk about missing the boat! Here's the real kicker, the first in the series is currently available for purchase on Region 1 DVD through the Navarre Corporation (aka BCI) here in the States, while this film (**THE LEGEND OF LA LLORONA**) is not, it's only available for streaming on Netflix. Go figure. The first you can purchase but not rent and the sequel you can rent but not purchase. Qué inconveniente! No matter, based solely on the concept of the sequel, I have every intention of purchasing the first film from Amazon. For $6 you can't go wrong, that's one less colon demolishing meal at McDonalds.

HorrorParents, your children will really enjoy this film (as will you), and like so many other oddball productions I enjoy watching, it's educational as well! That's right...no English dubbing! Make your children read, don't let them become "those" kind of Americans that refuse to see foreign films because they might have to...*gasp*...READ! This is a one-of-a-kind flash animated feature that's sure to entertain everybody in the household, even your youngest! My 2 year-old sat for the entire 81 minute runtime, truly a miracle, and enjoyed every minute, laughing during the comedic sequences and screaming (with glee) during the scary sequences. She even picked up on a few words and cheered on her favorite character Kika!

Cult cinema fans take note, the finale of this film hints at a new adventure, one that will introduce the team to a new foe...THE MUMMIES OF GUANAJUATO! Here's hopin' for a Blue Demon cameo!

Mexico, 2011. Director: Alberto Rodriguez

THE DEVIL'S SISTERS

Review by Greg Goodsell

Naive Mexican village girl Teresa (Sharon Saxon) leaves the arms of her macho boyfriend to seek

FROM THE DEPTHS OF HELL

Sisters of the Devil

work in Tijuana. Answering a classified ad for what she thinks is for a maid position, she is introduced to a blowsy Madame (Anita Crystal) who sets her up with her own apartment. All is well for the first 10 minutes until Teresa finds out that her new career is one of prostitution! Beaten and held against her will by Crystal's band of thugs, her life becomes one of an endless series of tricks fueled by a strict diet of cheap wine and cigarettes. Once Teresa complains too strongly, she is transferred to the brothel's barn, where pregnant and injured girls are forced to ply their trade for bargain basement prices. Teresa attempts escape – but is captured and forced to endure the tortures of "the marriage bed" – i.e., tied naked to a wooden table with barbed wire. In her final bid for survival, Teresa attempts to escape once again … will she be able to flee with her life and lead authorities to finally shut down this house of horrors once and for all?

Many lost films are lost for very good reason: they're not any good. Such curiosities remain out of reach but continue to inspire interest because of an odd plot detail or an early performance by a performer who went on to do bigger and better things. Many of these features, when they resurface, invariably disappoint. Such is not the case of **THE DEVIL'S SISTERS**, which has long remained lost until now. A rough black-and-white descent into depravity, **THE DEVIL'S SISTERS** is a rare case of a low-budget film that delivers more than it promises. It's easily one of this writer's favorite DVD releases of 2012.

Lensed by Floridian exploitation auteur William Grefe, **THE DEVIL'S SISTERS** took full advantage of the local displaced Cuban film community who had fled dictator Fidel Castro. With Cuban expatriates working on both sides of the camera, one could infer that the film functioned as a cathartic project for people fleeing repression. Based upon a true story that was still fresh in international headlines, that of two Mexican sisters accused of killing countless prostitutes who disobeyed their brothel's rules, **THE DEVIL'S SISTERS** melds together film noir, instant exploitation films torn from recent headlines, the "roughie" sub-genre of soft-core sex films and presciently offers up what goes on today as "torture porn." The overall grimness outstrips the earlier OLGA series with Audrey Campbell and is similar in tone to the ILSA films of the Seventies.

The independently released DVD release is stuffed to the gills with extras. There is an audio commentary by Grefe himself, who says that the film was produced hot on the heels of his goofy, colorful monster romp **DEATH CURSE OF TARTU**. Grefe offers up a wealth of detail on the film's production and seat-of-your-pants movie making of that period, all the more remarkable for a film nearing its fiftieth birthday that took all of 10 days to film! There is a detailed essay from sleaze historian Chris Poggiali that recounts the film's limited release and quick departure from screens and its "lost status." Grefe himself found a copy of the film from German collectors and supervised the transfer. There is a making of featurette, an introduction by Grefe, still gallery and a brief radio spot when it played under a different ad campaign and title, **SISTERS OF THE DEVIL**, tying it into the then-recent "devil craze" borne out of **ROSEMARY'S BABY**.

If there is one caveat to the collector of cult DVDs that must be mentioned in this review, is the fact that the film lacks its final seven minutes! Coming right at a climactic moment while Teresa is fleeing one of Crystal's henchmen through a swamp, the film just comically melts in the projector in the manner of grind-houses of yore! Never fear, the still-spry Grefe comes onscreen to describe the ending with the aid of some surviving storyboard panels. Rest assured, no one will be left wanting more, as any Grefe film, from the most threadbare – **STING OF DEATH**, with its jellyfish monster with a garbage bag for a head comes to mind – always delivered. If you like your sleaze regional, raw and real, there's no excuse not to cozy up to these **SISTERS**.

(For more information, go to www.realitysedgefilms.net)

USA, 1966. Director: William Grefe.

KARATE-ROBO ZABORGAR

Review by Brian Harris

SUSHI TYPHOOOOONNN! Oh yeah, just when you think this new wave of low budget Japanese genre films have reached the end of their tether, they breaks free and savagely grab you by the crotch. Whether you enjoy what the filmmakers from Sushi Typhoon produce or not is never the point, the question is always,"Did you see that coming?" I've heard some say that their films go overboard (and they do), focusing on unrealistic action (natch), actresses that are nothing more than masturbatory fetish dolls (what's wrong with that?) and finally that the gore is cartoonish (a gross understatement). All of that is valid. Why deny it, right? The films produced by Sushi Typhoon are wild and wacky genre films for people tired of mainstream muck

and indie home video drivel. Sure, they can be hit or miss at times but there's always something, even if its just a short little sequence, that never fails to amuse, entertain or titillate me. Case in point, **KARATE-ROBO ZABORGAR**.

Yutaka Daimon (Yasuhisa Furuhara/Itsuji Itao) is a special forces agent working with the Japanese police to fight crime alongside his trusted robot companion, Zaborgar. No job is too big, no criminal too bad but all of that changes when the evil organization known as SIGMA begins kidnapping Japan's biggest politicians in an effort to harvest their DNA for a secret project know as "Jumbo Mecha!" Lead by Dr. Akunomiya (Akira Emoto), SIGMA intends to rule the world, like any evil organization worth a damn, and they'll destroy everything in their path that offers resistance.

Having a painful past connection with SIGMA that resulted in the death of a beloved family member, Daimon and Zaborgar set out to foil Akunomiya's plans but neither are prepared for his beautiful henchwoman and robotic right-hand woman, Miss Cyborg (Mami Yamasaki)! Can Daimon go through with the job he was assigned to do or will he allow his disenchantment with the Japanese government's corruption and love for blossoming love for Miss Borg get in the way? Faced with an impossible decision, Daimon makes the wrong one, sending the mighty Zaborgar over the edge as well as ruining his career as a crime-fighting hero.

25 years later, SIGMA is now working hand-in-hand with the Japanese government and Daimon is a lowly (and bumbling) driver for the Japanese Prime Minister. With "Jumbo Mecha's" completion on the horizon and Zaborgar gone, Daimon realizes the world still needs him and nothing will stop him this time around from making the right decision.

Adapting the 1974 Tokusatsu television series "Denjin Zaborger" (Electroid Zaborger 7) for the big screen, writer/director Noboru Iguchi (**THE MACHINE GIRL**) deviates very little from the tone of the original series, opting instead to update the insanity with VFX/FX as only Sushi Typhoon can. Watching clips of the TV show as it played through the end credits, it was instantly apparent that Iguchi wanted to remain faithful to the show and I think he truly did it justice. Believe it or not, as I watched the clips I kept thinking,"I didn't see that in the movie!" **KARATE-ROBO ZABORGAR** is a frenzied campfest that is almost indistinguishable from 70's era Tokusatsu like "Spectreman," "Ultraman" & "Johnny Sokko And His Flying Robot," at least for the first half of the outing. The remainder of the film (25 years later) has Iguchi re-introducing us to established characters, now useless, old cripples, and that's where things get really fun. The mixture of old heroes and new villains worked incredibly well and made for some hilarious sequences, including a PSA for Diabetes!

I'd touch on dialogue and acting but seriously... this is **KARATE-ROBO ZABORGAR**, bitch. If you don't know what you'll be getting into after reading this review, my advice to you would be to expect over-the-top, way over-the-top, and you'll do just fine. That's the charm, and curse, of ST productions. Quite a bit of the action and fight sequences (robot vs. robot) were computer animated as well but it's all incredibly well-made, I very rarely took notice of anything I considered "cheap." All in all, this film is a keeper for fans of this type of cinema.

Japan, 2012. Director: Noboru Iguchi. Availabe from Well Go USA

MIRAGEMAN

Review by Brian Harris

Not sure about some of you out there but I've always wanted to be a superhero. I mean, what's not to like about a cool outfit, bad ass weapons, crushing hope and taking over the world? Hmm? That's a super VILLAIN, you? Oh…sorry. Anyhow, believe it or not, we do actually have men and women all across the America dressing up in colorful outfits and patrolling the streets seeking out crime and looking to do good works for the

community. Though ridiculed by the media and occasionally bullied by law enforcement, you can't fault them for wanting to make the lives of others better by giving them hope. It's not like our schools, churches and government has done the greatest job of providing it.

This is pretty much the premise of all these "real life" superhero films and, yes, this is also the premise of Chilean filmmaker Ernesto Diaz Espinoza's **MIRAGEMAN**. Similar to films like **KICK-ASS**, **SUPER** and **SPECIAL**, **MIRAGEMAN**'s protagonist is just an average guy with a tragic past and a sincere desire to make life better for everybody in Chile, as well as his disturbed younger brother. Spurred on to continue being a masked vigilante after successfully foiling a rape/robbery, our hero takes his superior martial arts training to the streets and begins thinning the criminal herd. While initially considered a joke, Mirageman captures the hearts and minds of citizens when he takes on a pedophilia ring in order to save the life of an abducted girl.

Shot on video, in an almost documentary style, **MIRAGEMAN** may be low on budget but it's big on exciting action sequences with a groovy 70's exploitation flavor. Lead actor, and Chilean martial artist, Marko Zaror does what athletes-turned-actors do best...which is remain silent, occasionally brood and whoop more ass than a crabby donkey farmer. Zaror has a great on-screen presence with an impressive physique and dazzling martial arts talent. In my opinion, outside of Scott Adkins, he's got the chops to be the next "big thing" in martial arts/action cinema. It's no wonder Espinoza has stuck with Zaror for three films, the guy does it all from acting to fight choreography and stunt work.

While it seems that the quality of this production took a bit of a step down from Espinoza's previous film **KILTRO**, **MIRAGEMAN** was still a respectable endeavor and an entertaining watch. I grew up reading comic books, like most genre film junkies, but I can't really say I'm the biggest fan of today's superhero cinema. If, however, you are a fan of superhero cinema then you're definitely going to want to give this a spin. No worries on having to order out to Chile for this either, it was picked up for U.S. distro by Magnolia's genre film label Magnet and released to DVD in 2009. It currently retails for about $9 so give it a shot!

Chile, 2007. Director: Ernesto Diaz Espinoza.

KEOMA

Review by Gary Baxter

Our Hero Keoma returns to his hometown to find its residents in fear and the evil Caldwell (Peter O'Neal) controlling things, to add to the mayhem his three despised half-brothers have joined the sadistic bastard's gang of bandits.

Keoma quickly upsets some of the gang when he stops one of their caravans taking plague carriers to the old mine, rescues a pregnant woman and shoots up the bad guys, he then takes her back to a saloon in town where the people want the woman killed. Another gun fight almost breaks out and Keoma soon finds the lady a room where she explains the situation and Caldwell's control of the town. We're then introduced to George (Woody Stroud), an old friend of Keoma's and a washed up banjo playing drunk, Keoma's father (William Berger) and the three brothers, these, along with Caldwell are the main characters in the following ballet of bullets and bloodshed that Castellari handles so well.

The action goes back and forth at a great pace all the while allowing the story by Luigi Montfori(George Eastman) to flow nicely. Castellari's use of flashback in this film is a touch of genius with memories coming to life in real time around the characters as they are now effectively highlighting the dynamic between Keoma, his father and the three brothers. Also used to great effect as is the appearance of the old crone any time danger is afoot. We also get the obligatory slow motion during the expertly crafted shoot outs of which there are many, the best of which being the final show down between Keoma and Caldwell's gang and the slow stalking of the three brothers led by Castellari regular Joshua Sinclair. Set design is amazing with gunfights taking place among ghost town style ruins which makes for some creative camera angles and really helps build the tension as does the score by Guido and Maurizio De Angelis. Another touch of genius during the final battle of brothers is the use of the pregnant woman's screams as the only audio source, haunting stuff indeed.

I've long been a fan of Castellari's work since seeing **ESCAPE FROM THE BRONX** as a kid so it was a great day when I found this Argent Films release. Presented in anamorphic widescreen the film itself looks great and comes complete with reversible sleeve with original poster art, an exclusive in-depth presentation by acclaimed filmmaker Alex Cox (**REPO MAN**, **SIX AND NANCY**) and a brilliant 15 minute interview with Castellari himself, top it off with the original trailer and trailers for some of Argent's other Spaghetti Westerns and it's a nice a little package that comes highly recommended.

Italy, 1976. Director: Enzo G. Castellari available from Blue Underground

BLOODMATCH

Review by David Zuzelo

Sometimes you put a disc in the player and know what you are going to get. Sometimes you put a disc in the player and you don't get what you expected at all. Many times this is very true with Albert Pyun directed slabs of cinema. You just never know. While the director is one of the most maligned in the business of cine-snark that has dominated over the years, I find a lot of fascinating movies have him at the helm. **BLOODMATCH** is one of these films. The rather nondescript US artwork makes this look like another Kickboxing Tournament of Doom film, complete with a cast of baggy pants toughs staring at the potential renter. I happen to love the tourney flicks but **BLOODMATCH** is not exactly typical of the genre. As a matter of fact, it isn't that at all!

Brick Bardo is one pissed off lead with an in-joke for Pyun fans (listen and you'll hear many Bricks over the years). I mean, the guy is well and truly ANGRY! Pyun and his viewers are lucky that Brick is played by Thom Matthews, who gets to put his Friday The 13th gained skills in to action as the damn near psychopathic fist n' foot flinging nutjob that is on a trail of deadly kung fu vengeance. After Brick's brother is killed for not fixing a kickboxing match the smashing sibling is out to find those bastards responsible for this offense against the shrinking American Kickboxing Family. The film kicks off by having Bardo torturing a guy in the middle of nowhere for the opening 10 minutes of the film until he acquires a short list of names belonging to soon to be VERY sorry Kickboxing Conspirators. Luckily, that short list consists of a bunch of fighters, all champions and all ready to participate in a Bloodmatch! Well, they better be, because Brick and his lady friend are setting them up and kidnapping them all. Some get sexed and snatched, others have family threatened and some are just damn curious as to why the hell a guy named BRICK is so pissed off and crashing through their window.

This takes about 45 minutes to play out and the action quotient is nil so far, no holds barring one nifty fight that includes Vincent Klyn as a bad guy. Talk about subverting expectations for **BLOODMATCH**, THE KUNG FU FLICK YOU THOUGHT YOU RENTED! But it isn't the action (in a kickboxing film??) that sold me on this film at all. Brick Bardo's mind is not so slowly unraveling in his quest for vengeance. The "protagonist" is blinded to the reality that he is now far worse than the people he is punishing and Matthews just devours up the script and spits it out with total commitment. And watch as Bardo smokes the best pro-wrestlers out there for putting on his "rrrrrrrrrr...I dislike you very strongly!!" face.

The titular Bloodmatch section of the film fills up the second half of the running time and to be honest it is a mixed bag of fighting fury. On the plus side we have a great bit of screen kicking and

47

battling as Brick faces off against Benny 'The Jet' Urquidez, and each fight does actually carry the story momentum that Pyun and crew have built up to a satisfying finish. Brick becomes more repugnant than the four "guilty" parties-which has a screwy twist in the end to boot. There is a bit of distraction there, but I am a firm believer that you can salvage a plot twist that goes awry with a slam bang fight sequence. It isn't a great final battle, but here is the cool trick that Pyun pulls off in a nutshell. The kickboxin' berserker that Matthews portrays is so demented by the end you can't help but root for the "wrong" side! I'm sure this intentional and the structure and execution of **BLOODMATCH** really plays in to my "Familiar Tropes, Strange Takes" theory of Pyunotronic Cinema-viewers looking for a fight flick to pass the time with may be surprised by what they have here. Disappointed? Possibly. But if you are in the Pyuniverse as a fan of his work you might be going in the opposite direction-avoiding it because it appears to be just another fight film. That would be like calling the earlier Pyun masterpiece Deceit a Trancers style film-sure you have cops from odd places and fight scenes and all the familiar side dishes, but the meals are nothing alike.

The strengths of the film consist of Matthews as Brick Bardo, easily one of the more memorable characters in 90s kickboxing cinema, some cool Tony Riparetti cues that are the standard from this frequent Pyun collaborator, cameos by Vincent Klyn (of **CYBORG**), Michel Qissi (ain't no Faux Tong Po here baby!) and the always welcome Urquidez. I've long believed that Albert Pyun is an ass man when it comes to sex scenes, because he loves to go from behind and finds women with bodies that are appropriate to the role. Marianne Taylor may not have done a heck of a lot, but George Mooradian and Albert Pyun could light and film her ass(ets) with great skill. While it is easy to declare this as a film that has enough strength to overcome the weak parts, there are one or two parts that erode the complete success of the film.

I'm not going to pick on Hope Marie Carlton too much here since she looks really good and handles most of the dialog she is given well enough. That final fight though...yikes. A Kickboxing champion is a tough sell for her. I do have to give bonus points to her for not being shy in front of the camera! So, one stand out actor can't sink a Bloodmatch, but some other things really can. The editing of the film by Paul O'Bryan, whose name I have seen in David A. Prior movies, is really odd.

First I wanted to put this in the category of Albert Pyun funk, editing the fights to a rock beat and blending the typical with the unexpected. However, I get very itchy when the CHOP/EDIT/CHOP/EDIT school of Kung Fu screen fighting is employed. And it is. **BLOODMATCH** has a very unique spin on that. Very unique. In most of the fights almost EVERY move is shown 2 to 4 times from different angles. Uh...once in a while to punctuate something is totally cool, I get it. I actually like it. Low kick (x4), Low kick (x4), punch (x2) and fall (x3) should be input for a Street Fighter game and not in the editing suite in my opinion though. Most of the fighters look way more proficient than this kind of cover up would imply and it becomes a complete distraction. I figure it could be a reflection of the mania and pre planned vengeance of Brick Bardo if I wanted to stretch things into storytelling technique, but it becomes really wearying on the viewer. Somehow, thankfully, the Urquidez fight overcomes the presentation. Maybe I'm just a big fan of The Jet and was missing seeing him in action and will take what I can get.

Overall, **BLOODMATCH** is not the greatest kickboxing movie you could find, but it is one of my favorite examples of dropping your cinematic senses needle to the Albert Pyun record. I can't imagine he set out to make a great kickboxing film at all! It is funky and odd and unique and ambiguous and well-acted for the most part. It has nudity. It has fights. It has you wondering what the hell is going on at times! I recommend it if you want something totally strange that also has kickboxing scenes to punch you in the face repeatedly from every angle after the half way point. Hell, it is worth watching just to see Thom Matthews grit his teeth...and then kick a bunch of other people's teeth OUT OF THEIR HEADS!

USA, 1991. Director: Albert Pyun

THE GOOD, THE BAD, THE WEIRD
(Joheunnom nabbeunnom isanghannom)

Review by Tony Strauss

In a dusty, dry, 1930s Manchuria filtered through a Spaghetti Western lens, the best bandit on the continent, cocky and cold-blooded Park Chang-yi (**I SAW THE DEVIL**'s Lee Byung-hun), is hired to steal a map being transported by train across the desert. But by the time he stops the train, it is already in the process of being robbed by bumbling small-time thief Yoon Tae-goo (Song Kang-ho of **THE HOST** and **THIRST**), who unwittingly acquires the map among his stolen booty. Also aboard the train is renowned bounty hunter Park Do-won (Jung Woo-sung from **THE WARRIOR**), dead set on collecting both the map and the hefty price on Chang-yi's head. The high-octane train robbery shootout sets the adrenalized tone for the non-stop thrill-ride that follows, as Tae-goo The Weird escapes with the map into the desert with help from his sidekick Man-gil (Ryu Seung-su), with not only Chang-yi The Bad and Do-won The Good in pursuit, but also the ruthless Ghost Market gang, who are after the map for their own purposes.

As Tae-goo and Man-gil sort through their loot, they discover the strange map with Russian writing, and Man-gil speculates that it could be a map to a legendary treasure buried somewhere in Manchuria before the Qing Dynasty's fall. After some rudimentary Russian-to-Korean translation work courtesy of Man-gil, they decipher the words "buried...excavation...large volumes." But before they can translate any more specifics, they're attacked by Chang-yi's men, and are forced to separate in the melee.

Tae-goo flees across the desert, only to be easily captured by Do-won (in a scene that gives a sly nod to Leone's **DUCK, YOU SUCKER**). When Tae-goo is informed that the infamous Park Chang-yi is also after the map, the two agree to form a tentative alliance in order to get to the buried treasure first.

Chang-yi's men report back to him that the person in possession of the map is none other than Yoon Tae-goo, and an old grudge resurfaces in Chang-yi. He is now determined not only to get the map for himself, but to kill Tae-goo in the process.

And then there's the whole business about the Japanese Army's interest in the map…

This, the fifth feature from South Korean director Kim Jee-woon (**A TALE OF TWO SISTERS**,

I SAW THE DEVIL), was at the time the most expensive production in South Korean cinema history, and every single won spent by the producers is beautifully-represented on-screen. From the lush period sets and costumes to the mind-blowing action choreography and cinematography, this movie presents some of the finest work yet achieved in the annals of Adventure cinema. You will be on the edge of your seat from the very start, with nary a moment to stop for a breath until after the film's roof-raising final battle.

While being an obvious tribute to Leone's classic, **THE GOOD, THE BAD & THE UGLY**, in both title and aesthetic, as well as the basic premise of three formidable gunslingers of varying moral fortitude vying for the same treasure, this film is very much its own beast. Even when making direct references to Leone's Westerns—and there are many such references—it is never derivative or redundant, but seems fresh and new at every turn while making an entry into a thoroughly-treaded genre. The script is witty, engaging and deceptively complex, and the characters are well-developed and played to utter perfection by the cast. Each action set-piece is bigger and more outrageous than the last, and the action never stops.

The methods through which said action was filmed delivers a connective experience for the viewer rarely found in Adventure films, wherein the usual technique generally involves editing room cunning and CGI trickery to avoid revealing the switches between actor and stunt-person, with much of the "good stuff" being played out in wide shots wherein you can't see the performers' faces, resulting in the loss of actual acting during the most intense sequences. No such distancing occurs here; the performers and stunt-persons are one and the same, and the cinematographers have obvious thrill issues, and all of this comes together in a big, delightful bundle of action-adventure wonderment. When watching the behind-the-scenes footage on the DVD, I was completely blown away by the revelation that all the scenes in which I was certain that CGI compositing and green-screen had been used had actually been accomplished through an insane sort of elaborate, Rube Goldberg-esque, wires-and-pulleys-and-prayers technique that was as hair-raising to witness as the resultant sequences themselves. Seriously, after you've watched the movie, watch the behind-the-scenes extras—the way they shot some of these sequences has to be seen to be believed.

Two versions of the film were released in cinemas—the Korean cut and the International cut—and although the Korean version runs approximately seven minutes longer, the International cut is the version that reflects the director's vision, and is the cut that was released internationally on home video. Though I was unable to review the Korean cut, reports seem to indicate that the extra footage was merely an extended epilogue that was superfluous and already hinted at by the preferred ending.

Though working in the Spaghetti Western world, Kim Jee-woon prefers to call this film a "Kimchee Western", believing that the story and film are spicy and vibrant, just like the Korean culture and people. Regardless of one's taste for Korean dishes made from fermented cabbage, this film is a wonderfully rich entrée that will delight the palate of the most jaded Action-Adventure and Western movie gourmets. Take a bite—it's delicious.

South Korea, 2008. Director: Kim Jee-woon
Available from MPI Home Video

THE WILD GEESE

Review by Douglas Waltz

THE WILD GEESE tells the action packed tale of a group of aging mercenaries that are hired to do one last mission. They have to train a squad of men to parachute into an African nation in turmoil and grab the deposed president out of a maximum security prison and out of the country to safety. And if that wasn't bad enough it doesn't take long before the double cross rears its ugly head.

Severin Video has taken this film that is described as a 70's British version of The Expendables and given it the royal treatment. First, it's a Blu Ray DVD Combo so you have a choice in how you watch it. If you have a Blu Ray player that is the way to go. The picture quality is gorgeous.

And the extras. Oh my, the extras are even better. There are lengthy interviews with the direc-

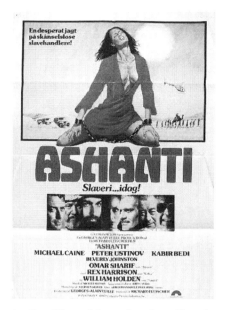

tor, the military advisor and producer. There is a newsreel of the premiere, a featurette on the making of the film and the audio commentary has Roger Moore in it!

But without a good film no amount of extras in the world would save this flick. Luckily, everyone brought their A game. Burton, Moore and Harris work so well together. This is old school action at its finest and it tears through it's over two hour running time like a bullet.

Severin should be commended on another fine release and I urge anyone who loves classic action films to get this DVD set.

UK/Switzerland, 1978. Director: Andrew V. McLaglen
Available from Severin Films

ASHANTI

Review by Douglas Waltz

Dr. David Linderby (Caine) and his gorgeous, exotic wife Anansa (Beverly Johnson) are vaccinating native villages in West Africa when she is abducted by Slave Trader, Suleiman (Ustinov). The rest of the film is David on the run trying to save Anansa before she is sold to Prince Hassan (Omar Sharif). Along the way he is helped by a human trafficking activist (Harrison) and a mercenary helicopter pilot (Holden).

But will he get there in time.

Severin Films release of **ASHANTI** is a beautiful print. Available as a Blu Ray DVD Combo, Ashanti is an epic adventure that runs through the exotic land of Africa in the 70's. Directed by the man who gave us Soylent Green and Mandingo, Ashanti, while slightly predictable never fails to be entertaining.

The only real failure might be that this release coincides with the release of **THE WILD GEESE**. That Combo pack has so many extras that it boggles the mind. This only has a single, brief interview with Beverly Johnson and, while informative, could have been a much longer piece for this release. A theatrical trailer is the only other

feature. This film deserves a lot more extras and the fact that there is no commentary is a crime. **ASHANTI** is a gorgeous, action packed film with more than enough movie stars to make it great, but I think people drawn to this would have liked to get more background information in the form of a few more extra features.

France, 1978. Director Richard Fleischer
Available on DVD by Severin Films

OS VIOLENTADORES DE MENINAS VIRGENS
(The Rapists of Virgin Girls)

Review by Brian Harris

Estupro! A small group of debauched millionaires, tired of whores with no traction left on the tires, has their slimebag pimp provide them with fresh young virgins. Naturally, finding virgins to satisfy their tastes is no easy feat as Brazil's female population is apparently comprised of women with no moral fiber. The pimp commands his crew to drive about the city, searching for young girls they believe to be suitably virginal and then kidnap them. If they prove to be pure, they're kept alive for a short period of time to serve their purpose. Once sullied by the moneybag molesters, they're brutally executed and their remains are unceremoniously disposed of.

During a harrowing kidnap, one of the thugs loses a button from his blazer and curious onlooker Pedro, played by director Francisco Cavalcanti, scoops it up. As luck would have it, Pedro isn't just any onlooker though, he runs the local laundromat with his best friend Shorty and Shorty's sister (and Pedro's fiancée) Suely. His access to all the clothing in the area may prove useful, especially if the kidnapper brings his clothing in to get cleaned and Pedro can match up the missing button. Which is exactly what happens!

Instead of waiting for the police to arrive on the scene, Pedro jumps in a car and follows the kidnappers through the streets of the city, hoping to tail them back to their hideout and the missing girls. It's a great plan but the two thugs get wise to it immediately, pull off to the side of the road, yank Pedro from his car and beat his laundry lovin' ass. Saved by the blaring sirens of the police, the two run off before they can be put into custody. Now Pedro, Shorty and Suely are now on the molestation & murder ring's radar and have made the shortlist for unmarked graves.

As the search to find the molestation & murder ring intensifies, the millionaires begin feeling the squeeze and decide it's time to pull the plug on their extra-virginal activities before they land in prison for life. Slapping the perverts with a $2 million blackmail, the pimp agrees to deliver one final rapefest, stepping up his virgin round-up rodeo and his assault on the only living witnesses able to identify hi crew...Pedro and friends! Can the police stop these monsters before more young girls are raped and murdered?

Was there any film industry sleazier than Brazil's during the Seventies and Eighties? The sheer amount of nudity, brutality, rape and offensive racial and sexual stereotypes in **OS VIOLENTADORES DE MENINAS VIRGENS** is staggering. Not only was I occasionally aroused, in a "I'm going to need a baptizing after this!" way, but I was blown away by the director's near-superhuman ability to stretch the barest storyline into a feature-length runtime. Seriously, about 20 minutes in and I was scratching my head and wondering what in hell he'd fill the rest of the film with. Boy did I underestimate Cavalcanti! HE FILLED IT WITH SLEAZE OF COURSE! Silly me. There was masturbation, panty-sniffing, strangulation, drowning, ass-eating, explosions and, yep you guessed it, nudity. If this film had an odor, it would stink of urine, pomade, Brüt and probably Astro-glide. A heady stink indeed, no?

Acting, terrible. Dialogue, terrible. Some of the sex sequences were unconvincing and the action was poorly staged, in other words, it was bad. And fantastic. But mostly bad. Readers, I won't lie to you, the women in this film were really ugly. "How ugly were they Brian?!!" The women in **OS VIOLENTADORES DE MENINAS VIRGENS** were so damn ugly I had to wait until bras and panties came off before allowing myself an erection! And even then I was cautious! [rimshot] But seriously folks, this flick does have a powerhouse final quarter that actually makes all the bad well worth wading through. I kept thinking,"Nah, there's no way this film is smart enough to 'go there'!" but "go there" they did and I'm a better man for having stuck with it. Right?

Yeah, maybe not.

Brazil, 1983. Director: Francisco Cavalcanti

A REENCARNAÇÃO DO SEXO
(The Reincarnation of Sex)

Review by Brian Harris

You know, the great thing about being a cult cinema wonk is that you don't need dubs and, by god, you don't need any freakin' subs either! Sure, we'd LIKE to have English subs for the foreign films we watch but that's not always possible with some of the way-out, far flung shit we get our pudgy hands on. Thankfully, most of it is poorly written with nary a plot or feature-length story to be found so following along without dubs or subs is a snap. Sorta. Hell it's probably better some don't, otherwise we wouldn't enjoy them half as much as we do! Sorta.

Case in point, Brazilian smut-peddler Luiz Castellini's erotic horror film, **A REENCARNAÇÃO DO SEXO**. Truly, if ever a film was made that needed no words, it is this very film. The VHS copy I was able to kick back with featured Portuguese audio and no English subs, which was fine, as the soft, swaying and rhythmic jiggling of breasts in this film slapped out everything I needed to know in a Morse Code of the carnal kind. Swack swack swack. That means,"My goodness I am having a wonderful time having intercourse with you. Perhaps you and I could have more later?" Ah yes, the international language of scuzz. Here's what I gleaned:

A farmer and his wife are awoken during the middle of the night by noises, leading them to the bedroom of their beautiful daughter. It appears the hired help has taken it upon himself to do more than just trim the hedges around the house and, from the sound of it, the farmer's daughter seemed to approve. Blinded by rage, and perhaps a little deep-seated jealousy, the farmer is determined to stop the humpy shenanigans from happening again so he grabs an ax and heads out in search of the farmhand. No good dong goes unpunished though and when he finds the young man, he lops off his head and chops him up but good!

Later that night, after a fitful sleep, the farmer's daughter is beckoned by her lover, from beyond the grave, to dig up his remains and put him to rest. I think. Anyhow, with the help of her mother, who may or may not have intimate knowledge of the dark arts, she brings his decapitated head in the house and there they bury the noggin in a large flower pot. Now, nestled within the dirt, with the roots of beautiful flowers burrowing into rotting flesh, the restless spirit yearns for his soul-mate. No sooner has the grotesque gardening been complete does the young woman fall ill and pass away, presumably from a broken heart.

Ten years later we're introduced to a new couple looking for a country home to settle in but their stay will be short-lived as the head begins a'callin', the farmer's daughter reappears and a whole lotta humpin' and dyin' goes on! Nobody that moves into the house is safe from the malicious (and horny) spirits' influence and the evil that dwells within!

Loosely inspired by Boccaccio's The Decameron (Fourth Day, Novel 5), Castellini's **A REENCARNAÇÃO DO SEXO** is both genuinely creepy and disturbingly arousing, combining bloody sequences of graphic murder with simulated sex that just barely toes the line between soft and hard. Throw in a disembodied voice, the knife-wielding spirit of an angry young woman and a ton of nudity, including an orgy of blood, and you've got yourself quite the sleazy Brazilian Sexploitationer worth tracking down and checking out, dubs and subs be damned. It's certainly not the best erotic horror film I've seen but it does generate a healthy amount of tension, something erotic horror films often lack. Once you've witnessed the unforgettable "DILDO OF DEATH" sequence, you'll be hooked.

I would mention the acting but everybody spoke in Portuguese and it was a softcore porn/horror film so there's bound to be all kinds of bad acting going on! From what I saw, most of it wasn't terrible, though I'm sure some of my Brazilian compadres would vehemently disagree with me. I guess that's just one of the benefits of not having any idea what the hell is being said and not giving two shits anyhow. I mean, the men were hairy, as to be expected from a film made in '82, and the women were stunning (and hairy as well), if you need to know more, you're probably out of your element and won't like this film. If, however, you enjoy a rousingly randy romp of red and dead, **A REENCARNAÇÃO DO SEXO** is tent-worthy. -

Brazil, 1982. Director: Luiz Castellini

SILENT NIGHT

Review by Brian Harris

A few years back, one of the bigger online review websites hailed Dimension Extreme's release of Steven C. Miller's **AUTOMATON TRANSFUSION** as "One of the best zombie films in decades" and the "Holy Grail of true independent horror films." While tastes may indeed vary and not everybody can be expected to agree with one another on something as subjective as art, Miller's zombie film was pure shit and anybody remotely familiar with good horror cinema would agree. I was genuinely baffled by Dimension's decision to pick it up for distribution when there were so many other, far more deserving, indie horror films out there just waiting to be discovered. Hell, Miller himself inadvertently confirmed it was trash by insisting consumers avoid renting his film as he claimed the quality of the rental transfer was inferior to the retail transfer! In other words, skip renting for $4 and just PURCHASE for $15. As you can imagine, it was the manufactured review hype and Miller's own antics that soured me on any of his future cinematic misadventures. Or so I thought. [RANT OVER]

SILENT NIGHT

Five years later, there I am sitting in front of the TV, cramming some trans-fat-dripping offal in my gaping maw, fixated on a "bad but entertaining" SyFy Original production entitled, **SCREAM OF THE BANSHEE**, directed by none other than, you guessed it, Steven C. Miller! I'm not one to hold grudges really, I mean, if you intend to entertain me and you do so, you're okay in my book. Miller did just that and though the film wasn't great, he had made noticeable strides in his filmmaking. Along comes his surprisingly well-received **THE AGGRESSION SCALE**, and Miller is starting to look like a solid genre director on the rise. Nothing meteoric mind you, but from **AUTOMATON TRANSFUSION** to **THE AGGRESSION SCALE**, he's certainly movin' on up! Taking on a remake of the beloved X-mas holiday horror film, **SILENT NIGHT, DEADLY NIGHT**, was one of those risky "make him or break him" deals, no doubt about it. The fans would either embrace his **SILENT NIGHT** as worthwhile (or at the very least better than the sequels) or, as most often do, buy tickets for a one-way bandwagon ride to Crucifixionville.

A small-town is overrun during the holiday season by a massive swarm of Santas (Santii?) preparing for the annual Christmas Santa contest and one St. Nick in particular is leaving mutilated bodies in his wake. The local police department are determined root out the killer but with hundreds of possible suspects, their task begins looking nearly impossible until two viable suspects come to light; a nasty character by the name of 'Santa Jim' and down-on-his-luck drug dealer Stein 'Mr. Snow' Karsson. Could Jim's proximity to a spate of X-mas slayings a few years back in another state be a coincidence? And how about Karsson's connection to some of the murder victims and his vicious attempt on the life of Officer Bradimore?

With two good leads but no hard evidence pointing to either, the police department just may have their eyes on the wrong men. The true culprit may be more of a legend than they'd anticipated.

From shit to shine! Steven C. Miller's **SILENT NIGHT** was bloody as hell and downright entertaining! Now, I've heard the complaints surrounding this film, outside the usual remake hate, and some of it is valid but, ultimately, I found this to be a better film than Sellier, Jr.'s **SILENT NIGHT, DEADLY NIGHT**. Don't even get me started on comparing this to a few of the **SILENT NIGHT, DEADLY NIGHT** sequels! Truth be told I'm surprised this didn't make it to the big screen as everything from the lighting and cinematography to the score and FX gave this production a slick, big budget feel. I'd easily put this up there with another gruesome little X-mas remake, **BLACK CHRISTMAS**.

Now, there's no getting around some of the script issues here and there as Malcolm McDowell's character was in desperate need of a re-write but the film as a whole works, and it works well. The tried and true slasher formula may not be looked upon fondly by cinema snobs today as it was 30 years ago but when it comes to a killer Santa film, "if it ain't broke don't fix it" would certainly apply. I can't say I'm much of a slasher film fan, or a born again Miller convert, but these days I'm all about the entertainment value and **SILENT NIGHT** is a film I'd happily watch again with friends and family. If you're able to look be-

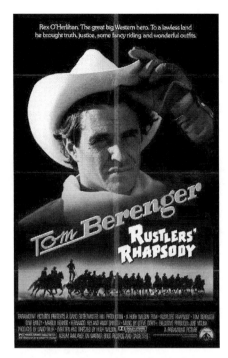

yond McDowell's atrocious dialogue and you're not opposed to nudity, graphic violence and the cattle prodding of young children, why not give it a shot. Be sure to pair this up with **RARE EXPORTS: A CHRISTMAS TALE** and you've got yourself a night of merriment sure to be approved 100% by Jesus Christ and Santa Claus!

Canada/USA, 2012. Directed by Steven C. Miller

RUSTLER'S RHAPSODY

Review by Tony Strauss

Pull up a rickety barstool, pour a glass of warm gin with a human hair in it, and take a bite of narcotic root—it's time for the rootin'-tootin' adventures of Rex O'Herlihan the Singing Cowboy and his Wonder-Horse, Wildfire, in this brilliantly subversive spoof of 1930s/1940s Western film conventions from writer/director Hugh Wilson (**POLICE ACADEMY, GUARDING TESS**).

Tom Berenger (**PLATOON, SOMEONE TO WATCH OVER ME**) stars as Rex, a White-Knight-style balladeer cowboy who, we're told, was the hero and star of some fifty-two cowboy movies made between the years 1938 and 1947—fifty-two movies that were exactly the same, as most of the cowboy adventures of that era were. In a contrived-yet-amusing introduction, voice-over narration wonders what things would have been like if those films were still being made today… and, as we watch a scene from one of Rex's old black & white adventures, the world suddenly begins to rumble as color and Dolby surround sound intrude into the picture, and the bad guys Rex is single-handedly chasing suddenly realize they have more firepower than their pursuer. The introduction sets up the film's premise in a usefully expeditious way, but is a bit incongruous with what is to follow, since what we're really getting with this Western spoof isn't so much a story of self-aware movie characters as a formulaic genre story played through a meta-world viewfinder in which every Western town is exactly like they were portrayed in the films of that era—therefore, all Western towns are exactly alike—and the only person who knows this is Rex, the Good Guy whose station in life is to travel from town to town and solve the same problems over and over again.

The plot itself is by necessity simplistic and familiar: Wandering good guy rides into a Western town overrun with corruption and violence, makes friends of the downtrodden and misunderstood, and challenges the corrupt forces lording over the citizenry, leading to a grand final showdown in which the town is freed from the clutches of evil. Where the film achieves its excellence is in its knowledge of every rule and cliché of the "Singing Cowboy" subgenre, and forcefully playing by those unbreakable rules within a real-world-logic context, to hysterical ends.

For example, we're all familiar with the handsome old-time cowboy movie good guys in the beautiful white western shirts, the ten-gallon Stetsons, the ornate leather gun belts with the giant silver buckles, and the shiniest polished boots. Rex O'Herlihan the Singing Cowboy is just such a Good Guy, so in order to maintain this iconic image, real-world logic dictates that he would travel from town to town with a massive 7-foot tall jumbo-size armoire filled with an impressive selection of the finest Good Guy wardrobe items in the West (with room for several guitars), which he does. Planning the perfect ensemble for each day is just part of the job.

Rex rides into the town of Oakwood Estates and strolls into the saloon, and is approached by Peter (**POLICE ACADEMY**'s G.W. Bailey), the town drunk, who offers to trade local gossip for drinks. Peter informs Rex that the power-mad cattle baron known as The Colonel (a hilariously effete Andy Griffith) lords over the town with an iron fist, and preys on the pacifistic local sheepherders ("They're the good guys. But they smell godawful…kinda makes you wanna kill'em", explains Peter). And right on cue, the Colonel's top henchman, Blackie (**DOWNTON ABBEY'S** Jim Carter), bursts in with his men and shoots one of the unarmed sheepherders, obviously ready to gun them all down. Rex steps in and warns Blackie that if he doesn't back down, Rex will shoot the gun out of Blackie's hand. You see, Good Guys never kill anyone—that wouldn't be nice—they just shoot the guns out of their enemies hands, and that's exactly what Rex does (this hand-shooting credo is one of the funniest running gags in the film, at one point sending the oblivious town doctor into a panic that the town might be overrun with a bizarre skin virus that affects only the hands of male adults). When The Colonel learns that this mysterious newcomer has killed his top man (and apparently, lover), he begins to plot Rex's demise.

But Rex can't be outwitted, because this is what happens in every single Western town…he knows every move before it's made against him. It's both his power and his curse. Nothing ever surprises him. When Peter challenges this claim, Rex rattles off specifics he couldn't possibly know about Oakwood Estates ("Is the owner of your newspaper a young idealist who hawked everything to buy his printing press?"). And yes, every single Western town does indeed have the railroad coming through. Every single one.

In an attempt to get rid of the seemingly unbeatable cowboy, The Colonel reluctantly decides to team up with the evil railroad men (led by Spanish legend Fernando Rey), who, it is hilariously revealed, live in a Spaghetti Western world…they all wear long dusters, have foreign accents, and have cooler theme music. After several disastrous attempts, they realize that their only hope is to concoct a plan so devious that Rex could never have encountered it before…but how do you out-think an adversary who knows the future?

Rex is a true Western Good Guy to the letter; nobody can outsmart him, and he never misses a hand. The only thing that ever does shake him is the advance of a beautiful woman, and both Miss Tracy (Taxi's Marilu Henner), the town prostitute, and The Colonel's daughter (**THE FUGITIVE**'s Sela Ward, demonstrating scene-stealing comedic chops) have set their sights on the handsome stranger. Unfortunately, all the Good Guy ever does is kiss the pretty girls before riding off into the sunset, and when Rex's masculinity comes under scrutiny (a Good Guy must be a "confident heterosexual", we learn), Rex begins to doubt his qualifications as a Western hero. This just might be a weakness the bad guys can use to their advantage.

Hugh Wilson's obvious passion and formidable knowledge of an outdated and laughably idealistic Western subgenre—combined with a wit alternately razor sharp and infantile—is what gives this criminally overlooked comedy its unique strength. Repeat viewings reward with new discoveries of jokes-within-jokes that will keep you coming back for more gut-busting fun. This is one of those comedy gems that deserve rediscovery; it's simply one of the funniest and most astute genre parodies out there. Whether or not you're an expert of Singing Cowboy cinema—or even a fan of Westerns—you'll recognize most of the tropes from pop culture and other parodies, and be able to laugh along at the world where only the Good Guys win, and every single stunt happens in slow motion.

USA/Spain, 1985. D: Hugh Wilson
Available from Paramount Pictures

MY WIFE'S MURDER

Review by Chaitanya Reddy

Police Inspector Tejpal Randhawa is assigned to investigate the case of the dead woman whose body was recovered from a small pond. Tejpal links this matter with a missing persons' report filed by Ravi Patwardhan and his father-in-law, and subsequently has the dead woman is identified as Sheela, Ravi's wife. According to Ravi, Sheela had left their home to go to visit her parents. When she did not arrive at her parents' 24 hours later, he himself went to their house, Still not being able to locate her, he accompanied his father-in-law to the nearest police station and filed a missing persons report. Tejpal would like to conclude that Sheela was waylaid on her way to her parents' by person(s) unknown, beaten, and her body was left in the pond. But this case

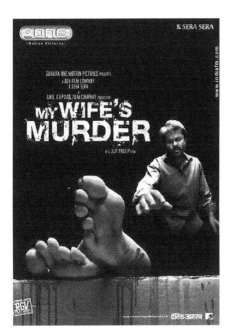

puzzles him, as there was no apparent motive for unknown person(s) to kill her, as no money has been taken, and her body has not shown any signs of sexual molestation. Taking these facts into consideration, Tejpal starts to suspect Ravi. But what possible motive could Ravi, a father of two children, have in killing his wife?

Anil Kapoor delivers one of his best performances as Ravi Patwardhan. He's got the perfect looks for a man with a nagging wife and a messy life. In the "man on run" scenes he does a great job with the stammering and the reaction after the accidental killing of his wife are just wonderful. This performance should clearly stand in his top five roles of all his 100+ movies. Boman Irani shines as a cop. He is just made for acting. From comic roles to a serious cop no-one has done a job better than him. Suchitra as a nagging wife suits the role, only Nandana Sen has little to offer.

MY WIFE'S MURDER is a definite an oddball flick to come out from Bollywood. Jijy Philip does a great job with his directorial debut, it was always going to be a better unusual flick since it came out from the infamous RGV (Ram Gopal Varma) factory . Though rejected by the Indian crowds this movie is a dark & gripping tale of emotions of a man who accidentally kills his wife and is running to save his life for his children. MY WIFE'S MURDER is a must watch if you are looking for something 'Unusual' from Bollywood that includes a stellar performance from Anil Kapoor.

India, 2005. Director: Jijy Philip
Available from Eros Entertainmen

DARNA MANA HAI
(Getting Scared is Forbidden)

Review by Chaitanya Reddy

Six city students take refuge in deserted ruins after they are stranded on a highway, and start telling each other scary stories to keep amused. The stories include: A husband trying to scare his wife; a man stuck at a creepy "healthy hotel"; a school teacher spooked by a child's homework; a housewife scared of apples; a bizarre lift on a freeway; and a college kid with an unusual power.

DARNA MANA HAI is the first horror anthology ever in Indian cinema, and is the best one when compared to the other two (one being the sequel to this movie). **DARNA MANA HAI** has an ensemble cast with stars that include Saif Ali Khan, Vivek Oberoi, Nana Paterkar & Boman Irani. The cast has some immense talent and each segment is very well acted. Coming to the segments of the movie, each segment does offer something fresh starting from ghosts in swamps to a bizarre story concerning apples. For the first time a movie from 'RGV' factory tries to scare the audience without the use of Sound effects and does it very convincingly. Segments like 'No Smoking' and 'Stop/move' draw inspirations from Hollywood flicks **PSYCHO** and **CLICK** but stay original. Prawaal Raman does a great job managing seven stories to complement each other and to maintain a good pace. **DARNA MANA HAI** paved path for a whole new sub-genre in Bollywood which only ended up with two more movies. On the whole the movie is a must watch for every horror fan (more or less). *And* there are no "dance and song numbers" in this Bollywood movie!

India, 2003. Directed by Prawal Raman.
Available on from Eros Entertainment

GEHRAYEE

Reviewed by Chaitanya Reddy

While the basic plot of the movie is about spiritual possession, **GEHRAYEE** is more about a happy family pushed into tragedy because of past deeds of the head of the family. It's a movie with a very serious tone which is very rare among the Bollywood horror flicks released during the 70's and 80's. Nothing really happens in the movie for the whole time other than crying, family dinners, breakfasts and occasional weird behavior from the possessed girl.

The possession of the young girl slowly starts to tear the family apart, constant son and dad fights, long discussions about to which doctor the girl should be taken to and what treatment she needs to have. As the movie progresses towards the intensity increases as all the plans to cure the girl's illness start to fail. Well the girl's possession comes to an end she is fine and everything appears normal, but still there are 20 odd minutes left in the movie which sort of act like a revelation behind the evil happenings and a disturbing climax which made me think of a David Fincher's 1995 film **SE7EN**.

GEHRAYEE is an absolute delight if you are looking for some serious acting in the 80's Bollywood horror. Starring Anant Nag (introduced in Shyam Benegal's 1974 movie **ANKUR**), Shreeram Lagoo, the talented Padmini Kholapure as the possessed teen, and a brief role by the greatest villan of Indian film Amrish Puri. The Directorial combo of Vikas Desai-Aruna Raje did a great job in making a two hour long intriguing supernatural horror. The music needs a special mention as it transforms from a brighter happy tone into a tragic unsettling tone as the movie progresses.

Overall **GEHRAYEE** is the best movie about possession that have ever come out Indian cinema, and needs to be seen by every genuine fan (everyone I say) of Bollywood horror flicks.

India, 1980. Directors: Vikas Desai & Aruna Raje
Available from Shemaroo Entertainment

SHAAPIT

Review by Chaitanya Reddy

Director Vikram Bhatt has had a great impact on Bollywood since he made film **RAAZ** (2002), and established himself as a horror movie specialist

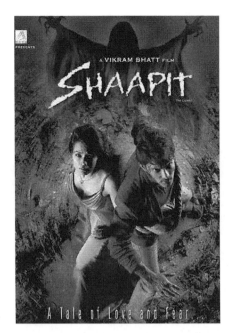

since then. But his movies weren't that great post-**RAAZ**. **1920** (2008), a thrilling tale of possession, ends on a bad note causing an audience backlash as Bhatt copied William Friedkin's **THE EXORCIST** (1973) scene per scene in the penultimate moments of the film. This was very frustrating since the movie was very good for most of the part. **RAAZ 3** (2012) was his only success post **1920**. Okay now I will end the banter and say that **SHAAPIT** is a midget in the world of "disaster movies".

The Concept of **SHAAPIT** is innovative and thrilling: a curse is carried through generations of a royal family, which is guarded by a ghost. Unfortunately Kaaya (our leading lady) belongs to be the third or fourth generation of the royal family and cannot get married to Aman (our leading guy) and keeps getting hurt by the ghost whenever she tries to get in contact with him because of the curse. Now Aman sets off on a journey with his friend and a Professor of Paranormal Sciences (is there such a thing?) to destroy the ghost guarding the curse and save the life of Kaaya. The story shifts to various places, and there is even a different time period during the movie. How could one make a mess of such a handsome looking story line???

Vikram Bhatt does have great skills and is an excellent storyteller when he is on his game. But makes up some seriously complex concepts for his movies which are totally illogical and are never understood. His scientific concepts are pretty far fetch as he uses theories by the Mayan, some kind of weird connection between solids, liquids and gases which ends up sending people to other worlds. This results in making **SHAAPIT** pretty dumb very irritating at times. Next comes the computer graphic effects, which has always been the biggest drawbacks of his movies. The CG is so bad that it's just ... well, *very bad*. He uses very cartoony GC even in his latest blockbuster **RAAZ 3D** which made the film laughable. Why not invest some money in your special effects it when a supernatural story calls for it?

Now moving on to the better parts of the film. The acting is believable, and that is the film's saving grace. Aditya Narayan does a good job and never looks like a debutante, and Rahul Dev as the Professor does an excellent job. Shubh Joshi and the others do their part well leaving no room for bad acting which could have made the movie almost intolerable. The soundtrack by Chirantan Bhatt is exceptional like in many other Vikram Bhatt movies, but could have been way better if it was cut short of at least two songs.

On the whole **SHAAPIT** starts well and reaches the climax by the end of the first hour. The last hour, though, is an endurance test, and non-Bollywood viewers may have a hard time sitting though all of the film.

India, 2010. Director: Vikram Bhatt
Available from Moser Baer Entertainment

KAUN...?

Reviewed by Chaitanya Reddy

KAUN...? is an unique Bollywood flick which belongs to the 'Whodunit' genre with the interesting point is that it has only three principal characters. Other than a group of people who make a brief appearance for 10 seconds and an unknown dead body, it's just about three people inside a house. Well, given that the third character enters the house after more than half of the movie is finished it's basically two characters in the movie, a Paranoid young woman and a Psychotic visitor. **KAUN...?** is movie which shows what happens inside a house can be far from human habitation. On a stormy day a lost psychotic looking stranger tries to intrude on a paranoid young woman who is home alone. Later on, a man calling himself a cop also enters the house.

After reading through the strange looking synopsis of the movie and observing Urmila and Manoj Bajpai in the casting it is obvious that this movie is directed by "Mr. Creative Genius" Ram Gopal Varma a.k.a. *RGV*. It's too bad that Varma does not do films like this anymore as **KAUN...?** is an absolutely brilliant experiment (considering Bollywood) which works for most of the part. Written by Anurag Kashyap (now called as the best Indian 'cult' director by most critics) this movie has every reason to make one curious before watching it, and your time won't be wasted. Sandeep Chowta provides the perfect sound effects and so does Mazhar Kamran with his camera work. The huge house, the dark attic, fishpond, stormy atmosphere, a little cat, and the constant audio from the television warning about a serial killer on loose play as their own subtle characters intensifying the climate inside the house.

As usual Urmila is at her natural best with her sexy curves and brilliant acting skills. She perfectly fits the role of ''Madam'' a confused and paranoid young woman. Manoj Bajpai is the standout performer in the movie. He displays everything from being scared to death to rib-tickling humor which suits the role of "Psychotic strangers" role without a doubt. Sushant Singh, as the cop, doesn't have much screen time, but did his best with what he was given.

Overall it is very hard to review a movie which is an experiment more than an ambitious project as **KAUN...?** The film is one of those rare experimental movies of Hindi cinema. It's a suspenseful thriller with subtle humor and strong casting, and great technical aspects. The film does have its flaws but is undoubtedly an entertaining and an enjoyable flick. Look out for inspirations drawn from Tarantino!!!

India, 1999. Director: Ram Gopal Varma

WENG'S CHOP ISSUE ZERO

The zine that started all this madness! Digest-size, 56 pages, color cover, reviews, articles, interviews! If you liked Weng's Chop #1 and #2 you'll go bonkers over SPECIAL ISSUE ZERO! Available from amazon.com -or- we have a limited supply of our first printing for only $5 PPD USA & Canada or $8 PPD overseas. Paypal: orlof@oberlin.net. Offer good while supplies last!

Cult Cinema Under the Gun
Reevaluating the Classics & More
• Danae Dunning

IN THE REALM OF THE SENSES and SADA

On May 18, 1936, Sada Abe strangled her lover, Kichizo Ishida, then removed his genitalia and carried them around in handbag, so he will always be with her. Sounds gruesome, right? But this is not fiction but fact, and this woman would be vilified by men and venerated by women. Her case has become legend and a treatise on a misogynistic culture.

IN THE REALM OF THE SENSES, directed by Nagisa Oshima, tells the tale of how Sada (Eiko Matsuda) and Kichizo (Tatsuya Fuji), meet when she works as a maid at his restaurant. Sparks fly right away and the two are consumed by their passion doing nothing but going from inn to inn, geisha house to geisha house making love practically non-stop even in the presence of geishas and servants. The escalating intensity of the affair and Kichizo's refusal to leave his wife drives Sada to contemplate the unthinkable...... with Kichizo's full consent.

This film was quite controversial for it's explicit, non-simulated sex scenes including penile penetration, which is strictly forbidden in Japan, even in their pornography. In fact, the censorship laws were so strict that Oshima had to send the film to France to be developed. It was actually banned in several countries, and the director faced obscenity charges, but the case was dropped after a four year court battle. When it premiered in Germany, it was seized immediately on suspicion that it was pornography, but it was re-released 18 months later uncut. In the end, it's a beautiful film with amazing performances by Matsuda and Fuji, who prove quite well that they can carry a movie with just the two of them in the last half. And the erotic atmosphere is so thick, you can even smell the sex.

Now we come to the less explicit **SADA**, directed by Nobuhiko Obayashi. While we get vague references to Sada's past in the previous film, this film is her story. Sada (Hitomi Kiroki) is raped at the tender age of 14, an experience that causes the normally well-behaved girl to skip school and go completely wild. She becomes a syphilitic prostitute moving from brothel to brothel under assumed names. She eventually tires of the lifestyle and becomes a waitress, which leads to her fateful encounter with Kichizo.

I really don't know what to say. This movie is all over the place. It changes from black to white for no apparent reason, characters break the fourth wall, and there's even musical numbers and inappropriate comic relief. The scene that blows my mind, and not in a good way, is when a hyperactive client dry humps Sada in several positions, and even she looks puzzled. In my opinion, subject matter such as this should be treated seriously, and not as fodder for an avant garde project. I was fascinated, repulsed, and aroused by the previous film. This one just left me scratching my head in confusion.

There is also an earlier version called **A WOMAN CALLED SADA ABE** (1975), but as far as I know, it's not available in the States yet. If my review of **SADA** has made you want to see it anyway, I would recommend starting with **IN THE REALM OF THE SENSES**.

Sada Abe: Love her, hate her, pity her. But you will never forget her.

Japan, 1976. Director: Nagisa Oshima
Available on DVD thru Criterion Collection

Japan, 1998. Director: Nobuhiko Obayashi
Available on DVD thru Home Vision Entertainment.

ASHURA
(Ashura-jô no hitomi)

Demons walk the earth in human form, causing mass destruction and it's up to a powerful band of slayers called The Demon Wardens to stop them. When one of The Wardens, Izumo (Somogoro Ichikawa) kills a child by mistake, he retires in shame. Even after five long years, as a beloved Kabuki performer in 19th Century Edo, he still has nightmares. However, when a demonic nun named Bizan (Kanako Higuchi), and renegade Warden Jaku (Atsuro Watabe) join together to to use beautiful acrobat Tsubaki (Rie Miyazawa) in a scheme to bring Demon Queen Ashura into the world, Izumo leaps back into action to save both his lady love and the human race.

Sound exciting, right? And it should be. The acting is the perfect blend for this type of genre film, both over the top and subdued at the right moments, and I ended up caring for the characters. I was even hoping that the evil Jaku would redeem him self at the end. The script by Sei Kawaguchi, Kazuki Nakishima, and Masashi Todoyama is tight and engaging, but the end result is a beautiful, but confusing mess.

Let's start with the running time. At 119 minutes, it's way too long. If it were a busy movie, I wouldn't care, but it's not. Long passages of people walking the streets, gazing at the sky, lounging in dressing rooms, etc. And while it is a part of his character development, a few of Izumo's stage performances could have been cut. I only hung on because I cared about the character's fates. If that's not fan love, I don't know what is. Also the comic relief characters of Magataro, Izumo's cross dressing manservant, The Master Playwright, and his two goofy assistants just get in the way. And if Ashura's so powerful, then why go through all this elaborate stalling when she could just zap Izumo anytime. Lord know, this movie doesn't need any padding.

Now the effects: the up close fight scenes are

beautiful, and the final battle between Ashura and Izomo features the awesome wire work that I so dearly love in these films. But when the camera backs away, it's obvious CG. Either they couldn't find convincing stunt doubles, or they couldn't afford any, convincing or not. It's gets even worse inside Ashura's castle. It looks exactly Izomo just stepped into a video game, and one with crappy graphics at that. I can be forgiving if I'm watching something put out by Troma, not a movie like this, especially when the rest of it looks so good. I can't honestly give this a total thumbs down, but I only recommend it to viewers who are infinitely more patient and a lot less nit-picky than I am.

Japan, 2005. Directed: Yôjirô Takita.
Available on DVD from Animeigo.

BLACULA

Of the many movies riding the '70's Blaxploitation wave, the horror classic **BLACULA** is definitely one of the best.

Our story begins in Transylvania in the 1800's. Prince Mamuwalde and his wife Luva of the African Ubani tribe visit Castle Dracula. The Count himself is a most gracious host until he finds out the reason why they are there. They want his help in abolishing the slave trade. Then Dracula becomes rather rude. "Slavery has it's merits.", He says slyly. " But not for the slave, of course." He adds further insult to injury by making lewd remarks toward the Princess Luva, which further angers the Prince. Drac sics his zombie minions on the couple, biting Mamuwalde before unceremoniously dumping and sealing him in a coffin. then both Luva and the now undead Prince are locked in a secret room to slowly starve to death.

Flash forward to the present (or 1972, actually). Two American antique dealers have arrived in Transylvania to buy furniture from Dracula's estate. One of their purchases just happens to be the coffin containing the extremely ravenous Mamuwalde.

Back home, in their warehouse, curiosity gets the better of our guys, and they just have to open the coffin. (It would be a very short movie otherwise.) Once our Prince is freed, he makes short work of the boys. Then he discovers a familiar looking cape at the bottom of the casket (I guess Drac didn't want his "guest" getting cold. What a guy!) Then the Counts last words come back to haunt him. " I curse you with my name!", Dracula taunts. "You shall be called Blacula!" (We can now add racism to the list of his rather unpleasant traits.)

With a title like **BLACULA**, it would be so easy to turn this movie into a total cheesefest, but director Crain avoided the temptation, which put this in the same class as such Blaxploitation classics as **SHAFT** and **SUPERFLY**. Part of that has to do with the casting. Mamuwalde is played by William Marshall (who unfortunately succumbed to Alzheimer's several years ago), a tall, handsome, Shakespearean actor who instills the character with both menace and sadness. Then, there's the stunning Vonetta McGee, who makes the transition from the aristocratic Princess Luva to Tina, her hip modern reincarnation with ease. And how can we forget Thalmus Rasasula and Denise Nicholas (of the '60's show "Room 222") as our resident vampire hunters.

That being said, **BLACULA** is not without it's B-Movie moments. The vampires look absolutely horrible! They're pasty gray with bushy eyebrows and fangs that look like the ones you can get at Walmart during Halloween. And, I swear that one of them looks like it's a mannequin rolled on wheels! And don't even get me started on the gay stereotypes!

All in all though, I would have to recommend **BLACULA** as a fun popcorn flick that just happens to tell a good, solid story.

USA, 1972. Director: William Crain
Available from MGM Home Entertainment

EXCISION

Pauline (AnnaLynne McCord of the "90210" revival) is not your usual angst-ridden teenager. She has an overwhelming desire to be a surgeon and she indulges this by practicing on roadkill. Not only that, but she has disturbing dreams containing mutilation and necrophilia that she finds arousing. Combine that with an overbearing, religious fanatic of a mom (Tracy Lords, who's proven she has left her porn past way behind.), a whipped dad (Roger Bart), and a much adored younger sister slowly dying of cystic fibrosis (Ariel Winter) plus being bullied at school, and Pauline is a ticking time bomb.

I went into **EXCISION** with an open mind; I really wanted to like it. It's well made and acted, but awfully unpleasant and depressing. There were a few times that I felt sympathy for the main character, but for the most part I found her highly unlikable. She's surly, filthy, and deliberately does things to put people off. We definitely have a budding sociopath on hand, but her school does nothing until she expelled for violent behavior, and her parents' answer is to send her to a preacher

(the "Prince Of Puke himself," John Waters), instead of a psychiatrist, and try to force her to attend cotillions to teach her to be a "proper" young lady, all the while ignoring the underlying problem. The scenes with her sister are touching, also the one where she's crying after overhearing her mother telling her father that she's hard to love, but other than that, it's hard to engage any sympathy for her.

I read that there have been several walkouts during **EXCISION**, and I can understand why. Having said that, there is no denying that this film is a labor of love, and I'm really looking forward to what Bates does next. Recommended only for those with strong stomachs and thick skin.

USA, 2012. Director: Richard Bates Jr.
Available from Anchor Bay

DJANGO

Django, (Franco Nero), enigmatic drifter who drags a coffin around with him, rescues the beautiful Maria (Loredana Nusciak) being beaten by a group of men and ends up being caught up in a war, led by the corrupt, racist Major Jackson (Eduardo Farjado) and a group of Mexican renegades in a semi-deserted town. It turns out he and Jackson have a history, but who is Django really, and what is his agenda?

Sergio Corbucci's **DJANGO** is one of a sub-genre know as Spaghetti Western, the more popular ones being Sergio Leone's Man With No Name trilogy (**THE GOOD, THE BAD, AND THE UGLY, A FIST FULL OF DOLLARS** and **FOR A FEW DOLLARS MORE**) starring Hollywood tough guy Clint Eastwood. I'm really not a western fan but I had first heard of in, believe it or not, Rue Morgue magazine, a Canadian horror periodical. It was featured in an article written on "ultra-violent" westerns, that, of course, intrigued me quite a bit. Ultra-violent, no, and this was the unrated version. Except for a scene involving a man getting his ear sliced off and forced to eat it, this film was pretty tame. (It does boast a body count of 138 and was banned in several countries, according to Internet Movie Database)

The film is pretty to look at and Franco Nero is handsome, charismatic, and morally ambiguous, but the rest of the characters are one-dimensional, and to be honest, I'm not really sure what the movie is about. It's rather convoluted. In fact, I rather enjoyed Takeshi Miike's homage/remake SUKIYAKI WESTERN DJANGO much better. If you are a spaghetti western fan, you will love this. If not, this is not one for beginners. Try THE GOOD, THE BAD, AND THE UGLY instead.

Italy, 1966. Director: Sergio Corbucci.
Available from Blue Underground

DEAD MAN

Mild-mannered accountant William Blake (Johnny Depp) heads out from Cleveland, Ohio to the small town of Machine to make a fresh start after the death of his parents. Murphy's Law goes into full effect when his promised job falls through then he's forced to shoot a man in self-defense, prompting him to go on the run. Injured, he is saved by an Indian named Nobody, (Gary Farmer in an unfortunately stereotypical role.) who's convinced that William is the English poet of the same name.

The first six minutes (though it seems longer) of the two hour running time is taken up by the train ride. William sleeping, staring at the passengers, playing cards, staring out the window, reading, yada, yada, yada. (I felt his boredom. I really did,) Then to add confusion to the mix, a filthy Crispin Glover shows up to ask probing questions and spout inane dialogue. And I'm afraid it doesn't get any better. Most of the dialogue throughout the movie sounds improvised from The Existential Handbook 101, if such a thing even exists.

The presence of Robert Mitchum in one of his last roles, as well as John Hurt, Billy Bob Thornton,

Iggy Pop, and genre faves Lance Henriksen and Michael Wincott (Top Dollar in THE CROW) should have redeemed this for me, but it didn't. As I have said before, I'm not a western fan, but I don't think that most western fans will get DEAD MAN either.

Jim Jarmush's films are an acquired taste, but as Bartleby says, "I do not wish to."

USA, 1995. Director: Jim Jarnmush

CURSE OF THE UNDEAD

In the rugged Old West, the Carter family is terrorized by a robber baron named Buffer, who wants their land. When the latest intimidation attempt ends in tragedy, Oldest sibling Dolores (Kathleen Crowley) hires mysterious black-clad gunfighter, Drake Roby (Michael Pate). Soon, she has more than vengeance on her mind as she slowly falls under the stranger's spell. Dolores' behavior and the mysterious deaths of the townspeople alerts her admirer, Preacher Dan (Eric Fleming), that there might be something more malevolent about Roby than just being a gun for hire.

Have I ever been wanting to get my hands on this ever since I read about in one of my vampire books, in spite of hearing how awful it is. Well, I'm happy to say that I scored a copy of of ioffer, and it was well worth the wait. When one hears the words vampire Western, they usually cringe because BILL THE KID VS. DRACULA or BLOODRAYNE 2 come to mind, but this gem in nothing like them stinkers. It is well acted, atmospheric, and Michael Pate makes a vampire who is both sympathetic and creepy. It's a damn shame that this baby has fallen by the wayside. CURSE OF THE UNDEAD is definitely worth checking out.

USA, 1959. Director: Edward Dein
MCA/Universal Home Video

HELLDRIVER
(Nihon bundan: Heru doraibâ)

A meteorite falls from the sky, spreading an ash that turns half the Japanese population into the walking dead,causing the government to have a wall built to keep the infected away from the uninfected. The country is also divided on how to deal with the creatures. Some want to keep them locked up until there's a cure, and some want to destroy them. The only way to accomplish this task is to get close enough to chop off the antenna- like horns that grow out of their forehead, which some are harvesting as an illegal drug. Meanwhile Kika (Yumiko Hara), a young girl who has had her heart literally stolen by The Zombie Queen Rikka (Eihi Shiina, Audition) , is chosen to lead a ragtag group of survivors into Yubari, the center of the infected half of the country. Given an artificial heart and armed with a chainsaw kitana sword (where can I score one of those?), Kika aims to settle the score and end the plague once and for all.

I have to admit it. Even after liking their Facebook

page and reading anything I can find on them, alas, I have been a Sushi Typhoon virgin. Sushi Typhoon, an offshoot of Nikkatsu Studios (notorious for their pinku ciga, or pink films), are the makers of such wild and wacky fare as MUTANT GIRLS SQUAD and VAMPIRE GIRL VS. FRANKENSTEIN GIRL (both co-directed by Yoshihiro Nishimura). Not only did he direct this film, he also supervised the makeup effects for HELLDRIVER, as well as Shion Sono's SUICIDE CLUB and NORIKO'S DINNER TABLE). And let me tell you that HELLDRIVER is one hell of a cinematic first time. This movie is totally insane in the best way possible. I have not been entertained this much in along time.

What can I say about this, What can't I say? What's not to love? These zombies are unlike any seen before and in various forms such as: six-limbed (two of the limbs are tiny arms stinking out of the zombie's cheeks armed with a knife and fork. A zombie chainsaw army, zombie that drive cars made of body parts. Zombies who chop of their heads and launch them at victims, and zombies who's spinal chords are protruding out their necks with the heads on top like stalks. They even round up survivors and take then to The Zombie Bar where they are used for food and sport. And that folks, is where we meet my favorite zombies: pregnant geisha whose hungry unborn babies have eaten their way out of their bellies, still attached to the umbilical cords and used as projectiles. Morbid sounding, I know, but these are actually the funniest scenes in the movie, and I am the LAST person I though would ever say that. All of this pandemonium leads to an absolute jaw dropping finale that has to be seen to be believe. If you are a fan of nonsensical, madcap gorefests, then HELLDRIVER is for you.

If any of their other movies are even remotely like HELLDRIVER, then I think I just might become a Sushi Typhoon slut. - Danae Dunning

Japan, 2010. Director: Yoshihiro Nishimura
Available from Well Go USA

THE DOGGIE BAG
INDIAN HORROR & FANTASTIC CINEMA PART 3

• Tim Paxton

Yes, I am obsessed with Indian horror films. I confess. It's an addiction. More specifically, I am fascinated with their creature features. Monsters are a very rare commodity within Indian films, and their appearances aren't typical of an A-grade picture. They lurk in the dark and dismal corners of Indian movie houses. Or they did, until the global interest in horror films over the past decade inched its way passed Indian Censors. While horror films have been a staple of European and American cinema for over a century (with a few minor exceptions), censorship in India is very strict when it comes to "Adult" subject matter. Emotional distress caused by action, foul language, partial nudity, and acts of extreme fear may be considered too much for Indian audiences.

For decades, the closest a director could get to making a horror film in India would be in the fantasy genre. There were a few early films about reincarnation and spooky happenings, and even a knock-off of James Whale's **INVISIBLE MAN** (1933). But extreme monster rampaging, as we saw from Universal Pictures with their Frankensteins, Draculas, Mummies, and Wolfmen (even after the Hays Code went into effect), would never have made it through Indian censors. Oddly, demons appear on a regular basis, albeit that is due to the always popular Hindu mythological genre. But truly ghastly stuff? Torture will always get an A-Certificate, and man, do the Indians love their violent movies, but supernatural horror is another thing altogether.

Government issued A-certificate for the film **PHOONK 2**.

The MPAA rating system and censorship in the USA film industry is (currently) a self-imposed and self-monitored (and some say, very abused) system. Our rating system was developed in 1966 with G, GP, R, and X after the Hays Code was deemed out of touch with modern audiences. The current G, PG, PG-13, R, and NR-13 system was set in stone by 1990. Prior to independence (1947), censorship in India was regionally controlled. The current Indian censorship code has been strictly enforced since the 1950s by the Indian government's "Central Board of Film Certification", which uses the following certifications: U – universal audiences, UA – parental guidance, A – Adults Only, and the oddball S certificate which is "restricted to any special class of persons" such as clerics and physicians.

Practically all Indian horror films over the past sixty years have fallen into the "A" certificate category because of the forbidden element of "adult and disturbing themes" that come with the territory. Many of the more famous Indian horror films were forced to cuts scenes or were banned outright by government censors. Despite intense pressure by the censors, the overall production of horror films has not ceased, as there has always been an audience hungry for all things monstrous.

Many early Indian horror or monster films have been hard to locate, and some have fallen into the official category of "lost." The number one lost film that I am currently after is an Indian *kaiju* flick. *Kaiju* is the Japanese word for any giant monster flick that includes Godzilla-size creatures. The film I am interested in is called **GOGOLA** (D: Balwant Dave), and was a minor hit in 1965. Not much is known about this South Indian production other than a popular regional LP release of its soundtrack. Assorted reports give the plot as thus: The monster Gogola rises from the ocean and threatens all of India; "[an] enraged Gogola charges into the city wreaking vengeance by destroying many public lives, buildings and properties…"[1] A scientist develops a poison that will rid the world of **GOGOLA** and the young hero of the film is recruited to dive below the waves to deliver the substance (echoing the original 1954 **GODZILLA**). Not much else has surfaced other than the LP and a pressbook which has an ad from the film... which is as close as we will get to seeing an Indian film devoted *entirely* to a giant monster. Other films have featured giant critters, but only in brief supporting roles.

Other giant monsters from the 1960s include the weird dinosaur dragon creature from **KING KONG** (covered in *Weng's Chop #1*), mythological monsters, and fantasy oriented fiends that appeared in films based on "Arabian" stories. Shreeram

---
1 From surviving elements of the film's pressbook; pedrotheapebomb.wordpress.com/2012/05/06/fun-with-filmi-ads-the-bollywood-godzilla-gogola/

1954 Newspaper ad from the English language newspaper "The Hindustan Times", featuring the adults-only mystery/horror film **BHAIRAB MANTRA**.

Bohra's 1968 Dara Singh action vehicle **THE THIEF OF BAGHDAD** featured many magical adventures and two giant-sized monsters. Singh stars as "The Thief," and in one very brief sequence towards the end of the film, he encounters a grinning, overweight *triclops* and a scaly, reptilian, horned devil. Both monsters were vanquished and the adventure continued. Being a family-oriented fantasy film this was granted a "U" certificate. Apparently, threatening monsters and loads of killing on behalf of the movie's hero made for great kiddie fodder (which I don't have any problems with).

As discussed in *Weng's Chop issue Zero*, hairy monsters have been the rage in Indian cinema from the very beginning (from what I can find) until the mid-2000s. Thereafter, monster-oriented horror films have become a rare species, with only a few popping up now and then. Supernatural spook tales are now all the rage, with the occasional monster. But hairy monsters. Yeah, with monkeys abundant in India, it's no wonder they were so often the paranormal villains in Indian cinema.

An early example of a hairy monster appeared in the unofficial Indian "Tarzan" film from 1934, called **TOOFANI TARZAN**. Tarzan is thrown into a pit with a crazy, hairy humanoid who is just about to munch down on the Indian variant of Jane. Tarzan leaps to the rescue and demolishes the creature.

THE THIEF OF BAGHDAD.

Issue Zero also covered the hairy giants that appeared in Rajkumar Kohli's **JAANI DUSHMAN** (1979) and Shyam Ramsay's 1991 yeti film. **AJOOBA KUDRAT KAA**. The costume designers for both of these monsters must have been recipients of a large part of each film's budget - by Indian film standards anyway. Great care was put into their horrid appeal. As for this type of monster, I'm going to examine a few of the creatures that populate that lower end of the cinematic spectrum: the "C" grade variety.

There have always been films made on shoestring budgets in India. In fact, since so many movies are made every year in that country, it's hard *not* to have a slew of bottom-of-the-barrel productions (and in India, that barrel is always nearly full). These films are the creations of renegade filmmakers who produce films out of nothing; genuinely independent filmmaking misfits working outside of the Bollywood system with pathetically low budgets.

An early entry made after the Ramsay family began the boom in the late 70s is **SAU SAAL BAAD** ("One Hundred Years Later," D: Mohan Bhakri, 1989), a "*tantrik*" horror film. That is, all of the problems caused in the film come from a sex-crazy, magic hoodoo man who, in this case, has a monstrous hairy sidekick. The film opens a hundred years or so ago, when an evil *tantrik* woos and then commands the heart (by magic of course) of a royal maiden. The wizard brings the girl back to his cave where he plans on consummating their unholy union. The local raja, who happens to be the girl's father, arrives on the scene bringing *his* holy man to the party. The unlucky girl is magically transformed into a statue and the tantrik is killed. Afterwards, the raja orders that the tantrik's lair be walled up and a symbolic holy weapon, Shiva's trident, be used as a seal.

A hundred years later, a group of folks manage to unleash the tantrik from his tomb, who then uses his magic to conjure up his hairy henchman. The huge, skull-faced creature runs rampant, killing random people. The monster kidnaps a woman who has a resemblance to the long-petrified princess. The film ends where it began, in the cave of the tantrik. Unfortunately for our re-animated wizard he runs afoul of a male Naag (snake) demi-god, who is possibly sent by Shiva (again, no subtitles) to destroy the monster and his master. The final ten minutes is a wild throwdown between good and evil.

SAU SAAL BAAD is not a bad film, although it does foreshadow some dreadful films to come. The utter cheapness almost ruins it, but, luckily, the plot is rather old skool and doesn't rely too heavily on sleaze to push the envelope. There are some wet sari sequences to keep the rabble in the theatres fixed to the screen, but it isn't as scuzzy as later films by filmmaker Kanti Shah and his cronies.

Director V Prabhakar's 1998 film **HAIWAN** is yet another low-budget horror film with a furry beast that terrorizes a young woman. Apparently this was a direct-to-video release that has a bit of mystery behind its production. There is an odd history behind this film. First off, the date of release is 1998. That's nothing unusual unless you take into consideration that the film bills Silk Smitha as the star, even though the real star of the film is the actress Gowthami. Former "adult" film star Smitha died under mysterious circumstances in 1996 (she was in negotiations that would have seen her return to Indian cinema as a producer rather than a star). Her appearance in the film is *very* brief. My guess is that **HAIWAN** was partially in the can when she died and it sat around until Gowthami was found to replace the dead starlet. Or, since Smitha's role is pretty vague, her scenes may be inserts from a previously unfinished film (something that is not uncommon with cheap Indian productions), as there are a few post-1996 films which "star" Silk Smitha in musical numbers.

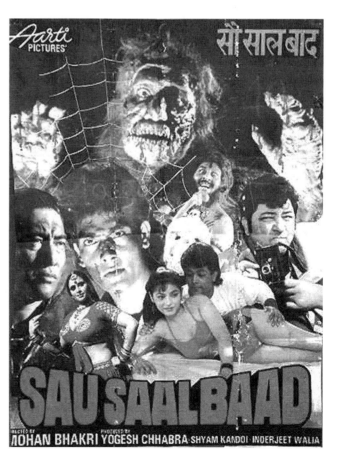

the serum that created the monster also made it indestructible even after being shot repeatedly and burned to a crisp (he regenerates). As luck would have it, a local police officer uses his unique kung fu abilities to catapult the giant into an abandoned well. The well is capped and everyone exhalations a sigh of relief.

Roll the title credits. Yes, all that action happened within the first five minutes of the film! Which leads me to believe that **HAIWAN** is a sequel of sorts to a previously unknown film. The pre-credit intro is a direct rip-off of Michael Miller's 1982 Chuck Norris film **SILENT RAGE**. In that film Norris, as a small town sheriff, battles an indestructible madman portrayed by a robotic Ron Silver. Was there an Indian **SILENT RAGE**? Not that uncommon as the Indian cinema is full of such rip-offs.

Years later the old well, overgrown with weeds and vines, long forgotten as the resting place of the monster, is disturbed by a violent thunderstorm. Aww geez, wouldn't you know it: the giant emerges from the pit. But instead of a human emerging from the pit, a hairy creature with fangs and claws is freed. The monster crawls from the well, bellows and screams, then ambles into the darkness not be seen again for about 40 minutes. In the meantime, there are a few saucy musical numbers and then the monster reappears to kill a few guys and snack on their bones before the next song and dance interlude.

Just as **HAIWAN** threatens to get bogged down in the typical miasma that is Indian cinema (i.e. insufferable comedy and convoluted sub-plots) the plot picks up steam. There are a few additional random killings, another musical number and then the final fun begins. The monster lunges into a non-stop killing spree in the last 25 minutes, annihilating folks (including the comic relief, thank god) before turning its attention to our heroine (played by the lovely Telugu actress Gowthami). She flees in terror as the furry fiend stalks after her. The film kicks the terror up a notch with mildly effective cinematography and some fairly decent action sequences.

The shaggy creature chases our heroine out of her house and eventually into an abandoned gas station. There she manages to lure the monster into the building and then sets the station on fire. The resulting explosion catches the creature, setting it ablaze. The crispy critter falls to the feet of the terrified woman only to rise to its feet, and the chase resumes. She flees to a nearby factory where the monster follows and searches for her (**TERMINATOR** style) throughout the building. In the end, the monster is finally vanquished when a police officer shows up with special bullets that blow the seemingly "indestructible" monster away.

Oh, this could have been a doozy of a film if only the producers weren't so occupied with the comic relief and half-baked musical numbers. From the looks of the effects department, money was spent on the creature, but its appearance in the film wasn't properly exploited. Sources around the Web say that this was a "made-for-video" release. But it just doesn't look like it.

Earlier I mentioned Kanti Shah and his films so I should give a nod to his production company's 2003 hairy monster movie **DUPLICATE JAANI DUSHMAN** ("Duplicated Killer," D: J Neelam). I bought this film (went out of my way to purchase it from an even more obscure website than I usually frequent) because it was a "duplicate" of **JAANI DUSHMAN**. I had to see how Shah was going to mangle one of my favorite Indian films. Oh, and it also stars the bodacious Sapna Tanveer playing one of her tough-as-nails female hellions. I couldn't miss that!

However, upon closer examination of the film, other factors surrounding the release date just don't gel. While the film is mentioned as one of the few Hindi productions on Gowthami's bio, it doesn't appear on her official filmography. **HAIWAN** was "made" in 1998, a time period where she took time off from film to start a family. There was little information on this film other than the same incorrect stats regurgitated over and over no matter what site I visited.

But enough of those oddball facts, on with the monster movie.

The film opens as a group of scientists inject an experimental serum into the body of a corpse. The dead body is revived and goes on a killing spree. Nothing can stop this giant crazy undead man as he rampages. Apparently

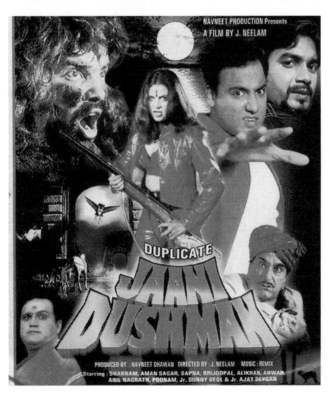

If you are familiar with the original film, then you know the plot. A hairy werewolf-cum-bigfoot monster terrorizes a village of brides-to-be, murdering the women one by one. Neelam's "duplicate" version sort of follows **JAANI DUSHMAN**... kinda... just barely. There is more of Sapna and her amazing bosoms than a hirsute critter. But as this is a film produced by... yep... an associate of Kanti Shah (or maybe Shah himself under some pseudonym), that's to be expected.

I was hoping that the monster would be more than just a guy in a gorilla suit with fake hair glued to his face. I was not that lucky. And the sequences that do involve the monster are very badly handled... which was not all that unexpected when you consider the director, Neelam, a man responsible for numerous other atrocities. On a happy note, he does manage some two okay musical numbers and allows the always sassy Sapna to ham it up, which is always a pleasure.

The plot is very simple: young women who are about to marry are killed by a hairy monster. Turns out the creature is a malignant spirit that just hates seeing a wedding take place. Tracking the killer down is somewhat tricky, as the monster can transfer its essence from one man to another, turning its host into a hairy horror. See the original **JAANI DUSHMAN** if you can, as it has a better monster AND a better soundtrack.

With the hirsute horrors behind me, let's take a gander at what else I've managed to unearth:

BHAYAANAK MAHAL
Director: Baby (1981, VCD, no subtitles)
"Terrifying Mansion" is definitely a film where you wish the sourced video element was something better than a cruddy VHS tape. This is an ambitious horror film that, simply put, lacked the budget it needed to pull off all its plot. Still, for this type of zero-budget production, the effects are imaginative, even when spooky scenes are direct rip-offs of **POLTERGEIST**, **THE EVIL DEAD**, and even Albert De Martino's brilliant 1974 **L'ANTICRISTO** (itself a rip-off of the **EXCORCIST**). Malayalam director "Baby" was someone who had an eye for the unusual but lacked the financial resources to make an exceptional film. Baby's other films, **VEENDUM LISA** (1987), **AADIVARAM AMAVASYA** (1993), and his last film to date that I know of, **BHAYANAK BHOOTANI** (2002), remind me of dark and gooey Taiwanese and HK black magic horrors from the 80s.

BHAYAANAK MAHAL's opening sequence has all the hallmarks of a cheap Indian horror film: the omnipresent lightning and thunder, a spooky fog-shrouded mansion, and a Panama Cigarette ad – say what? Apparently to offset the cost of this already thread-bare VCD release, ads for various products have been added every twenty minutes. Damn.... well, at least the advertisements are as entertaining as the film itself.

The rather subdued soundtrack contains bits and pieces of possibly popular Pakistani psyche-guitar pop, non-intrusive traditional instrumental pieces, *and* a well scored spooky soundtrack from Guna Singh (which has delightful science fiction hints of Alexaner Laszlo's **NIGHT OF THE BLOOD BEAST**). Singh also scored the musical numbers, which are surprisingly good (despite a lackluster attempt to make them into spectacular sequences), having a delightful cinema verite/home movie feel.

The first half of the film drags plot-wise as we are introduced to the characters in the film. It isn't until the dramatic exorcism during the final 30 minutes that we see what director Baby may have been up to. A possessed young woman is tied down to a chair while a holy man attempts to free her of the demon that inhabits her body. It pains me to see someone like our director working hard and attempting to make **BHAYAANAK MAHAL** into something, but not having the budget to do so.

MAIN PHIR AAOONGI
Directed by K.I. Shaika (VCD, 1998, No subtitles)
You know as soon as has-been actor Harish Patel waddles into the first scene that you are in for a shit hole of a film. Even the acting chops of Kiran Kumar, star of some excellent films in the 70s and 80s, can't save **MAIN PHIR AAOONGI** ("I will return") from its lack of originality: the ghost of a murdered girl returns to take the lives of those who killed her. As usual, the canned soundtrack is unrelenting and cranked so loud at times that it drowns out the dialogue. The film's only saving grace is the lead Telugu actress, Shraddha Sharma. Sharma, who plays the mournful but vindictive ghost, appears in two of the musical numbers that, for the budget and type of film, are not half bad (albeit they seem to have been edited for this VCD release).

SHAITAANI KHAZAANA
Directed by Thai. Prakash (VCD, 1999, no subtitles)
A yogi master and his female companion disembark from a bus in a haunted region of India. Their destination is a spooky deserted temple atop a small mountain. Their mission is to collect data about possibly supernatural goings-on in the temple. The first ten minutes of the film are very moody and atmospheric, and one would assume that the rest of the movie would be the same. But **SHAITAANI KHAZAANA** is a cheap *horror filmi masala* and it quickly devolves into a bullshit comedy adventure epic with horrible musical numbers. However...

The plot thickens: a group of thieves plans on raising a local temple in search of treasure, but unbeknownst to them, a team of rival criminals plan to beat them to the loot. Uninspired dance numbers and comedy ensues, including extended kung fu battles that are very Sammo Hung in execution. Just when you thought all was lost, the supernatural element makes a surprising return when a young woman is possessed by a vengeful spirit.

Terrified that his girlfriend is killing people with telekinesis, the possessed woman's boyfriend flees to the abandoned hilltop temple where he encounters the young holy woman. She informs the worried man that his girlfriend is possessed by the restless soul of a woman who desires reincarnation. It takes over an hour, but **SHAITAANI KHAZAANA** ("Demonic Treasure") kicks into high gear when the Goddess Durga Maa makes an unexpected appearance and kicks butt. I totally didn't see that coming.

Director Thai Prakash attempts to save the film with imaginative special effects that must have cost him an arm and a leg. We're not talking mind-blowing work, but some stop-motion effects as well as primitive computer graphics. Making **SHAITAANI KHAZAANA** must've been very frustrating for its director. He faced the same daunting reality that Baby did with his films: there just wasn't enough in the budget to make a top-notch horror film. The final battle between the boyfriend and a reincar-

Actor, writer, and director Joginder as the loud-mouth demon in **AADAMKHOR HASEENA**

nated evil of an ancient tantrik was pretty ambitious. The scene didn't work on many levels, nevertheless Prakash tried, and that's what I find important.

AADAMKHOR HASEENA
Directed by Joginder (VCD, 2002, no subtitles).

Wow. Seriously. This is a film that defies explanation. But I will attempt to do so. I'm never a person who likes a film because it's bad. The so bad it's good branding just doesn't fly with me. If a film is crap I'll say so; usually watching it once and then never again. However, many films are train wrecks, and they are hard not to watch. This film, made by actor Joginder (he's in **SAUL SAAL BAAD**), falls into my category of so weird it rules. I wouldn't call it horrible – just misunderstood.

I reviewed another of Joginder's productions in *Weng's Chop Zero,* a strange mash up of an old film with newly shot horror footage with stolen sequences from Western films spliced into the mix. That was **SHAITAN PAYYAN**. A true classic of insane cinema. **AADAMKHOR HASEENA** was made a decade or so later and it is full-on nuttiness without the backbone of an old film graphed onto it. The film is a potpourri of disjointed effects, an over-driven, distorted canned soundtrack, and horrendous acting ... however, you make it past the first four minutes of the film, then you may very well be hooked for the remaining two hours.

A balding loud-mouthed, one-eyed demon (Joginder) bellows and pontificates about possessing the soul of a young woman and making life miserable for her family. There are unbelievable scenes of crazy no-budget special effects throughout, including one head-scratching effect that has two evil dijin servants of the demon "swimming through the air" by way of having the actors rolled in front of a bedsheet with moving pictures of clouds projected onto it. No luxury of a green screen for director Joginder. As dumb as it may sound the entire sequence, complete with cheaply animated "energy bolts", works in a funky manner. This is a true fantasy film, and there is nary a dull moment. **AADAMKHOR HASEENA** ("The Man-Eating Sexy Girl") stars Kanti Shah regulars Amit Pachori, Poonam Das Gupta, Raza Murad, as well as Joginder.

THAT WAS THEN... THIS IS NOW

Not one to dwell too much on the past, I've tried to keep up with recent Indian horror and fantasy. The sad fact is that the amount of such monster-genre films has dwindled dramatically from three to four dozen a year in the late 90s thru the early 2000s, to about ten to twenty a year thereafter. And that is not the work of the censors either. Are folks just not into cheap horror films anymore? It seems that the populace is now expecting more sophisticated films than the once mighty Grade C film industry used to churned out on a weekly basis. More than likely it is the fact of higher production costs, as well as a hunger for Western horror films, that has fueled the no-budget filmmaker's demise.

As the old adage goes, "Fool me once, shame on you. Fool me twice, shame on me." The modern Indian audience apparently isn't into the rubber mask silliness anymore, and I doubt there will ever be a return to the abundant insanity that was the Golden Age of Indian Cheap Cinema.

Director Ram Gopal Varam has made over 35 films in his career so far, and he was one of the early horror breakout directors from the 1990s. **RAAT** (1992) helped pave the way for this modern take on Indian horror. No rubber masks, no singing and dancing, and only a tiny bit of comedy that usually ruins such films. Varma was one to be typecast as a horror director so he made thrillers, comedies and dramas. His more successful films fall into the fantastic genre. **RAAT**, a possession film, was followed by **BHOOT** in 2003 and **DARLING** in 2007 (both ghost films) and with **PHOONK** in 2008, a black sorcery film. Recently, he returned to the genre with **BOOCHI 3D** and **BHOOT 2,** both released in 2012.

PHOONK is the one up for review this time around, as is the sequel **PHOONK 2,** directed by Milind Gadagkar.

PHOONK: successful land developer and all round family man Rajiv is a happy guy who is loved by his family, even though he is an atheist. While Hanuman and Ganesha are the household gods, these deities can't protect the man from the evils of Madhu, a witchy woman, and her creepy husband. Rajiv discovers that as business partners, the two have been giving him false information leading to an unfortunate call from a group of financiers. Rajiv looses the backing of his latest construction plan, and he attacks the two cheats, publicly embarrassing both of them. Bad move, Rajiv.

Licking their wounds the two witches muster forces of black magic and possess the soul of Rajiv's young daughter Raksha. All sorts of nasty things happen as the child levitates, curses, and gets physically and mentally weaker within days. Nothing can be done medically, and at the pleas of his family he turns to religion. Rajiv seeks out Manja, a blind tantrik. Manja leads Rajiv to Madhu's lair where a supernatural battle for Raksha's soul takes place. Madhu is killed when a ceiling fan falls and decapitates her. All is back to normal, except that Rajiv is no longer an atheist.

PHOONK is a horror film chock-full of flashy cinematography, some fancy effects work, and a subtle score which features two songs, but no dance numbers. And no comedy. Thank Hanuman! Varam instead concentrates on

the horrible aspect of black magic and its effect on the family. That's not to say that the end result is exceptional, as **PHOONK** relies on numerous possession film clichés rather than really digging deep into India's supernatural folk rituals. There is little in the fright department, as the film is all gloss with very little substance.

However, **PHOONK** was a runaway hit and that fact usually sparks sequels. **PHOONK 2** was rushed into production in 2010 with Milind Gadagkar at the helm as both writer and director (he was one of three contributors to the first film's screenplay). Reportedly Milind wasn't happy with how **PHOONK** turned out and wanted to make a better film.

After two years of successful construction projects Rajiv and his family, wife Arati, son Rohan, daughter Raksh, and the family maid are on their way to a newly purchased summer cottage for a much deserved vacation. Upon their arrival to the remote bungalow weird things begin to happen. Raksh finds a spooky looking plastic toy baby doll in the woods. She takes the doll back to the house ... along with the attached ghost of Madhu. Strange and horrible events occur and family members and friends begin to die one by one as the malevolent spirit takes possession of Arati in a bloody act of vengeance.

PHOONK 2 turned out to be a superior supernatural chiller than its predecessor. Gagagkar borrowed cues from previous low-budget thrillers from the 90s with the inclusion of both a marauding ghost *and* a killer baby doll. The doll in particular is a fun throwback, as the toy torments the family and, in one scene, kills a good ascetic hired to dispatch Madhu's ghost. The doll beats the crap out of the holy man tossing him up into a tree where is skewered by a branch. The film takes an even darker tone when bodies begin to pile up and only Arati's death ends the curse.

Sadly, Gagagkar's film bombed and Varma is working on the third installment of the series.

So where does this leave the future of Indian horror? Another director that has had some success with the genre is Vikram Bhatt. His 2008 film **1920** was a run away hit, as was **HAUNTED 3D** which holds the record of the highest grossing horror film in Indian history. The recent addition of **RAAZ 3D** in 2012 has added fuel to his popularity.

Other recent films that promised more than they delivered were P. Vasu's **NAGAVALLI** (2011), a *Nagin* (snake goddess) film that opted for bad CG rather than old fashion real cobras to deliver the chills; and Nitish Roy's **GOSAIN BAGANER BHOOT** (2011), sentimental kiddie fare about a boy and a ghost. Puja Jatinder Bedi's **GHOST**, Anik Dutta's **BHOOTER BHOBISHYOT**, and S. S. Rajamouli's **EEGA** are exceptional stand outs from 2012.

Director Puja Jatinder Bendi is one of those rarities in horror films, no matter in what country they're made... Bendi is a woman. Her film **GHOST** has been labeled the most violent film in Indian history. While I think that's way off the mark, as I've seen much more extreme Indian gangster and daaku (bandit) films, **GHOST** is pretty gruesome. Government censors heavily edited the film before it was allowed to be released in the theatres and on DVD. Critics of her film wondered how a woman could make such a blood thirty ghost film. Well, hell, Kathryn Bigelow made **NEAR DARK** in 1987, and it's one of the best vampire movies ever. I'm not going to compare Bigelow's film with Bendi's work, as there is no similarities, but Bendi made a film that was outside her country's normal parameters of good taste. Bigelow's **NEAR DARK** is an excellent film, but Bendi's **GHOST** was more daring... if you take into consideration where it was made.

There were a lot of government edits and alterations before the film was allowed to pass with an A Certificate. The film's monstrous protagonist is the vengeful spirit of a woman who was crucified by a group of thugs. She was murdered on the orders of a rich man who didn't want a Christian marrying his son. I admit what saw on the DVD was excessive, but no more so than what I've seen in a lot of western horror films. The witch/ghost, a *chudail*, delights in tearing its victims hearts out and splattering their entrails all about. Most of these blood-drench sequences where re-edited as color reversal making all the gore a negative blue. A cheap way to obscure the gore effects without all the red blood.

Exploding heads and dismemberment aside, what bothered the government censors the most was the brutal crucifixion of the woman. "It's a scene where the ghost gets crucified like Jesus Christ," she told the *Times of India*. "The

scene was very pivotal for the screenplay."[2] But the government censors didn't see it that way. Part of their job is to keep the peace in a country composed of volatile religious groups. Bendi explains, "The censor board felt that the crucifixion would hurt religious sentiments of the Christian community."

The film also featured a weird half devil/ half saint figure that prowled the plot, sending evil souls of the recently departed to hell. That was also high in the censor's list of no-nos, but those scenes seem intact.

Effects-wise the *chudail* is a frightening creature and the gore effects are surprisingly effective considering what I am used to from Indian productions. But bloody dismemberment doesn't make it good, only interesting. Bendi pushes and pulls her limited budget to the breaking point in an attempt to make an original monster movie. There are moments where she almost succeeds. One sequence wherein bodies of the dead are floating in the still atmosphere of a large cafeteria is very effective. However, as far as the rest of the story goes, I've seen enough of the desi-horror from the classic period of 1980-2000 to know that all she has done was to recycle the tale of the *chaidul*.

NAAN GOWRI ("Chemistry") is a 2009 film from Malayalam director Vinu Kiriyeth, and is a prime example of low-budget modern day Indian horror. Parvati, a young female college student is possessed by the spirit of Gowri, a girl who mysteriously died while attending the very same school. It seems that Gowri and two of her friends may have committed suicide because of being involved with three "bad boys." In a fairly exciting climax Aayoung is successfully exorcised by a tantrik, aided by the fact that the young woman is a devotee of Shiva (that always helps in these supernatural matters). The film has a nice look about it despite the cheap CG effects and funky editing. Had **NAAN GOWRI** been made in the 1990s its well worn plot elements surrounding the motif of a vengeful female ghost wouldn't have been too out of place. It seems that no matter what decade an Indian horror film is made, the popular element of spiritual possession has always permeated the horror genre.

The Bengali spooky drama/comedy **BHOOTER BHOBISHYOT** ("The Future of the Past") is another matter altogether. Director Anik Dutta's film

---

[2] articles.timesofindia.indiatimes.com/2012-01-09/news-interviews/30607239_1_snips-scene-ghost

features an old family mansion full of ghosts who are determined not to have their home torn down and turned into a shopping mall. I was hesitant to buy this as its trailer was questionable. Drama? Comedy? Horrible new wave Indian Cinema? Nevertheless, I was pleasantly surprised that it lacked the artsy-fartsy elements of other supernatural films like **RAAZ 3D**, **KAALO**, and, heck, characters briefly discussed a Ramsey horror movie in the first 35 minutes. I chuckled and nodded at that reference. **BHOOT BHOBISHYOT** was very good.

A young director is scouting locations in the heart of Kolkata (Calcutta) to shoot his first film. While checking out an old mansion he encounters a middle-aged man who tells him a ghost story about the building. The mansion is called Chowdhuribari, and it is haunted by a gang of ghosts from different eras in India's history from the 1700s to modern times. The *bhoots* (spirits) have taken shelter at the mansion over the past few decades to escape gentrification of their old haunts into condos and malls. Witty script, fine character development, subtle acting, and some low-key musical numbers help make this one of the best *filmi masala* I've seen in ages. Besides the spooks, the audience gets a brief bit of Indian history and even a brief behind the scenes look at the film industry.

If fantasy is your thing, then definitely set up a double bill of **BHOOT BHOBISHYOT** with another new film called **EEGA** (2012), a fun and adventurous production by Telugu director S. S. Rajamouli. Rajamouli has had a number of hits over the past few years with and assortment of science fiction and action adventure films. He is a special effects guy ... but one of the few effects men in India that manages to blend effects work with good acting and direction. His most successful films to date have been his modern/mythological mash up **YAMADONGA** (2007) and the time-tripping historical drama **MAGADHEERA** (2009).

As a side note I'd like to say that **YAMADONGA** is S. S. Rajamouli's variant of the classic Telugu satirical-fantasy film **YAMADONGA** from 1977 (D: Tatineni Rama Rao). That film was later remade as **LOK PARLOK** in 1979 by the same director, this time in Hindi, and is one of the best Bollywood fantasy films ever. This matter of multiple versions of the film (like the original **YAMADONGA**) for different Indian ethnic and language markets is also worth researching, and could possibly merit a future article in *Weng's Chop*. If I have time.

In **EEGA** ("The Fly") Rajamouli again takes to using excessive amounts of computer graphics to tell the tale of a young man who is murdered and returns for revenge as a housefly. The film is ludicrous and absurd, and it is those elements that help make **EEGA** very entertaining material. Not a horror film, but a fantasy with a wonderful script, good acting, some restrained musical numbers, and only a smidgen of the usual horrible comedy bits I so abhor in *filmi masalas*[3].

A few of you may have issues with the computer effects in the film. Me? For a production like **EEGA**, I don't need super realism when it comes to a fly seeking vengeance. Weird fantasy is what I expected and I was more than pleased with what I saw. **EEGA** is prime fodder for a Hollywood remake and there are more than a few American "comedians" who would fit the bill as the fly ... even though the insect has no spoken lines.

Tune in next issue for another exciting installment of Fantastic Indian Cinema as I tackle the oddball Jungle genre as well explore the filmography of the bodacious Sapna Tanveer.

...

---

[3] K. Moti Gokulsing, K. Gokulsing, Wimal Dissanayake (2004). *Indian Popular Cinema: A Narrative of Cultural Change.* Trentham Books. p. 98, [The fourth influence on masala was Parsi theatre, which] "blended realism and fantasy, music and dance, narrative and spectacle, earthy dialogue and ingenuity of stage presentation, integrating them into a dramatic discourse of melodrama. The Parsi plays contained crude humour, melodious songs and music, sensationalism and dazzling stagecraft."

BHOOTER BHOBISHYOT

THE BOOKSHELF

MUCHAS GRACIAS, SEÑOR LOBO
Second Edition
Creepy Images Publications

If you are reading an issue of Weng's Chop I'm fairly certain that you are familiar with Paul Naschy and his astounding cinematic legacy. I'm also going to wager that you enjoy them, because I certainly do. But Naschy films have always been doubly amazing in that they generated some of the all-time coolest Spanish horror artwork not just in his home country, but around the world! Several years ago I was delighted to get the original edition of *Muchas Gracias, Senor Lobo* and to see a checklist of all these amazing pieces. If you gave a distributor a chance to put monsters, beautiful women, Yeti, swords, Samurai or anything else on the SAME poster you were bound to make magic. And many artists, both illustrative and commercial, did.

This is the book you NEED to appreciate it. The second edition is much larger and loaded with color images that include poster art, lobby cards, cast lists, pressbooks and even some original sketches by Paul Naschy! If you want to have a labor of love for a subject in your hands, this is for you. Jammed to the edges of each of the 390 pages (!!!) with gory glory, I can't recommend it enough. It's hard to really do it justice with a review, because my eyes just glaze over when I open the book, at any page really. It's an instant transport into the world of Paul Naschy that you can go back to anytime you would like.

After an introduction, 30 individual films memorabilia are cataloged and reproduced in varying amount, with the horror films getting the Lobo's share of the spotlight as you would hope. But this isn't just a collection of pictures. The text by Thorsten Benzel is presented in Spanish and English (with solid translations) and document the marketing history of the films in good detail—Pakistan loved HELL CREATURE I hope! This opens up a new world for this Naschy fan, going not just into the films and my feelings on them, and not just on the way I get a crazy tingle in my cine-schlong when I see an amazing piece of art for La Orgia de los Meurtos in gruesome color...but in how these audiences first saw the film before even entering a cinema. The promise of many of these images is met in the films for sure, but ranging from Ultra Shock to Shocking Beauty, there are many truly stunning pieces of work that were tied to the Naschy legacy.

If you are at all interested in European Trash Cinema artwork, the films of Paul Naschy or just want a coffee table book loaded with lobby cards for Hunchback of the Morgue, I would recommend picking this up regardless of the price tag. Hell, I sold a few things just to get this myself. This is an enduring piece of work that you'll pull off the shelf many times. I only wish that the people at Creepy Images had as much love for Joe D'Amato or (dare I dream?) Jess Franco!

Uncluttered by opinion, loaded with eye catching art and in a package that screams QUALITY...you'll be saying Muchas Gracias, Creepy Images!

~ David Zuzelo

Available directectly from **creepy-images.com** or Amazon.com.de or assorted Ebay sellers.

CINEMAGFANTASTIQUE
Issue #2

From Belgium, here comes the latest issue (number 2) of *CINEMAGFANTASTIQUE*. Written by Francophile bloggers and film historians, the full color 62 pages covers news on the latest horror and fantasy films available. This issue also has an in depth history of Italian exploitation films from Sword-and-sandals to Horror, with unpublished interviews of Umberto Lenzi, and Ruggero Deodato, as well as career article on Fulci, Massimo Pupillo and Lenzi.

This is also the only magazine to uncover the local Belgium film oddities **HAPPY BIRTHDAY MR ZOMBIE** and **SLUTTERBALL**. For those interested in the erotic arts, they will also read the erotic section developed by the « Loup dans la bergerie /wolf in the henhouse » website, here devoted to the **CAFE FLESH** trilogy.

You can order the magazine from their website **cinemafantastique.net/shop.html**. Although there is no button to order it in English, I have been told that, with postage, issues would cost 11 Euros for the USA, due to the cost of postage overseas. *~ Lucas Bulbo*

Drilling for Oily
The Oily Comix Primer

Whenever I'm a bit blue about where American comics and comix are going, messages and minicomics from the universe arrive via different venues, and my faith is restored. Amid the swill and backwash of the current "mainstream" (actually, no-longer-mainstream: DC and Marvel are now the fringe, as far as I can see, of comics) industry, fresh voices, visions, and air arrives unbidden—or, at least, unexpectedly.

Oily Comics as a positive force, a positive sign, of the collective future of comics. I've met and spoken to a number of young cartoonists who are already inspired by what Charles Forsman and his partners in Oily Comics have started—and that's a good, good thing, my friends.

I could argue I was the first subscriber to Charles aka Chuck Forsman's Oily Comics. Full disclosure: Chuck and Melissa are Center for Cartoon Studies alumni—I was their teacher—and I love their work, and have for years.

I so loved what I saw of Chuck and his partner Melissa Mendes's post-CCS graduation work whenever it popped up that I finally just mailed a fat check to Chuck and Melissa with a note saying, "please, send me everything you do! When this money runs out, tell me when I need to send more."

In 2011, Chuck announced the formation of Oily Comics. "There were two factors that spurred me on to make Oily," Chuck told me in December 2012. "One was the inspiration I got seeing Max de Radigués' *Moose #1*. It wasn't the first mini comic I had seen by any means, but it was the satisfaction Max was able to get into just 12 pages. A few months later I was finishing up a rather laborious comic and I wanted to jump into something without expectations and something that I could work on with more speed and not toil over large pages. So I started T*he End of the Fucking World*. I soon asked Melissa Mendes' to do a comic and she delivered the fantastic *Lou*." And the rest, as they say, is history-in-the-making.

The origins of Oily are thus tied to the beginnings of Max's *Moose*. According to Max (who ought to know), "I started *Moose* while staying for a few month in Montréal. The first issue was done a week before TCAF [Toronto Comics Art Festival] to have something [to sell] over there. I had no idea of what I wanted to tell. I just wanted to make a zine out of nothing, a guy runs for 8 pages, no text, but still make it look like I was telling a story. I started issue two not knowing if it was happening before or after issue one and have been working on [it] loose that way." Max now has over a dozen issues under his belt, and *Moose* has grown into its own as a unique narrative about a bullied boy and his plight.

Melissa Mendes' *Lou* is both a companion and tonic, if you will, to *Moose*, focusing on its tomboyish heroine and her immediate circle of family and friends. Anecdotal and forever attentive to its (and her) own internal music and muse, *Lou* is forever a treat.

Where did *Lou* come from? "Chuck and I moved into my childhood home about a year ago," Melissa recalled just before this past Christmas, "and I think that has inspired *Lou* especially—it's set in rural New England."

As Max allowed for *Moose*, Melissa has given *Lou* her own space and time to grow. "I thought I had a plan," she notes, "but a lot of times when I am working I will have an idea in my head, or an overarching storyline, and then the characters just take on a life of their own and become something completely unexpected. *Lou* started out as a story about a girl and her dog, but is becoming just as much about her brothers as it is about her. Eddie (the oldest brother) is very much based on stories Chuck has told me about himself as a teenager. I am having so much fun doing it. My cartooning is growing and changing in ways that I didn't expect. And the end might be just as surprising for me as it is for everyone else."

Then there's Chuck's devastating serialized teen-fugitives-on-the-run graphic novel *The End of the Fucking World*—but I'm getting ahead of the oil and ink flow.

Early in 2012, Chuck formalized actual Oily Comics subscriptions via a special offer (which they again offer every three months or so; see website/url link information at the end of this article, below), so I formally subscribed and signed up for the longest program offered (one year). I'll be renewing in a heartbeat, when the time comes. So, now, every month, a modest white business envelope of engaging minicomics just show up in my mail, and my heart soars whenever I get 'em. Chuck and his team have standardized their mailing to five minicomics per monthly mailing, and it's always a rich blend of visions and voices. For instance, the October 2012 mailing offered *Moose #11* by Max de Radigués—I should add that Max was our CCS Fellow three years ago, and his comics come winging to us from Belgium, by way now of Oily (and in English), and I'm absolutely addicted to Max's *Moose*.

All of Max's comix (that I've seen and read) are about life, pure and simple—particularly the life of young people, coming of age. *Moose* is Max's (autobiographical? Semiautobiographical? He hasn't said) chronicle of a lad on the bottom of the bully pecking-order at school has been a heartfelt, leisurely-paced read thus far, closely and lovingly observed and rendered, but it shifted into a new gear with the 11th issue.

"Working on one issue after another not really planning the 'big' story," Max recently explained to me. "Still it became clear from issue 8 where the story was heading and what the end would be.

For that story, one of the things I wanted to do, that I had never manage to in the past, is to have a character who's bad, almost evil. I always smooth the edge of those characters. They end up being 'people with problems' rather than bad guys. I wanted Jason to be a bad guy and readers to hate him. I don't know if I completely succeeded but is pretty bad, no?

As far as influence for the story, I clearly thought of New England and the main character is called Joe because I think he is influence by how Joe Lambert draws. But Maybe I'm the only one to see that..." Joe Lambert, a classmate of Chuck's who also graduated from CCS, has been making his own distinctive mark in the contemporary comics scene, with work in many anthologies, his own collected edition *I Will Bite You! And Other Stories* (2011, Secret Acres), and the recent acclaimed graphic novel *Annie Sulliven and the Trials of Helen Keller* (2012, Hyperion).

Also in its 11th issue as of October—and, I hasten to add, in polar extremis in the familiar "we've all lived this one way or another" emotional realms of Melissa's and Max's comix—is Chuck Forsman's slow-simmer, occasional-boil-over/bloody eruption account of a rootless, homeless teen couple on a harrowing tear in *The End of the Fucking World*.

It's fascinating how focused and unblinking (well, you'll blink, but Chuck sure doesn't) *TEOTFW* has been since its first page—hell, its first cover image—while maintaining a perfectly measured, dispassionate, steady, and secretive rhythm and pace that is oddly quite attuned to Max's *Moose*.

Frankly, Chuck's comix are unlike any I've ever read before, and at 57 years of age, I've read a fuckload of comics and comix. Ever since his participation in a Lynda Barry workshop busted open some kind of internal beaver dam of self-expression, Chuck's comix have been among my favorite pen-and-ink experiences.

What started in the pages of his self-anthology *Snake Oil* (which is ongoing) has blossomed into something far darker than his earlier, often surreal works; *TEOTFW* is a different brand of storytelling altogether, with a different approach to visual narrative as well. This seems natural enough, particularly given his chosen genre this time around (another echo, in more ways than one, of the arid wake of Charles Starkweather and Caril Ann Fugate's 1957-58 infamous Nebraska and Wyoming killing spree, though there's plenty of pop cultural and real-life successors to Starkweather and Fugate to fuel Chuck's possible role models for his *TEOTFW* couple-on-the-run).

Given the December 2012 school shooting atrocities still sending shockwaves through the collective American soul and psyche, it's an understatement to note Chuck has tapped a still-beating black heart of America, but I think anyone diving into *TEOTFW* will be surprised at how, when, and where the spillage takes his characters, and the along-for-the-ride reader (I don't want to reveal too much, but I do want to communicate some of what *TEOTFW* is about). Me, I'm in to the bitter end, Chuck—where ever this leads.

Maybe it's purely the coincidence of their cozy companionship in the Oily envelopes every month, but I've come to look forward to the ying/yang opposition and complimentary clockwork of *Moose* and *TEOTFW*, working in synch and out of synch with one another. It's patently unfair to compare the two works: they're totally unlike one another, save in their spare lines, crystalline clarity, and surgical simplicity and precision of effect.

But man, oh man, do they sing—together and apart.

Joining *TEOTFW* and *Moose* in the fall of 2012 was *Dumpling King #1* by Alex Kim (another CCS alumnus), which establishes its own identity in short order; I'm also familiar with Alex's work (see *Sundays*), but *Dumpling King* is unlike his earlier creations to date.

Again, though I made time to read *Dumpling King* an hour or two apart from my readings of *Moose* and *TEOTFW*, I can't help projecting a bit. Alex is finding fresh kinks and corners in another patch of urban blight: fast-food delivery, a disappearance (murder?), hard-edged shadows, splinters of memory. But Alex is mighty playful with his ink-slinging, dialogue, and narrative shards, and it's way too soon to tell where Alex is taking me/us, but again—I'm in for the long haul, where ever we're headed.

The self-standing minicomic autopsy *Flayed Corpse* by Josh Simmons left me a bit punch-drunk, which was clearly the intention. Successful, Josh, and I'm a tough customer with thick callouses. I think I have defensive palm-cuts myself after spending time with it (and that's a compliment, coming from me).

More mysterious and tantalizing still is the dreamy *Close Your Eyes When You Let Go #2* by James Hindle, which I'll hold off saying much more about until you can savor his *"Father Don't Know Best"* (in fact, it seems Father Don't Know Shit) pastoral suburban paranoiascape for yourself. Aaron Cockle's *Word & Voice* series likewise begs a longer steeping, as if my mind were a teabag brewing in Aaron's cup of hot water—just a couple more cups, Aaron (who, BTW, is also a CCS alumnus), and I'll have more to offer by way of comments. Keep pouring.

And that's not all. Reaching far beyond their immediate CCS circles, Chuck has added to the Oily mailings Jessica Campbell's T*he Public Life of Bees*, Zach Worton's *Blood Visions*, Benjamin Urkowitz's *Real Rap*, Michael DeForge's *Elizabeth of Canada*, and others, with more to come. I have to also bring to your attention the ambition and scope of the entire Oily Comics experiment in distribution, which is the second eruption from the CCS community I know of (the online distribution/mail order venue "I Know Joe Kimpel" was the first; there may be more, that I've missed—more than a few CCSers have arrived already part of various self-publishing and/or collective experiments and venues, a trend I hope will continue) positing a self-made, self-propelled alternative to the limbo I keep seeing the current generation of cartoonists and self-publishers consigned to.

It's a fine bit of synchronicity that renegade orphans and runaways are the nominal "stars"

CLOSE YOUR EYES WHEN YOU LET GO
Part Three of Three   By James Hindle

of what may well be Chuck's breakthrough work—*The End of the Fucking World* has already been contracted by Fantagraphics for future publication in collected form (but please, please don't let that stop you from subscribing to its minicomic original serialization; I, for one, am eager to see how and what revisions may be in store between the serialized and the collected incarnations, and there's much to be savored and learned by investing yourself in that process, too). But it must be noted that *Moose* is the first offspring of the Oily Comics line to graduate, so to speak—from the minicomic format—and in Europe, no less. "*Moose* is now done as a zine," Max explains. "I added a good 30 pages with a different ending for a book version in French that will published by Delcourt, Lewis Trondheim's collection *Shampooing*, in May 2013. I still got the rights for the English language so I hope to have the book out in the US too."

Still, they began their print lives as orphans, of a kind. After Chuck "adopted" *Moose*, the rest followed.

Orphaned by the so-called "industry," increasingly reliant on regional independent comics and comix conventions/shows that function more and more like seasonal craft fairs, Chuck and Melissa and their creative Oily Comics compatriots have decided it's high time they carve out their own niches and solutions, and thus Oily Comics was born. Others in the CCS community and the much larger national and international creative communities (remember, Oily Comics opened its subscriptions as an international collective, given Max's active participation and role) have little choice but to essentially reinvent the wheel—or, more to the point, invent their own wheels—to get their work out there to its potential readership.

In the context of the market realities, *"Flayed Corpse"* is an appropriate moniker for what remains of the once-vital marketplace my own generation of self-publishers were able to work within. It's dead and buried, what once was self-interred and embraced exclusion of the new generations, as far as I can see. The Diamond Comics monopoly

that has strait-jacketed the once-thriving "industry" simply isn't open to Chuck and his creative confederates (until those contracts and projects with the likes of Fantagraphics make it possible to enter that closed-shop marketplace—but they still have to work and self-publish to get to those "opportunities" and contracts).

Given the ramshackle and ever-changing nature of what means of (what we laughingly call) distribution remains for the current generation of self-publishers and non-superhero-obsessed cartoonists to tap, I'd say they've been left little choice: "make your own" applies as much to distribution as it does to publishing.

So, here we are. Oily Comics is one hopeful seismic eruption in a landscape hungry for creative volcanoes. There are more I know of (though I can't speak or write of them now), some of which, yes, I've already by-proxy subscribed to.

They're coming. Meet them with open arms. Send

them what money you can; believe me, they aren't asking much for their labor, and the fruit is mighty tasty, inexpensive as it is. Selling you their work via the internet and mail is also way, way less expensive (in time and money) than waiting for convention season. In fact, sans the internet and mail support, it's mighty tough to afford the travel, room & board, and table space at those regional indy comics and comix shows, folks. You want to support the new generation? Invest. However modest your investment, however little or much you can afford, invest. They are the future.

For what frankly amounts to a fraction of the cost of my monthly cable/internet/phone service—for less than what I spend in two weeks going to see theatrical movies—for far less than I pay on occasion for largely unsatisfying "meanstream" comics, when I'm moved to sample those overpriced color ad-packed mongrels—I've been enjoying a monthly harvest of Oily Comics.

It's been sweet.

It gets sweeter every month.

Go to http://**oilycomics.com**

When asked how long Oily will be pumping comics gold out of their hands, Chuck concludes, "As far as the future. I hope to keep this ship afloat until people get sick of it or I do."

I, for one, will be sticking with Oily until the end of the fucking world...

© 2012 Stephen R. Bissette,
Mountains of Madness,
December 2012

MATT BAKER: THE ART OF GLAMOUR
Edited by Jim Amash and Eric Nolen-Weathington

I have always loved Matt Baker's comic book art from the Golden Age; nobody could draw the female figure like he could. *Phantom Lady, Alani- the South Sea Girl* and countless damsels from the St. John romance comics all proved his prowess with portrayals of four-color pulchritude. But other than knowing he was an African American toiling in a predominately Caucasian industry and that he died from a heart attack before he turned 40, I knew absolutely nothing about the man.

Amash and Nolen-Weathington's new book from Fantagraphics clears up all of the mysteries about Baker, his life and his art. Stuffed to the gills with strips, original art pages, sketches and photos, Baker is finally brought out into the open for all of us to learn about. Interviews with his peers, friends and family reveal him as a dapper, generous man with an amazing sense of style and taste. (More than one interviewee mentions that "canary yellow convertible Oldsmobile"!) Handsome and smiling, the photographs show a man happy with his life, even though he knew it wouldn't be a long one.

There are also some full stories to drool over Baker's art with; *Phantom Lady, Canteen Kate, Sky Girl* and *Tiger Girl* among them. Some of the sexiest women ever drawn for comics, with long, panel-bursting legs and flowing hair, are lovingly reproduced here. And they were drawn by a man that lived his short life to the fullest. I think I fell in love with Baker's abilities even more after enjoying this essential book.

And thanks to the complete checklist of all of his published work, I have plenty of comics to keep an eye out for.

~ Mike Howlett

Available now through Amazon.com and other vendors of fine literature -- like Weng's Chop!

RIGOR MORTIS #4

($3.50 to PO Box 11064, Baltimore, MD 21212; livingdeadzine.blogspot.com) – *Rigor Mortis* is part of the recent wave of horror movie (and literature) zines that re-ignited my desire to bring my zine *Exploitation Retrospect* back into print. Deadvida, Dread Sockett and crew have produced a handful of issues tackling everything from zombies and vampires to creature features, the sexiest monsters in filmland, **WILLARD**, Crispin Glover, queer horror and much more. Tons of book and graphic novel reviews, original artwork and more round out every thoughtful 50+ page issue.

ROGUE #1
BETTY PAGINATED #32

(contact Dann Lennard at danhelen@idx.com.au for price and availability) – While I was taking a 13-year hiatus from doing a print version of my zine, Dann Lennard was cranking out the excellent *Betty Paginated* (the best-looking zine this side of Rod Lott's late, lamented *Hitch*) from his homebase of Australia. The mag was a cheeky appreciation of junk culture with a particular focus on rock, comics, trash cinema, wrestling and curvy lasses (no wonder I always dug the mag!). I'm bummed to report that *BP* is no more but the publisher has already unveiled *Rogue* – which debuted in early 2012 and has more of a "zine" feel despite Lennard's always strong layout. The focus is on many of the same topics that would have been right at home in *BP* and the first issue also includes a chat with infamous Aussie criminal Mark "Chopper" Read. Dann promises a new issue soon so don't miss out!

SPRAK! VOL. 2, NO. 8

(contact Kami McInnes, PO Box 278, Edwardstown SA 5039, Australia or cammy@arcom.com.au – Here's more thunder from down under courtesy of Kami McInnes, who has been at this zine game for about as long as I can remember. McInnes laughingly (lovingly?) refers to the issue as "the best toilet read you will ever find" and he's right on the money. This 32-page, digest-sized installment runs about as wide a gamut as you can find, diving into everything from a 1940s Phantom serial and 70s nunsploitation to Bigfoot cinema, Eurotrash classics, erotic sleaze, micro-budget trash and much more. As if that's not enough for you to throw the man some trade goodies (or "nek-kid pics"), there's a time-travel surf comic, a review of some sonic sludge and McInnes' look at the book 'Mail Order Mysteries: Real Stuff from Old Comic Book Ads!'. I've always loved getting zines from Kami as it's like reading a trash culture brain dump committed to the printed page and the latest *SPRAK!* is no exception.

LUNCHMEAT #6

($6 to 710 Glendalough Rd., Erdenheim, PA 19038; lunchmeatvhs.com) – It feels like VHS is the new 8-track but the guys behind *Lunchmeat* are no johnny-come-latelies to appreciating the maligned-but-still-loved media. When I received *Lunchmeat* #1 back in 2008 my biggest complaint was that the reviews tended to lean heavily on plot descriptions that would spoil potential viewing and the writing seemed to lack the enthusiasm for the subject matter that it seemed to deserve. But that was then and I have to say that the zine has grown and improved with each subsequent issue. #6 is probably the best yet, mixing the "meat" (VHS reviews) with interviews (including **DUDES** co-star Daniel Roebuck and 3-D pioneer Gene Quintano!), articles on 80s teen sex comedies and interactive VHS games like Doorways to Adventure and other thrift store mainstays.

TAPE MOLD #1 & #2

(2105 West 29th Street, Erie, PA 16508; vhshitfest.com) – Reading through *Tape Mold's* two glorious issues takes me back to that golden age of trash film and pop culture zines, when daily trips to the PO Box yielded a treasure trove of reading material from publishers with passion. I never knew what I was about to get edumacated on… Hong Kong cinema? Spaghetti westerns? Eurotrash? Christina Lindberg? 8-tracks? Board games? Cereal collectibles? They all had zines devoted to them and *Tape Mold* – from VHShitfest.com co-creator Dan Kinem – is probably the closest thing I've seen to something from that era. Each issue is packed with Kinem's fascination with the VHS format and those who inhabited its universe, whether it's obscure video labels, BBW star Big Bad Bertha, pumpkin carving craftsmen, or an ultra-obscure shot-on-video anthology flick like **SOUTHERN SHOCKERS** (whose awesome Spanish box art graces the cover of issue #2). An excellent companion to the more review-oriented *Lunchmeat*, *Tape Mold* is a must have even if you probably have no chance of finding many of the tapes discussed between its covers!

~ reviews courtesy of Dan Taylor

CANNIBALE FANZINE #3

52 pages, black and white photocopy, color front sheet and back cover, shipped for 7 € euros (9 USD). In this issue:

* 27-page feature dedicated to French director Daniel Daërt including a 16-page interview, complete filmography and reviews of five of his films: **CAÏN DE NULLE PART, LE DINGUE, LES FÉLINES, LES FILLES DE MALEMORT, FUREUR SEXUELLE**.
* Interview with French director Marc-Henri Boulier about his multi-award winning short film: **TOUS LES HOMMES S'APPELLENT ROBERT**
* Reviews of documentary Nollywood Babylon and Nigerian dilogy 666 (Beware the End is at Hand) 1 & 2.
* Article on French theater company The Brooklyn Rippers bringing back Grand Guignol to stage with André de Lorde's play: *Un crime dans une maison de fous*.
* Retrospective of the screenings organized by French association Cannibale Peluche in Le Havre during the 2010-2011 season (**CRUISING, DON'T LOOK NOW, THE HEROIC TRIO, I WALKED WITH A ZOMBIE, BAD BIOLOGY, DAISIES**…)
* Review of John Woo's war / exploitation flick **HEROES SHED NO TEARS**

Cannibale Peluche – 13 passage Gavarni 76600 Le Havre, France
cannibalepeluche@hotmail.fr

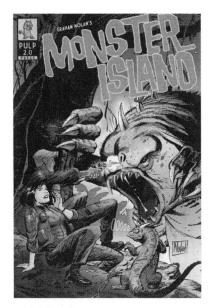

MONSTER ISLAND
Written and illustrated by Grahm Nolan

Growing up I was hooked on the comic strip pages within The Cleveland Plain Dealer and The Elyria Chronicle. Back in the 1970s both newspaper had two *entire pages* dedicated to the comic antics of Peanuts, Hägar The Horrible, Dick Tracy, Calvin and Hobbs, Buzz Sawyer, etc. What a second... Buzz who? For me Buzz Sawyer was one of the best action comic strips ever ... both in its daily pacing and the over all look. I LOVED it. And apparently Grahm Nolan did too, because from the very first time I laid eyes on the promotional material for his trade paperback "Monster Island" all I could think of was Roy Crane's "Buzz Sawyer." According to the bonus interview with Nolan was also a big fan of film magazine *The Monster Times*, comics *Werewolf by Night* and *Fantastic Fou*", and building Aurora monster model kits. I knew there was a reason I was drawn to this book!

Monster Island started out in 1997 as a comic strip for possible syndication through newspaper. Sadly, that didn't fly (I would have bought a daily just to read that strip!). Luckily, Nolan was cool enough to include them as a bonus in the back pages of "Monster Island" which also includes a great "How to Make a Monster Island Comic Book!" section, character design, reprint cover the Compass Comics original, and...

... Oh, and then there's the book itself! Thrill to the adventures of Duke and Mac as they transverse an island full of Fing Fang Foom-sized monsters, weird aliens, and a sexy princess. Fun stuff! Now, where's book 2?

Available for $7.99 from Pulp 2.0 Press @ pulp2ohpress.com or Amazon.com. Worth. Every. Penny!

HULK
Written by Tony Lee

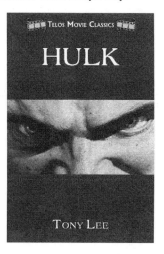

From its 1962 comic book origins in *The Incredible Hulk* by Stan Lee and Jack Kirby, director Ang Lee's classic movie **HULK** (2003), updates and re-invents the story of how scientist Bruce Banner is transformed into a giant rage monster, and becomes a new antihero for the 21st century. This book reviews the movie's narrative complexity and its varied genre elements, which include science fiction, tragic drama, action thriller, doomed romance, and a modern fairy tale with mythological references, energized by an artistically innovative editing style, and realized by ground breaking visual effects.

As a neurotic 'puny human' changes into the unstoppable 'Angry Man', *Hulk* offers a study of dysfunctional family relationships, and monster-movie rampages with tank-busting, helicopter-crashing mayhem in 'hulkgasm' adventures, that results in a final confrontation of cosmic proportions. A unique aesthetic spectacle, and extraordinary makeover for Hollywood blockbuster cinema, **Hulk** is the greatest screen adaptation of a comic book and it rediscovers the enduring legacy of a green-skinned 'superhero' without a costume.

HULK is published by Telos, and can be ordered direct from – http://www.telos.co.uk/

The GIMP book series can be purchased through AMAZON.COM and BARNESANDNOBLE.COM!

GIMP: THE RAPENING VOLUME UNO

Join legendary (not really) cult cinema critic and published (barely) author Brian Harris has he introduces readers to exclusive online reviews spanning almost a decade of writing. From the sublime sleaze of European exploitation to the gag-inducing underground gore of Asia, Mr. Harris paints a picture of unhinged cinema the likes of which only the most depraved genre fans are capable of enjoying. GIMP: THE RAPENING VOLUME UNO collects together the first five previously published GIMP film guides into one massive tome of useless opinions. Never has a book more deserved to be purchased, read and burned than GIMP: THE RAPENING VOLUME UNO.

GIMP: THE RAPENING VOLUME DEUX

Back again with a book sequel nobody in their right mind would demand, Brian Harris returns with yet more cinema reviews, this time collecting together unpublished material. Originally meant to be released as the next five installments in the original GIMP film guide series, GIMP: THE RAPENING VOLUME DEUX offers up even more senselessly offensive and unbelievably unnecessary opinions on films only the dregs of society could enjoy. Now with more potty language and references to midgets, GIMP: THE RAPENING VOLUME DEUX takes the success of the first book and squeezes consumers for just a bit more support and money. Purchase a copy now!

GIMP: THE RAPENING VOLUME TRE

Seriously, nobody asked for this. No publishing company forced him to complete this. GIMP: THE RAPENING VOLUME TRE is a money grab, plain and simple. Take it. Take it all. You're going to love it, Brian Harris swears he'll only stick the tip in. Once you think it's not all that bad, he'll plunge it in, leaving you physically tattered and emotionally betrayed. It doesn't get better than this, forget WATCHING exploitation, now you've got the chance to BE exploited! COMING SOON!

Made in the USA
Charleston, SC
05 March 2014